THE ALAMO DEFENDERS

A Critical Study of the Siege of the Alamo
and the Personnel of its Defenders

BY AMELIA W. WILLIAMS

Edited by Michelle M. Haas

Copano Bay Press
2010

Originally published in 1931 as <u>A Critical Study of the Siege of the Alamo and the Person-</u>
<u>nel of Its Defenders</u> as Ms.Williams' doctoral dissertation at the University of Texas.

New material copyright 2010 Copano Bay Press

ISBN: 978-0-9822467-7-1

CONTENTS

PUBLISHER'S NOTE

The time period that contains the Alamo saga and the Texas Revolution is a fertile historical landscape that has continued to sprout fresh theories and debates for the last 175(ish) years. And why shouldn't it? Those events, after all, are the very reason that we can proudly call ourselves "Texans." Our Revolution sets our history apart. It makes us unique. We've continued to contemplate it, to study it, to kick the dirt around hoping news facts or artifacts will surface. We've continued to debate the minutiae of the events of the siege and the defenders of the fort. We continue to publish books on the subject. We remember the Alamo!

In the century that passed between the fall of the Alamo and the writing of this text in 1931, a multitude of books were written on the Texas Revolution. Some were meritorious or at least made an effort to be. Others were overtly romanticized accounts, brimming with legend and sticky with the syrup of lore that will always cling to all of Texas history. Eyewitness accounts, both Texian and Mexican, also appeared on the scene. Memoirs were written. Collections of historical documents were donated to the University of Texas and the papers of prominent early Texas statesmen were compiled and published.

A fine body of material had come together on the Alamo and the Revolution, and along came Amelia Williams to tackle it. She had already immersed herself in the issues surrounding the Alamo and its defenders in preparing her Master's Thesis. Now she would dig deeper in pursuit of her Ph.D. The pre-Centennial environment in which this work was prepared was wrought with the celebration of grand Texas legend, lore and song. Ms. Williams, however, was in the business of facts and primary research. She set out to do what she felt had not yet been done adequately in print or in granite: to accurately enumerate and name the Alamo defenders, to place facts neatly on the shelf where conjecture previously sat. The staggering amount of research, as she briefly and modestly describes it, in the old Land Office sounds almost physically painful to us now in an age of online books and research. The fruits of her labors, however, became the basis for most subsequent lists compiled of the Alamo men and her work is most likely cited in nearly every post-1931 Alamo book that you have in your collection right now.

In the intervening decades between when Ms. Williams wrote this study and when I edited it, a few new Alamo controversies have erupted. The accepted verified Alamo roll has changed, but only slightly. I have not attempted to update Ms. Williams's findings, to add or subtract men from her verified list. I believe that it stands alone as a sturdy foundation for future researchers and students of Texas history.

Though I much prefer, as the early settlers of this place did, the term "Texian," I resisted temptation to add that significant lowercase "i" each time Ms. Williams referred to the "Texans." Spanish language words, such as alcalde and ayunta-miento, normally italicized because they don't appear in our standard English dictionaries, are not italicized here. I feel that these words are likely familiar to the ilk of person who would purchase and read a tome such as this one. And, finally, it is worth noting that certain words appear in this text that are deemed racially charged today but were not so in 1836, nor would they have created a stir in the first half of the 20th century. These terms have not been changed or omitted.

I would like to lovingly dedicate this edition of *The Alamo Defenders* to my dear-est friend, Mark Pusateri, who, a long time ago, fostered my love of Texas history and who continues to passionately cultivate his own.

Michelle M. Haas, Managing Editor
Seven Palms - Rockport, Texas

PREFACE

For almost a hundred years the story of the siege and fall of the Alamo has been told and retold; the theme has so often been woven into poetry, legend and romance that practically all the world has heard of this dramatic and tragic episode in the war of Texas independence. But the very completeness of the Mexican victory, the utter despoliation of the fort and the burning of all Texan muster rolls, gave rise to a number of puzzling problems concerning this event, questions that have never been satisfactorily answered. How many Texans died at the Alamo? Who were they and whence had they come? How many Mexicans died there? When did David Crockett arrive at Bexar? Was he accompanied by a band of his Tennessee friends, or did he come alone? Who were the brave men from Gonzales who went to Travis's aid on March 1? Where were the ashes of the Texans finally buried? Questions such as these have remained unanswered for almost a century, and this study was begun with the aim of investigating all documents and accounts which could be found that would shed light on these dark spots in the Alamo story. The majority of the questions have been answered with a fair degree of certainty, but others will probably remain unsolved for all time.

The materials for the study are voluminous. There are several great collections of official documents. Both at the State Library and at the General Land Office there are two or three large collections of manuscripts; there are in the University Archives memoirs, reminiscences and records left by contemporaries and the Mexican participants, besides the many histories that have been written concerning the Texas Revolution, of which the fall of the Alamo was a key event. Moreover, there are the newspaper accounts of various phases of the story. All this material was carefully investigated, brought together, compared, paralleled. Where it has seemed possible or wise to do so, conclusions have been drawn and brief statements made, but throughout the pages of the study, an effort has been maintained to present the original document if it would carry forward the narrative.

My greatest acknowledgment is due to a number of persons who have given me advice and assistance in the solving of these problems. To Dr. Alex Dienst, Professor Samuel E. Asbury, and Mr. Harbert Davenport, all Texas historians of recognized ability, I am indebted for much information and encouragement during the early period of my research. To Mr. Davenport, especially, I owe thanks for a careful, rather drastic, but, on the whole, constructive criticism that he found the time and patience to write on my Master's thesis on this same subject. While I have not been able to accept his views in many instances, his criticism has made my later study of the subject far deeper and broader than I should have deemed otherwise necessary. Without the friendly spirit and helpful attitude of the men at the General Land Office, I could never have reconstructed the Alamo muster roll, for the file clerks, Mr. Joe McKinney and Mr. Bobby Robison, literally pulled thousands of files for my benefit, and the commissioner, Mr. J. H. Walker, gave me invaluable assistance in the interpretation of the documents. To Mr. E. W. Winkler, librarian of the University of Texas, and to Mrs. Mattie Austin Hatcher and Miss Winnie Allen, archivists, also to Miss Harriet Smither, archivist of the State Library, I am grateful for many kindnesses in locating materials. To Dr. C. W. Ramsdell, I also wish to extend my thanks for a friendly interest and for helpful suggestions. Finally, I am especially indebted to Dr. E. C. Barker for his consistent, patient kindness throughout my study and for the careful reading and the scholarly, constructive criticism of my work. I shall always consider that one of the greatest privileges of my life is the fact that I have had the opportunity to pursue my graduate studies under his direction.

Amelia Williams
The University of Texas
February 17, 1931

CHAPTER I
STORM CLOUDS OVER MEXICO

The siege and fall of the Alamo is the most dramatic and the most generally known of any single event in Texas history. The very completeness of the Mexican victory, the stubborn defense of the fort by the gallant Travis and his brave men, are deeds that have so stirred human imagination and sympathy that practically all the world has heard the story of this heroic feat in the cause of Texas liberty. And today whenever the name "Texas" is called, it is likely to bring back to memory Thomas Jefferson Green's brief but graphic account of this heroic tragedy: "Thermopylae had her messenger of defeat, but the Alamo had none."

To say one will defend a thing "to the death," has, for ages, been a figure of speech to express extreme resoluteness. The Texans brought that phrase to fruition at the Alamo, and a cause for which nearly two-hundred men literally fought till they died is one to stimulate the imagination and to enlist the sympathetic admiration of mankind. It is not, however, the purpose of this study to stress the dramatic element of the subject, nor to paint a word picture of that brief but awful carnage of March 6, 1836. That service has already been rendered and with great skill. Rather, the purpose of this study is to construct from all sources now available a clear, unimpassioned account of that event, and to compile as complete and correct a list as possible of the names of the men who fell with Travis. In order that the significance of the fall of the Alamo may be clearly and fully appreciated, the conditions that antedated and led up to the Texas Revolution of 1835-1836, of which movement the siege and fall of the Alamo was but one episode, must be understood.

In 1800, in the Third Treaty of San Ildefonso, Napoleon Bonaparte regained the Louisiana territory from Spain and reunited it to France under the pledge that it should never again be alienated. The terms of the treaty did not specify the boundaries of the lands being returned, however. In 1803, the territory was sold to the United States in the Louisiana Purchase and those undefined boundaries became a point of contention between the United States and Spain. The question of boundary continued to be a matter of dispute until 1819, when the United States, in negotiations which resulted in the purchase of Florida, gave up all claim to Texas lands lying west of the Sabine River.

Long prior to this event, the population of the United States had been moving ever westward, and especially after the American Revolution, the march continued with ever-increasing momentum. As early as 1785, we find the cross-boundary horse trader, Philip Nolan, in Texas, where he was killed in 1801 by the Spanish. He was followed by a group of adventurers whom Spain was ever on the alert to circumvent, but who were men of no great political ambition, like Sibley, Banks, and Davenport. Then came the more dangerous lot, whose projects, although they did have political significance, were abortive; these were men such as Aaron Burr, Magee, and Long.

In the face of this westward movement on the part of the Americans, the Spaniards in Mexico became troubled. They feared American aggression into their rich mining districts and, as early as 1806, relations between the United States and Spain were at the breaking point over the boundary between Louisiana and Mexico. For a time war seemed inevitable. Spain stubbornly claimed that her territory extended to the Arroyo Hondo, a creek seven miles east of the Sabine River, while the United States contended that its boundary reached the Sabine if not the Rio Bravo. War was averted by a personal agreement between General Wilkinson, the American official in command of the Mississippi Valley, and the Spanish officials in Mexico. By this arrangement, the Neutral Ground, a sort of no man's land, was created between the Arroyo Hondo and the Sabine River. It was agreed that in this strip of territory neither country should exercise authority. Consequently it was devoid of law and government and it became the refuge of desperadoes and criminals of every type.

This condition of affairs held for fifteen years, when Spain and the United States ended it by the negotiations in 1819. During this time many of the men from the Neutral Ground drifted into east Texas and made illegal settlements. Thus it was that conditions engendered in this lawless land were partly responsible for the Fredonian Rebellion, the catastrophe that first aroused the suspicions of Mexico against her Anglo-Saxon settlers.

From 1808 to 1821, Mexico was fighting her own war for independence from Spain. During this struggle, the United States sympathized with Mexico and helped her in an indirect way, for while American pirates under the leadership of Jean Lafitte merely harried other commerce on the Gulf, they practically destroyed that of Spain. Upon gaining her independence in 1821, Mexico set up an empire with Iturbide on the throne. This new emperor's career was short and stormy, and by 1823 another revolution had upset his throne and had driven him from the country. But before that fleeting empire's laws were entirely suspended, a colonization grant had been made to the Austins to settle families from Louisiana in Texas under the empresario system.

The Mexicans now declared for a republic. But what kind of a republic? Should it be federal, or centralized? Over this fundamental point of difference, two bitterly opposed political parties developed: the Federalists and the Centralists. These two parties were destined to keep Mexico in the throes of revolution, and her government in chaos for more than half a century, but in 1824, the Federalists won the argument temporarily and adopted a federal constitution, closely patterned after that of the United States. In order to establish this constitution, however, Mexico took nearly an opposite course than had the United States took in the adoption of its government. In Mexico the highly centralized nation had to disintegrate itself so that states could be created. The states, thus created, then federated into a union. The public lands, the possession of the central government, were distributed among the various states for administrative control.

From 1824 to 1825, colonization laws—both state and federal—were enacted which opened up the unsettled lands of Mexico to foreign colonization on very liberal terms. Both the nation and the states cordially invited settlers to come. Land was granted almost free for the taking, with the governments pledging to the settlers a guarantee of safety and security of person and of property. Moreover, the newness of the land and the lack of developed resources made it seem reasonable, also, that these newcomers should be free for a period from taxation and tariff duties. Accordingly, they were granted immunity from these contributions for a period of seven years. Indeed, the only requirements demanded of the immigrants were that:

(1) They be Catholics, or willing to become such

(2) They show certificates of good character and habit

(3) They take the oath of allegiance to the newly established republic[1]

The avowed object of the government in making these laws was "to control the savage Indian and to build up a strong, productive frontier that would serve as a sort of buffer territory between Mexico and the United States, to ward off the cupidity of the latter."[2] To these ideas was joined the notion that the plains of Texas were barren of real value, and that the gain that Mexico would derive from settling them with Americans and other foreigners would be a return of protection for nothing invested. Whatever of self-deception or of true policy there may have been concerning the matter, these laws were the letting down of barriers that permitted a perfect flood of immigration, previously dammed against the eastern border, to overflow into Texas. Sooner or later these hardy, adventurous frontiersmen, under some pretense, legal or otherwise, would have possessed themselves of these coveted lands anyway, but the Mexican colonization laws of 1823-1825 certainly hastened the process of the taking. By 1834, flourishing settlements had been planted from the Sabine to the Colorado, and in this same year, Colonel Juan Almonte, whom the federal government had sent to inspect these colonies, reported a population of 36,300, of whom 21,000 were civilized and 15,300 were Indians—10,800 savage and 4,500 friendly.[3] Kennedy and Yoakum both think that Almonte's estimate of the colonial populations is too low,

1 William Kennedy, *Texas*, II, 4.

2 *Ibid*, II, 3.

3 Homer Thrall, *Pictorial History of Texas*, 175.

and they declare that at this time the Anglo-American population in Texas aggregated 30,000, exclusive of more than 2,000 negroes.[4] Dr. Eugene C. Barker agrees with this estimate, for in speaking of the number of colonists, he says: "My impression, derived from a somewhat minute acquaintance with the field, is that the total population in 1835, when the Texas Revolution began, was around 30,000—men, women, and children."[5] Although a few of these immigrants had come from Europe, the majority were from the United States, and no doubt a considerable number had arrived after Almonte's report was made.

They had settled under two systems: (1) that of the independent colonist, by which system each settler got his grant of land directly from the government and had all transactions concerning it directly with the government; (2) the empresario system by which empresarios, or land agents, got from the government permission to settle, at their own expense, a given number of families on unoccupied lands. For each hundred families settled, the empresario was given for his own use five square leagues of land (22,142 acres) of grazing quality, and five labors (885 acres) of arable land.

During the colonial period, twenty-six empresarios took out grants. By far, the most conspicuous and well known of these men was Stephen F. Austin, whose first grant was made by the Spanish government in 1821, ratified by the empire under Emperor Iturbide, and reaffirmed by the republic. Under the colonization laws of the republic he took out several other grants, formed a total of four colonies and, in all, brought in 1,540 families to Texas.[6] Austin was the leading figure of the entire colonization period and by his wonderful sagacity, his diplomatic genius, and his long and patient service, he well deserves the title "Father of Texas."

For the most part, the early Texans were typical American frontiersmen. They were hardy, bold, aggressive, self-reliant men, engaged chiefly in farming and cattle raising. There were to be found, however, in every settlement, a few professional men, especially doctors and lawyers, as well as shopkeepers, tavern owners, horse traders, and others who could thrive by supplying the needs of a simple agricultural community. The opinion commonly held in the United States and in Europe was that the Texans were all criminals and fugitives from justice, and that belief was erroneous. These men were industrious, productive and, on the whole, their morality ranked high.

Austin attests to the group's overall character in a letter penned March 31, 1829. In his letter to Thomas White, he says, in part on the subject:

4 Kennedy, *Texas*, II, 79-80; Henderson Yoakum, *History of Texas*, I, 327.

5 E. C. Barker, *Mexico and Texas, 1821-1835*, 21.

6 Report made by J. F. Perry and Henry Austin, legal representatives of Stephen F. Austin, Empresario, to the Senate of the Republic of Texas, November 18, 1836, *Domestic Correspondence* (1836), State Library.

> The settlers of this colony, taken *en masse*, are greatly superior to
> any new country or frontier I have ever seen, and would lose noth-
> ing in comparison with some of the oldest counties of many of the
> Southern and Western states...in proportion to our numbers, we
> are as enlightened, as moral, as good, and as "law abiding" men as
> can be found in any part of the United States...

They were not very religious, however, according to the ordinary interpretation of the word. To enter the country required a certificate of Catholic faith, but
there were few true Catholics among them. They as well as their leader, Austin,
interpreted this governmental requirement liberally. In a manifesto issued to his
colonists Austin said: "I wish the settlers to remember that the Roman Catholic
is the religion of this nation. We must respect the Catholic religion."[7] So after
having furnished a certificate of that faith for purposes of entering the country,
the colonists were very apt to practice none. One observer in 1831 noted:

> The people of this country seem to have forgotten that there is such
> a commandment as "Remember the Sabbath Day"...They spend this
> day visiting, driving stock and breaking mustangs. I have not heard a
> sermon since I left Kentucky except at a camp meeting in Arkansas.[8]

They had taken the oath of allegiance to the Mexican government, and the
majority of them honestly meant to be loyal to their adopted country. They appreciated their beautiful and rich lands, given to them on such liberal terms; at
the same time they fully realized that only by their own trials, privations and
hard work had they built their homes and changed the land, valueless before
their coming, into prosperous farms and ranches. They attended to their own
business and did not participate in the muddle of Mexican politics, since the seat
of their state government was far removed at Saltillo, and local government was
slow in being organized and was poorly established. The central government was
in constant turmoil, under the control of the Federalists one month and under
that of the Centralists the next. The Mexicans were simply not prepared for
the complexities of federal government. For more than three centuries, their
political training had been under the highly centralized system of one of the
most absolute monarchies of Europe, and so they should not be too severely
blamed for not immediately learning the meaning of democracy. Even to their
educated men—men who professed republican principles and who were leaders
of the Republican party—self-government, freedom of speech, of the press and
of conscience were but sweet sounding phrases of whose practical application
they knew next to nothing.

---

7 Dudley G. Wooten, *A Comprehensive History of Texas*, I, 494.
8 W. B. Dewees, *Letters from Texas*, 137.

Although the Texans took little part in Mexican politics, they had not left behind them their democratic principles and ideals. To them, self-government, liberty, freedom of conscience and speech were as necessary as the air they breathed; moreover, the conditions of their lives forced them to be self reliant. They were ready to conform to laws in the making of which they'd had a voice, or in which they saw justice and equity. They had come to Texas expecting that a republic which modeled its constitution on that of the United States would practice the same free institutions, and so they stubbornly refused to accept the principles of centralism that were set up in the face of the Constitution of 1824.

Furthermore, these colonists were of Anglo-Saxon descent, and it is the nature of the Anglo-Saxon man to refuse to be dominated by an inferior race. Long before 1836, the settlers had come to consider the Mexicans an inferior race, to despise them as they did Indians and Negroes and to ignore Mexican law. For the most part, the colonists saw the Mexicans at their worst. It is true that in the distinctively Mexican settlement at San Antonio de Bexar, there were a considerable number of high class Mexicans, men of high principles and of keen intellect and fair education. The majority of these men were willing and eager to do what they could to further the interests of Texas; they were staunch Republicans, and later joined hands with the Anglo-American Texans in their battles for independence. But few of the colonists ever had the chance to come in contact with these Mexicans in San Antonio, and the few native settlers that Mexico was able to introduce into other parts of Texas were ex-convicts and the very dregs of the country. The soldiers in the garrisons in Mexican Texas were of the same type.

This difference of race, of language, of ideals, of laws—this general lack of understanding between the two peoples—developed conditions bound to produce conflict—and it started very early on. As early as 1827 or 1828, the Mexicans were already suspicious and jealous of the rapid increase and prosperity of the American settlers. Trouble had arisen over land grants. Notorious for this trouble were the grants made to Hayden Edwards in 1825. Before the year had passed, this empresario quarreled with many early settlers already living on his lands before he took out the grant, but who had not made the proper arrangements with the government to secure title to their holdings. Edwards refused to recognize the titles of these colonists. This squabble over land titles was followed by disputes over supposed usurpations of the powers of the state by this empresario. The result of the matter was that Victor Blanco, the vice-governor—then acting as governor—banished Edwards from Texas in 1826.

This disturbance brought on the ill-fated Fredonian Rebellion, led by Edwards who drew some of the Cherokee Indians into his scheme by a proposal to divide Texas between the new state (Fredonian Republic) and the red men. Edwards had taken it for granted that the other colonists would support him. Instead, the

Austin settlers joined the government forces to quell the insurrection; the Indians were separated from the project and the leaders were forced to flee. Austin then secured amnesty for those who would surrender. Nothing had been gained. Although the bulk of the American colonists had proved their loyalty to their adopted country, the incident still looked bad. The Mexicans had a just cause for suspicion and mistrust.[9]

Thoroughly frightened by the Fredonian Rebellion, because it showed to what lengths many of the American settlers outside Austin's colony would go to effect their ends, the Mexican authorities decided that they would have to adopt a policy of repression if Mexico were to remain dominant in Texas. Accordingly, two acts, hateful to the colonists and aimed, at least on the surface, at abolishing slavery, were passed in order to check or to completely stop immigration from the United States. The first was the Emancipation Act of 1829, urged on by General José María Tornel, and the other was the Decree of April 6, 1830, proposed by Lucas Alamán.

After the senate had refused to pass an emancipation bill, Tornel persuaded President Guerrero to issue the emancipation decree of 1829. It aimed to limit the growth of farming immigration by forbidding the settlers to possess slaves. But owing to the firm and friendly cooperation of the local Mexican officials at San Antonio with Austin, this decree was soon set aside, so far as it concerned Texas. It seems that the Mexicans were not so averse to the *condition* of slavery as they were to the word "slavery," so when the slavery question again became the target for Mexican opposition, the Texans continued to import negroes but called them "indentured servants." Thus while the development of the slavery system in Texas was curtailed, it was never absolutely abolished at the hands of the Mexican government.[10]

Neither was the settlement of Texas a pre-organized plot of the "slavocracy," as several American writers have claimed.[11] The slave question at this time was merely an economic incident in the internal history of Texas.

Another threat that loomed on the horizon and fueled Mexican suspicion of the loyalty of the colonists (and rightfully so) were the repeated proposals of the United States to purchase Texas. To Mexican statesmen, it seemed a grave error and a real danger to continue to permit the influx of such great numbers of Americans into a territory so eagerly desired by their mother country. Hence, the Decree of April 6, 1830 as proposed by Lucas Alamán, Secretary of Foreign Relations, at the instigation of General Terán. This law, in general terms, did the following:

9 E. C. Barker, *Life of Stephen F. Austin*, 192-199; G. L. Rives, *The United States and Mexico*, 191-192; Yoakum, *History of Texas*, 230-250.

10 Lester G. Bugbee, "Slavery in Early Texas," *Political Science Quarterly*, XIII.

11 Barker, *The Life of Stephen F. Austin*, 203-260.

(1) Encouraged colonization of Mexicans in Texas

(2) Forbade the importation of slaves

(3) Ordered independent settlers, not on regular grants, to be ejected

(4) Required passports for entrance from the northern frontiers

(5) Prohibited emigrants from settling in Mexican territory contiguous to the nation from which they had come, and moreover, all contracts not already completed and not in harmony with the law should be suspended[12]

Although it was never efficiently enforced, the Decree did materially check immigration and it aroused a tremendous amount of ill feeling. General Terán himself was sent to enforce it. His plan was to establish a number of military posts within supporting distance of each other, and to introduce large numbers of Mexican colonists. But it was difficult to get Mexican colonists for Texas. Convicts and the most undesirable class of peons were sent. The ayuntamiento of Bexar plead against the sacrifice of public money for the purpose of bringing Mexicans to Texas as colonists if they had to be roped together to be brought there.[13] Concerning the soldiery in the new garrisons, H. H. Bancroft says, "they were for the most part convicts and the worst class of men in Mexico."[14] A decree passed on April 29, 1826 indicates a preference for this class of men to bolster the Mexican muster rolls. It allowed the ayuntamientos, with the assistance of the armed forces, to set conscription quotas. The preferred men to fill these quotas were "vagrants and disorderly persons," followed by single men who could be spared by their families. When all else failed, recruits could be obtained by "entrapment and decoy."[15] These were the soldiers who were to enforce the unpopular colonization Decree of 1830. The Mexican government finally came to the realization that the law was an impossible measure and it was rescinded in 1834. It had served little purpose except to arouse the indignation of the American settlers against the Mexican government, and to cause them to manifest a resentment that bordered on rebellion.

It will be remembered that an Act of September, 1823, had exempted the settlers from duty on certain necessary articles for a period of seven years. This exemption lent itself to much abuse. Smuggling was popular among the colonists so, when in 1831 the term of the exemption expired, there was widespread dissatisfaction at the enforcement of the payment of duties. Kentucky native turned Mexican soldier, John (Juan) Davis Bradburn, was seen as a particularly obnoxious figure to the Texans. Sent by the Mexican government to locate a site for a customhouse and fort near Galveston Bay, Bradburn established Anahuac,

---

12 Alleine Howren, "The Origin of the Decree of April 6, 1830," *Texas Historical Quarterly*, XVI, 416-422.

13 Vicente Filisola, *Guerra de Tejas*, I, 162-165, 289.

14 H. H. Bancroft, *North Mexican States and Texas*, II, 15.

15 H. P. N. Gammel, *Laws of Texas*, I, 42.

formerly Perry's Point, at the mouth of the Trinity River. He assisted George Fisher, the collector of customs at Anahuac, in employing arbitrary and retroactive collection methods with ships already in Galveston Bay and on the Brazos River. These practices were of great offense to the colonists, but the outrages of Bradburn and his soldiers were many.

Bradburn pressed supplies for his garrison and used slave labor in the erection of military buildings without compensating the owners of the slaves. He encouraged a spirit of revolt among the slaves by telling them that it was the intent of the law to make them free. He harbored two runaway slaves from Louisiana, enlisted them in his detachment and refused to surrender them to the owner, who demanded their return. Several colonists were arrested on Bradburn's order on various pretexts and held in the guardhouse awaiting military trial.[16]

The trouble culminated in 1832 in an uprising of the colonists under the leadership of John Austin; and this disturbance finally resulted in Bradburn's removal from his command, in the prisoners being released to the civil authorities for trial and in the payment for private property that had been appropriated. The garrison declared for Santa Anna and left Anahuac to join the Liberal Army.[17] Colonel Mexía was sent from Mexico to investigate the affair, but Stephen F. Austin, who was returning from Mexico on the same ship with Mexía, succeeded in convincing the Colonel that the Texans were not to blame.[18]

The colonists, in the meantime, fearing the consequences of their actions, had held a meeting and declared for Santa Anna—at this time, the leader of the Mexican Republicans, leading a revolution against President Bustamante—and for the Constitution of 1824. Colonel Mexía, finding the Texans pacified, loyal and properly enthusiastic for his chief, induced most of the soldiers in the Texas garrisons to adopt the cause of Santa Anna. He carried them off, leaving Colonel Piedras at Nacogdoches as the only adherent to the Centralist administration in Texas. Piedras, also, soon surrendered to the new movement. Thus, in 1832, all Mexican troops were taken from Texas with the exception of a few soldiers left at Bexar and Goliad to protect those places against Indians.[19] The collectors of customs also withdrew, unable, as General Filisola states in his memoirs, "to endure the untamable spirits of the inhabitants."[20]

16 Barker, *Mexico and Texas*, 111-112; Kennedy, *Texas*, II, 5-7; Mary Austin Holley, *Texas*, 322-323; Henry Stuart Foote, *Texas*, II, 8-16.

17 Bancroft, *North Mexican States and Texas*, I, 119; E. C. Barker, "Development of the Texas Revolution," *Readings in Texas History*, 165-168.

18 Barker, *Mexico and Texas, 1821-1835*, 116.

19 Filisola, *Guerra de Tejas*, I, 127-135; Foote, *Texas*, II, 8-26; Kennedy, *Texas*, I, 361-364.

20 Filisola, *Guerra de Tejas*, I, 301.

CHAPTER II
COAHUILA, CONSULTATIONS, CONTROL

Lack of representation was a nagging thorn in the colonists' sides. In 1824, Texas had been joined to Coahuila, and this union had continued to be a source of growing aggravation to the Texans. In the first place this dual state was administered by a large Mexican majority, since of the twelve members of the single house of the state legislature ten were allotted to Coahuila and only two to Texas.[1] The capital, Saltillo, was so far removed that the Texans experienced great inconvenience in transacting the legal business necessary for their welfare. This state of affairs kept ever prominent these questions on the minds and tongues of the colonists: What is to be the future of Texas? Shall it remain a province of Mexico, subject to the hazards of an ill-defined, arbitrary jurisdiction by military officers? Shall it seek to become an independent nation? Or shall it ask for annexation to the United States?

Piedras, Bradburn, Terán, Filisola and other intelligent Mexican officials in Texas honestly believed that there was a strong sentiment throughout the American settlements for separation from Mexico.[2] The colonists, no doubt, did discuss the question among themselves. There was a good deal of loose talk on the part of hot-headed persons on both sides of the American boundary line that did much to stir up the desire for independence, and many were in favor of breaking away. But the great majority of Texans were loyal and sincerely desired to remain a part of Mexico, and in 1832, there is good evidence of a strong sentiment against independence.[3] But the Texans *did* want separation from Coahuila, and they meant to have it, for they believed that as a separate state they could set up a local government that would give them the political freedom to which they were accustomed and for which they longed. Accordingly, a call was made for a convention to meet at San Felipe on October 1, 1832.[4] The reasons for the meeting as stated in the call were twofold—to stem the tide of current misrepresentations concerning the desire of the Texans for independence, and to devise means for quelling the frequent Indian raids.

Fifty-six delegates, representatives of all the primarily Anglo-American districts except Goliad, assembled. San Antonio did not send delegates. The Goliad delegation arrived after the sitting was complete but offered their approval of

1 Gammel, *Laws of Texas*, I, 157.
2 Barker, "Stephen F. Austin and the Independence of Texas," *Texas Historical Quarterly*, XIII, 261-262; Ethel Zivley Rather, *Ibid.*, VIII, 247.
3 Barker, *Ibid.*, XIII, 261-264; Jonas Harrison to Austin, November, 30, 1832, *Austin Papers*, III, 895-896; also December 8, 1832, *Ibid.*, III; John A. Williams to Austin, December 18, 1832, *Ibid.*, III, 903-906.
4 John Henry Brown, *History of Texas*, I, 195.226.

what had transpired, then waited at San Felipe several days in hopes that San Antonio might choose to send a delegation after all. None was forthcoming. In the course of six days' session, the body adopted the following resolutions:

(1) To provide for the collection of customs until the government could send out new collectors.

(2) To ask for a grant of land for schools.

(3) To ask for a reform of the tariff.

(4) To pray for the repeal of the law of April 6, 1830.

(5) To petition for separate statehood.

It also appointed a central committee to correspond with local committees and to keep them informed concerning questions of general interest, and to call, if need be, another meeting.[5]

Conditions did not improve and another convention was called to meet six months later on April 1, 1833. The delegates were elected in March and the convention duly assembled on the day appointed. Only about a quarter of the delegates to the earlier convention assembled at the Convention of 1833. Among the sea of new faces were William H. Wharton and Sam Houston. The petitions to the central government were about the same as those adopted by the Convention of 1832, but this body, in addition, drew up and adopted a tentative constitution for the proposed new state, as well as an address to the Mexican Congress requesting its approval.[6]

Three men were appointed to carry these resolutions to Mexico City but Stephen F. Austin was the only man to go. He arrived on July 18, 1833 to find that Santa Anna, the President, had retired to his country home, leaving the government in the hands of Vice-President Gómez Farías. Although a strong federal-republican by profession, Farías opposed separate statehood for Texas. After a long wait for a formal hearing, Austin wrote a letter dated October 2, 1833 to be circulated among all the ayuntamientos in which he advised the settlers to proceed with the formation of a state under the law of May 7, 1824, even though Mexico would likely refuse to assent. The ayuntamiento of Bexar, to whom the letter was addressed, saw in it intemperance if not treason and, fearing to involve Bexar in brewing trouble, forwarded the letter to the authorities of the national government. In the meanwhile, Austin had finally effected the abrogation of the hated eleventh article of the Decree of April 6, 1830 and, feeling that this was all he was likely to accomplish, was returning to Texas when he was arrested and carried back to Mexico City. No specific charges were brought but by February of 1834, Stephen F. Austin was incarcerated in a dungeon of the old inquisition building where he remained in close confinement for three months. He was

5 Gammel, *Laws of Texas*, I, 477-503; Brown, *History of Texas*, I, 197-213.

6 David B. Edward, *The History of Texas*, 196-205; Yoakum, *History of Texas*, I, 469-482.

never given a trial but was held a prisoner, part of the time out of confinement under bail where he was only free to move about the Federal District of Mexico, until July 1835.[7]

The state government of Coahuila y Tejas was in a chaotic condition due to a squabble between the cities of Saltillo and Monclova over the location of the capital,[8] but, during 1833-1834, the legislature passed a number of state laws beneficial to Texas, so the tensions in that quarter were somewhat relieved. Among these new laws were measures creating several new municipalities, thus making the local condition somewhat better. Texas was divided into three executive departments, each under a *jefe político*, who was to act as the direct representative of the government within the department. Two of these new departments were American in population and, in them, English was made coordinate with Spanish for legal usage. A new judicial system was also adopted which gave the Texans the right of trial by jury.[9] This system was never enacted, however, due to subsequent events.

In May of 1834, Santa Anna succeeded in dissolving the National Congress and many of the state legislatures. He then made himself dictator through the work of a council, subservient to his bidding. When Austin was finally given a hearing in November of 1833, he had eloquently pled the cause of Texas, urging the repeal of the Decree of April 6, 1830 and begging separation from Coahuila. As has been stated, the government had consented to abrogate the Decree, provided no good reasons could be found for continuing it. The new dictator and council in 1834 decreed that the law should be repealed but denied Texas separate statehood; furthermore, Santa Anna decided to send 4,000 soldiers to San Antonio "to protect the coast and frontier."[10] This decision cause grave apprehension in Texas. By the time Stephen F. Austin was released in July of 1835, he had become thoroughly convinced of the futility of hoping for stable conditions in Texas under the operation of the existing Mexican government.[11]

Austin arrived in Texas in September of 1835 to find a revolution brewing. There had been a good deal of local squabbling during his absence and two strong, well-defined parties had developed among the Texans since the initial Convention of 1832. One, the peace party, was composed of conservatives. These were the calm-minded men who believed with Austin that their differences with Mexico could be ameliorated and the Mexican officials conciliated. Thus they could

7 "The Prison Journal of Stephen F. Austin," *Texas Historical Quarterly*, II, 184, 196; Rives, *The United States and Mexico*, I, 223-255.

8 Bancroft, *North Mexican States and Texas*, II, 143-145.

9 Gammel, *Laws of Texas*, I, 197, 242, 254-255.

10 Yoakum, *Texas History*, I, 325-326.

11 "The Prison Journal of Stephen F. Austin," *Texas Historical Quarterly*, II, 183, 210; "Release of Stephen F. Austin from Prison," *Ibid.*, XIV, 155-163.

remain loyal to their adopted country. The other party, composed of the hotspurs of the colonies, wanted to fight for what they regarded as their rights. The peace party was undoubtedly in the saddle during the middle and latter part of the summer of 1835.[12] Nevertheless, there was need for concerted action, and so a number of local meetings were held in order to discuss the situation. The most noteworthy of these meetings was the one at Columbia where it was decided to make a call for a general consultation to meet at Washington on October 15.

When Austin arrived back in the colonies, a dinner was given in his honor at Brazoria. The Texans were somewhat doubtful that he approved of their doings and were eager to convene with him and learn his attitude toward the condition of affairs. They greatly rejoiced that he favored the calling of the General Consultation and, on September 12, a Committee of Vigilance and Safety was organized at San Felipe with him as a member. From this time until the revolution was well advanced, Stephen F. Austin was at the head of affairs. His motto seems to have been, "Texas first—under Mexico if possible—but always Texas."[13]

At this point, it is well to remember that when Santa Anna became dictator of Mexico and dissolved Congress, Texas and Zacatecas were the only states to protest and resolve to make a stand for the republic under the Constitution of 1824. Both of these states again sent up protests when the law of March 31, 1835, which reduced each state militia to one militiaman for every five hundred inhabitants,[14] was enacted. Zacatecas flatly refused to obey; whereupon Santa Anna marched some three to four thousand troops against that state and, on May 10, in a bloody battle followed by brutal butchery, Zacatecas was crushed. Now, General Cos, with an army fresh from victory, was on his way to force the Texans to obey the laws which they had either been evading or disregarding. The Texans were now facing a question that required a speedy and determined answer. Should they, too, submit to the tyranny of Centralism? Should they yield to the will of the dictator, give up their arms and suffer their country to be garrisoned with strong military posts? Should they weakly consent to live under the rule and sway of the military? They must do this, or they must prepare for war and prepare without delay, for the enemy was advancing upon them.[15] In the face of such alternatives, war was inevitable.

---

12 E. C. Barker, "James H. Miller and Edward Gritten," *Texas Historical Quarterly*, XIII, 145-153.

13 Yoakum, *Texas History*, I, 325.

14 Foote, *Texas*, II, 89.

15 R. M. Williamson, "July 4th Address, 1835," *Lamar Papers*, I, 207-213.

CHAPTER III
TO CAPTURE, HOLD & NEGLECT

The first shot of the Texas Revolution was fired over a cannon at Gonzales on October 2, 1835. In pursuance of the Mexican policy to disarm the Texans, Colonel Domingo Ugartechea had demanded the gun. The Texans outright refused to give it up. The engagement that resulted was rather trivial, but it ended in victory for the Texans. Six days later, October 8, the fort at Goliad was attacked and taken by the Texans. On the 28th of the same month, James Bowie and Colonel James Fannin with a small company, met a body of Mexicans under Ugartechea near Mission Concepción and completely routed them, killing about one hundred and capturing their field pieces.[1]

On October 4, Austin had sent out a circular letter to the committees of safety announcing that war had been declared against military despotism. On the 8th, he sent out a general appeal for volunteers, appointing Gonzales as army headquarters. Men flocked to Gonzales and, by the 13th, a small army of about 350 men had been formed. These men marched to an area within about eight miles of Bexar and pitched camp to await reinforcements. With the exception of the battle at Concepción, there was no fighting on any scale until December. By that time, Stephen F. Austin had left the army to serve as Commissioner to the United States, and General Burleson was the ranking officer.

Burleson commanded an army of about 800 men, divided into two divisions, commanded by Colonel F. W. Johnson and Benjamin R. Milam. They led their divisions to Bexar and, between December 5th and December 10th, stormed the town, compelling General Cos to surrender. After some haggling over the details, articles of capitulation were signed, allowing the Mexican officers to retain their arms and private property in exchange for their promise to retire into the interior of Mexico and not to oppose in any way the reestablishment of the Constitution of 1824. The six hundred convicts-turned-soldiers who had arrived at Bexar as reinforcements to Cos just before the surrender were to be taken back beyond the Rio Grande, accompanied by a small escort of armed soldiers. The rest of the Mexicans were free to remain in Texas or to go with Cos as they pleased. Private property at Bexar was restored to its owners; private citizens were not to be molested, and Texas was to furnish Cos with provisions at the prevailing prices of the day. Cos's losses are not known exactly but were relatively large, perhaps 200 men. According to Dr. Amos Pollard, chief surgeon at Bexar, the Texan loss was one officer, Milam, and a private killed. Four officers and twenty-one men were wounded.[2]

1 Bowie & Fannin to S. F. Austin, October 29, 1835, *Archives of the State Dept.*, Book No. 3, p. 13.
2 Amos Pollard to Governor Smith, February 13, 1836, *Army Papers*, State Library.

Having given up their munitions of war, Cos and his soldiers were allowed to retire, under parole, beyond the Rio Grande. Thus, by December 15, 1835, the Alamo, destined ere long to be the scene of the tragic events of our main narrative, was in control of the Texans, and was occupied by their volunteer army.

The proposal for a general consultation of all Texas had been made in August, 1835. It was to meet October 15, but there was, in the first place, some misunderstanding concerning the place of meeting. Moreover, by October, many of the elected delegates were in the army with Austin, so that those who did come together on the appointed day agreed to postpone the meeting until November 1. In the meantime, Stephen F. Austin had founded at San Felipe a sort of executive committee, composed of the representatives of the local Committees of Vigilance and Safety. This committee styled itself the "Permanent Council." It took charge of the work of organizing the defense against the Indians and in raising and supplying volunteers for the army. In fact, the Permanent Council was the only government that Texas had during October of 1835.[3]

By November 3, a quorum of delegates had arrived in San Felipe and the consultation began. First up for consideration was to decide whether to proclaim independence from Mexico, or merely to stand up for the Constitution of 1824. By this time a strong independence party had developed. It was composed chiefly of the radicals who had made up the old war party of the previous two or three years; but the majority of the fifty-six delegates assembled in this convention were conservatives— members of the old peace party. Most of these men, perhaps, believed that sooner or later independence would come, but they deemed it inexpedient to take the steps at this time. They argued that those who had elected them had not instructed for independence, nor had they intended it. They felt that a premature declaration for independence might alienate sympathy from their cause in the United States, and that a declaration to uphold the Constitution of 1824 would enlist the sympathy and assistance of the Mexican Federalists.[4] Consequently, the declaration adopted merely proclaimed the causes for taking up arms and asserted the Texans' claim to sustain, by force of arms, their rights and liberties under the federal constitution of Mexico as adopted in 1824.[5]

Having defined their objective for taking up arms, the Consultation proceeded to organize a provisional government. This was to have a twofold nature, providing for both the civil and the military organization, later described as "triumphs of potential confusion and conflict of authority."[6]

3 Barker, "The Texas Revolutionary Army," *Texas Historical Quarterly*, IX, 227; Rives, *The United States and Mexico*, I, 286.

4 Gammel, "Journals of the Consultation," *Laws of Texas*, I, 16-22.

5 Gammel, *Ibid.*, I, 522-523; E. C. Barker, "Declaration of Causes for Taking Up Arms Against Mexico," *Texas Historical Quarterly*, XV, 173-185; Filisola, *Guerra de Tejas*, II, 173-176.

6 George Pierce Garrison, *Texas*, 197.

The civil government was to consist of a governor and a lieutenant-governor, both elected by the Consultation, and a council, made up of one member from each municipality and elected by its delegates. But the powers of the government were ill-defined. The governor was to be "clothed with full and ample executive powers," and was to be the commander-in-chief of the regular and volunteer armies and the navy. The lieutenant-governor was to preside over the council, and to perform the duties of the governor in the event of his absence, death or other inability to serve. The council's functions, although chiefly legislative, were to be also partly appointive and advisory. It was to enact such laws "as in its opinion the emergency of the country required, ever keeping in mind the army in the field," and advise and assist the governor in the discharge of his duties. Provisional courts were also created. These were to administer the Common Law of England in all criminal cases, and grant writs of *habeas corpus*—all trials to be by jury.[7]

The Consultation of November 1835 also adopted provisions for the organization of an army, and for military defense. There was to be a regular army composed of 1,120 men, enlisted for two years and an indefinite number of volunteers, variously organized.[8] A major-general, chosen by the consultation, was to be the "commander-in-chief of all the forces called into public service during the war." He was to be appointed by the Consultation, commissioned by the governor, and subject to the orders of both the governor and the council.[9] The powers of commander-in-chief were granted to the governor upon the creation of the provisional government, but similar powers, seemingly only over the regular army, were conferred upon the major-general later in the Consultation. There was an air of ambiguity over who was in charge of whom and this resulted in many a squabble later, especially during the Alamo siege.

Henry Smith of Brazoria was elected governor receiving thirty-one votes against Austin's twenty-two. Smith had been a resident of Brazoria since 1821 and was a member of the Convention of 1833. He became an alcalde and acting political chief in 1834. Smith was a radical, outspoken leader of the war and independence parties. He was known for his quick-tempered nature and obstinance. The fact that the radical Smith defeated the conservative Austin—that farsighted statesman and genius of diplomacy—shows clearly that the sentiment for independence was already strong. James W. Robinson was elected lieutenant-governor, while Sam Houston was made major-general of the Texan armies. Branch T. Archer, William H. Wharton and Stephen F. Austin were appointed agents to the United States in the hope that they might negotiate loans and induce other means of assistance.

7 Gammel, "Journals of the Consultation," *Laws of Texas*, I, 539-542. Brown, *History of Texas*, I, 394; Garrison, *Texas*, 197.

8 Barker, "The Texas Revolutionary Army," *Texas Historical Quarterly*, IX, 227.

9 Gammel, "Journals of the Consultation," *Laws of Texas*, I, 543-544.

While the Consultation was in session, the volunteer troops, with Austin in command, were still camped near Bexar. Austin was an organizer, a diplomat and a statesman, but he was not a fighter. The duties of a military leader were irksome to him, so he was glad to be relieved of the command of the army in order to prepare for the duties of diplomatic agent to the United States. The command of the troops in the field was left to General Burleson, but it was "Old Ben Milam" who led the Texans into San Antonio and compelled the surrender of Cos on December 10, 1835. Milam was killed just as victory was assured and Francis W. Johnson took his place as leader. After the taking of Bexar, most of the Texas colonists, who had been in the army since October, were discharged and hurried home to Christmas dinners. Most of the foreign volunteers, however, remained in possession of San Antonio and of them there were a considerable number.

By the time Cos had evacuated Bexar, the provisional government had been in operation for about a month. Already, the murmurs of the jealous bickering and ridiculous squabbles between the Governor and the Council that would make the entire 107 days of the provisional government's existence a farce, were being heard. The fundamental cause of all the trouble was the fact that a majority of the Council differed from the Governor in their opinions concerning the best policies for the new government. It was largely a difference of judgment concerning the wisdom of adopting an offensive or defensive policy for the army. For the most part, the Council was composed of conservatives who were in favor of living up to the plan adopted by the Consultation in its pronouncement of November 7. They also believed in the "Federal Party of the Interior," and desired to cooperate with these Mexican liberals in restoring the Constitution of 1824. The Governor, on the other hand, was a most radical advocate for Texas independence. He did not trust Mexicans at all and wanted no dealings with them, for he honestly believed that "in the end they would all prove inimical and treacherous."[10]

Petty jealousies also sprang up concerning the exercise of authority in matters of detail, such as methods of drawing on the treasury and appointment of offi-cials.[11] As has been said before, the powers of the Governor and Council were ill-defined; they were practically coordinate. For instance, the plan of government as drawn up by the Consultation had not given the veto to the Governor, but in passing an ordinance to govern the method of legislation, the Council made pro-vision for the exercise of this power and thus conferred it.[12] Strangely enough, the Governor vetoed the ordinance itself, but henceforth exercised the power it conferred, and the Council made no protest except when he used the power

10 Smith to Council, December 9, 1835, *Governor and Council Papers*, State Library; Brown, *His-tory of Texas*, I, 443. Gammel, "Proceedings of the General Council," *Laws of Texas*, I, 644.

11 W. Roy Smith, "The Quarrel Between Governor Smith and the Provisional Government of the Republic," *Texas Historical Quarterly*, V, 292-296.

12 Gammel, "Proceedings of the General Council," *Laws of Texas*, I, 583-584.

against their appointments. Vetoes fell thick and fast, but the Council easily found the two-thirds majority necessary to overrule them. The Council itself changed with great frequency containing few of its original members and, according to Yoakum, "the change had not been for the better in either wisdom or integrity."[13]

It was concerning the army and military affairs that the controversy burned the hottest. The Council believed in and supported the local volunteers. The Governor was convinced that the state government should "bring everything under its own proper control," which meant that all the volunteers should be placed under the control of the commander-in-chief.[14] Moreover, the Council, possessed with the idea of sending troops into Mexico and filled with the same love for meddling in military matters that has historically characterized American legislative bodies, undertook to appoint officers in the Texan army, and to direct campaigns, without deference to the views of the Governor or the Major-General. The quarrel finally centered itself around a potential expedition into Matamoros.

Before the capture of Bexar, even before Austin had left the army, a plan was brewing for the capture of Matamoros. Matamoros was a town of good size not far from the mouth of the Rio Grande. It was a town of great strategic importance to the Mexicans, for all of the supplies for Cos's army which were sent by water entered its port. The proceeds from its custom house were a most important source of revenue. Here, too, were to be found carpenters, blacksmiths, shoemakers and other skilled workers necessary to the welfare of an army.[15] Colonel Guerra was in charge of this post and, in the early part of November of 1835, he had an army of less than 200 men consisting of mostly raw recruits who had never been under fire. The permanent battalion of the city had been sent to join Sesma's division, and the cannon and ammunition had been sent to Cos. There were but two small cannon left with no artillery men to work them.[16] After reports began coming to him of the increasingly precarious condition of Cos at Bexar, Colonel Guerra repeatedly asked for reinforcements for Matamoros. In October, Francisco Fernandez, the governor of Tamaulipas, had been instructed to send two companies of civic militia to strengthen Guerra's position,[17] but after about three weeks, the governor reported that he had not been able to raise the militia.[18] Finally, Fernandez went down with his poorly organized civic militia (just how many men could not be ascertained), forces that afforded no real protection to Matamoros.

---

13 Yoakum, *History of Texas*, II, 44.

14 Smith to Council, December 18, 1835, *Governor and Council Papers*, State Library.

15 Filisola, *Guerra de Tejas*, II, 266.

16 Guerra to the Minister of War, November 15, 1835, University of Texas transcriptions, Guerra, Frac. 1, Leg. 2, Op. Mil. 1835, Texas, Exp. 11.

17 Instructions to Guerra, October 23, 1835, Ibid., Leg. 1, Exp. 10, No. 4.

18 Francisco Vital Fernandez to Minister of War and Marine, November 14, 1835, Ibid., Leg. 1.

The scheme for Texan forces to attack Matamoros seems to have originated with Dr. James Grant, a Scotchman by birth but a resident of Mexico for many years. Grant was a radical federalist and had been a member of the dispersed legislature of Monclova. He had been arrested with Viesca and Milam by General Cos but, like the others, he escaped and joined the Texans who were then besieging Bexar. Here he was severely wounded while fighting in the Texan army. He was not, however, interested in the Texan cause. His desire was to reestablish the old order of things, the Federal form of government under Mexico, so that he might have the chance to redeem his vast estates which lay in Coahuila, near Parras. Grant was well-educated and an accomplished conversationalist. His highly colored descriptions of the interior of Mexico had excited among the foreign volunteers at Bexar a desire to march against Matamoros. Grant assured them that the majority of the inhabitants of Matamoros and of the interior were opposed to Santa Anna and his central system, and would gladly join a Texan army upon its approach. Grant may have had valid reason for this argument for, in January of 1836, on his march from Saltillo to Matamoros, General Urrea reported that "there were many supporters of the Constitution of 1824 in the northern towns from Matamoros to Rio Grande, and they were more or less in sympathy with the Texans."[19]

After the fall of Bexar, there was a general feeling that a march on Matamoros would be expedient. There were, at the time, in the town of San Antonio more than four hundred foreign volunteers, restless at inaction.[20] Others were arriving daily from the United States. They had come to help Texas in her cause and were eager to fight Mexicans. In order to hold them and to encourage the continual coming of others, they needed to be engaged so that the people of the United States would not be possessed of the idea that Texas no longer needed help. Accordingly, as early as December 2, 1835, Captain Philip Dimmitt, in command at Goliad, urged this expedition against Matamoros. In consequence of Dimmitt's urging, on December 17, General Sam Houston, under instructions from Governor Smith, ordered Colonel James Bowie to organize an expedition against that place.[21] If the reduction of Matamoros was not practicable, Bowie was to secure the most eligible point on the frontier and hold it. Additionally, the order was given that under any and all circumstances, the port of Copano was to be held.

Pursuant to this plan, Houston ordered to Copano all volunteers who should arrive at the Brazos, and named Goliad and Refugio as places of rendezvous for the troops. He instructed agents at New Orleans to ship provisions and munitions to Matagorda and Copano, and he stationed Colonels Travis and Fannin at

19 José Urrea, *Diario de los Operaciones Militares de la Division que al Mando del General Jose Urrea Hizo la Campana de Tejas*, 7.

20 Yoakum, *History of Texas*, II, 46.

21 Johnson & Barker, *Texas and Texans*, I, 364-365.

San Felipe and Velasco, respectively. Thus the Governor and the Commander-In-Chief made their arrangements for the expedition. Before Houston's letter reached Goliad, however, Bowie had gone to Bexar and so did not receive the order of December 17 until January of 1836. He then took no steps toward executing the order since the opportune time for the expedition had passed.[22]

In the meantime, Colonel Francis W. Johnson, who had been left in command at Bexar, espoused the plan as proposed by Dr. Grant. On December 18, Johnson wrote to Governor Smith asking, because of the threatening condition of affairs in Mexico, that the frontier outposts be strengthened. The letter was referred to the Council and on Christmas Day, the Committee on Military Affairs recommended concentration of troops on the frontier.[23] General Houston immediately protested against being ordered away from a central position at San Felipe to an outpost where he claimed "a subordinate could discharge every duty," but he failed to name the subordinate for the place.

On January 3, 1836, Johnson came to San Felipe and reported that he had already ordered the expedition to Matamoros under the authority of an official letter directed to General Burleson, his predecessor at Bexar, and that the troops had chosen him as their leader. The troops were already on the march from Bexar to Goliad.[24] He asked the Council to ratify his plan. This it did, and took steps to give him cooperation by sea. The Governor bitterly opposed the Council's actions and promptly vetoed them; the veto was overruled. Johnson, however, was so upset by the Governor's opposition that, on January 6, he withdrew from the entire affair. On the 7th, he changed his mind again and notified the Council that he would go. But in that intervening day, the Council had appointed James W. Fannin, Jr. as a special agent of the government, and had authorized him to lead the expedition. Nevertheless, upon receiving Johnson's letter of the 7th, the Council restored his authority without revoking Fannin's. On January 8, Fannin, in the execution of his orders, published a call for volunteers to rendezvous at San Felipe between the 24th and 27th of January. On January 10, Johnson issued his own call for volunteers, stating that the "whole of the volunteer army of Texas" was expected to leave San Patricio between the 20th and 30th for Matamoros.

As this juggling of plans and orders played out, Houston, on January 6,[25] began to protest against how Johnson and Grant had stripped Bexar of "both troops and supplies," also complaining that his authority as Commander-In-Chief was being superseded. The quarrel between the Governor and the Council was now on in earnest. The event that brought matters to a head was a report made by Lt. Col. J. C. Neill, who had been left in charge at Bexar with a handful of volunteers.

22 Bowie to Smith, February 2, 1836, *Army Papers*, State Library.

23 Johnson to Smith, December 18, 1835, *Governor and Council Papers*, State Library.

24 Johnson & Barker, *Texas and Texans*, I, 365-367.

25 Houston to Smith, January 6, 1836, *Army Papers*, State Library.

Commandancy of Bexar
January 6, 1836

To the Governor and Council at San Felipe de Austin:

Sirs:

It will be appalling to you to learn and see herewith enclosed our alarm-
ing weakness. But I have one pleasurable gratification which will not be
erased from the tablets of my memory during natural life, viz.: that those
whose names are herewith enclosed are to a man, those who acted as gal-
lantly in ten weeks' open-field campaign, and then won an unparalleled
victory in five days' siege of this place. Such men in such a condition and
under all the gloomy embarrassment surrounding, call loud upon you
and their country for aid, praise and sympathy.

We have 104 men and two distinct fortresses to garrison, and about
twenty-four pieces of artillery. You doubtless have learned that we have
no provisions or clothing since Johnson and Grant left. If there has ever
been a dollar here I have no knowledge of it. The clothing sent here by
the aid and patriotic exertions of the honorable Council was taken from
us by arbitrary measures by Johnson and Grant, taken from men who
endured all the hardships of winter and who were not even sufficiently
clad for summer, many of them having but one blanket and one shirt, and
what was intended for them [was] given away to men, some of whom
had not been in the army more than four days, and many not exceeding
two weeks. If a divide had been made of them, the most needy of my
men could have made comfortable by the stock of clothing and provisions taken from here.

About two-hundred of the men who had volunteered to garrison this
town for four months left my command contrary to my orders and
thereby vitiated the policy of their enlistment.

I want here for this garrison, at all times, 200 men, and I think 300 men,
until the repairs and improvements of fortifications are complete.

Yr. obedient servant,

J.C. Neil
Lt-Col. Commanding[26]

---

26 Johnson & Barker, *Texas and Texans*, I, 370, 383. Johnson here says in his own defense, and that
of Dr. Grant, "Whatever was taken from Bexar for the use of the army was authorized, and then
properly receipted for. Dr. Grant took by authority of the proper officer one six-pounder gun,
and one 6 or 8 inch mortar, with suitable ammunition for same. As to supplies and comforts,
there were none to take, the quartermaster's department being as empty as the treasury of
Texas...Not a thing was taken from Colonel Neill in the shape of supplies. He was left in possession of a full portion of what had been surrendered by the enemy."

The Governor received this letter on Saturday, January 9. He became thoroughly enraged and asked that a secret session of the Council be called for Sunday. To this session, the Governor presented Neill's report with a violent message of his own in which he used the most intemperate language, calling some of the members of the Council whom he did not name "Judases," "scoundrels," and "parricides," together with other offensive expressions. In conclusion, he notified the Council that the body was to be adjourned until March 1, unless it should be convened by proclamation at an earlier date, and that he would continue to do his duty as commander-in-chief of the army and navy, and as chief executive.[27]

The Council felt itself grossly insulted. The message was referred to a committee which reported on January 11. The reply was severe. Smith was denounced as a man whose language and conduct proved "his early habits of association to have been vulgar and depraved;" his charges against the Council were termed an outrageous libel; his style and language condemned as "low, blackguardly and vindictive." Furthermore, the committee declared that Governor Smith was suspended from the exercise of his functions, and that he be held to answer to the Council on an impeachment to be brought against him by that body. This report was unanimously adopted.[28] Lieutenant-Governor Robinson was recognized as acting governor and a proclamation explaining their action was made to the people.[29] Charges and specifications were made out against the Governor and a copy was sent to him. He was informed that he might, if he preferred, answer for his conduct to the convention that would meet March 1.

This reply shocked Smith out of some of his rage and, on January 12, he sent to the Council another message, intended to be conciliatory but the Council replied that the time for conciliation had passed. Robinson took up the duties of acting governor, but Smith refused to relinquish the executive records, the seal of office and the archives, declaring that he would defend them by force. In his turn, he called for certain papers, saying that if they were not given up forthwith, he would arrest the members of the Council and send them to Bexar for courtmartial.[30]

This miserable quarrel, a disgrace that will always cling to both the Governor and the Council, went on, each side surfeiting the people with their explanations. The effect was disastrous. Houston, siding with and representing the authority of the Governor, went about making speeches to the volunteers, in which he declared to them that the proposed Matamoros expedition was unauthorized and unwise, and that only he had the right to command them.[31] Johnson, repre-

27 Gammel, *Laws of Texas*, I, 759-761.
28 *Ibid.*, I, 762-764.
29 *Ibid.*, I, 764-769; W. B. Dewees, *Letters from an Early Settler of Texas*, 161-163.
30 Gammel, *Laws of Texas*, I, 768, 778, 804-805.
31 Barker, "The Texas Revolutionary Army," *Texas Historical Quarterly*, IX, 255; Kennedy, *Texas*, 496.

senting the authority of the Council, contended that Houston had no authority except over the "regular" troops. Fannin, the agent of the Council, said he would serve under Houston, but only if Houston would obey the Council and lead the expedition to Matamoros.[32] It is clear that the prerogatives of the Commander-In-Chief had been encroached upon, for the organic law of November 13 had declared that "the major-general should be commander-in-chief of *all* the forces called into public service during the war."

By this time, the spirit of independence among the Texans had developed considerably. Even the conservative Austin had written from New Orleans on January 7, "I now think the time has come for Texas to assert her natural rights, and were I in the convention, I would urge an immediate declaration of independence."[33] Fortunately, the Consultation had authorized the provisional government to provide for the election of a convention, and so the Council on December 10, 1835, had passed over the Governor's veto a call for such a meeting to be convened at Washington on March 1, 1836. But the quarrel between the Governor and the Council had produced bitter political factions among the Texans. Even the soldiers in the army took sides, and party conventions were prominent in all quarters. Governor Smith and General Houston were openly champions for an immediate declaration of independence, but those pledged to the Matamoros campaign opposed such a step, as it would surely cut off all hope of getting aid from the Mexican Liberals south of the Rio Grande.

It was a well known fact throughout Texas that Santa Anna would lead an army into Texas in an effort to subdue the rebellious spirit of the colonists. He had marched against and utterly destroyed Zacatecas in May of 1835 and, as early as June of that year, it was common talk in the cafes and other public places of the capital that the President's next achievement would be the subjugation of Texas.[34] Now rumors were daily arriving that he was actually advancing with a large army to retake Bexar. But why was the old fort of any importance?

San Antonio de Bexar, called indiscriminately San Antonio and Bexar, is situated on the San Antonio River, the San Pedro Creek lying on its southern side. To the northeast on the opposite side of the river was the old fortified mission of the Alamo. The ground was generally level in the neighborhood of the mission, though somewhat rolling on the west side. A number of irrigating ditches along the river afforded some defense to the town whose principal building had thick stone walls. The town proper was oblong in form and, on the east, it extended into a horseshoe bend in the river. There were two public squares, or plazas; one the Military Plaza, and the other the Plaza de Constitución, laid off in 1731.

32 Fannin to J. W. Robinson, Governor, and to the General Council, January 21, 1836. *Archives of the State Department*, Book No. 3, pp. 216-218.

33 Stephen F. Austin to Henry Austin, January 7, 1836, *Austin Papers*, III, 297.

34 Barker, "Stephen F. Austin and the Independence of Texas," *Texas Historical Quarterly*, XIII, 273.

These squares were separated by the church and other buildings. On the north side of these squares ran the main street. On this street, east of the river, was the *garita*, or look-out station, and the bridge across the river at the main street was the only one in town.

San Antonio was settled in 1718 and, from 1773 to 1824, it had been the capital of the province of Texas. In 1824, when Texas and Coahuila were joined in statehood, San Antonio lost its importance as a capital but remained the chief Mexican stronghold in Texas, and the head of the local government. The commandant and the political chief of the Department of Texas both had their headquarters there. Although some American colonists went to live in Bexar, the town never became a part of any American colony; the Mexicans always dominated there both in population and in political control. So when the town fell into the hands of the Texans in December of 1835, that event not only meant that the Mexicans had lost the last foothold in Texas that could be advantageously used as a base of military operations against the colonists, but it was also considered a humiliating defeat for them to have to surrender a stronghold which they had held for more than a century.

Thus, Bexar became the "key to the situation" in Texas, a point to be held at all hazards since, if the Mexicans could retake and hold it, they could more easily make inroads into the colonies—inroads that might possibly only be checked at the Sabine. At least this was the general opinion among the Texans. Even before the Texans had conquered Bexar in December of 1835, the *Telegraph* of San Felipe opined:

> Let Bexar fall and Santa Anna's power in Texas falls with it. Dislodge the enemy from that stronghold and all attempts to invade us from that quarter will be ineffectual. But should the expedition fail, our enemy will take fresh courage, *and the theater of war may be in the heart of our country*; and instead of our troops being fed at the expense of our enemy, the whole burden of supporting our own forces and those of the enemy will fall upon our citizens. But, by meeting the enemy on their own ground, in their own stronghold, we avoid the devastating effects of the war, we preserve our dwelling houses from the flames, and our families from the unrelenting cruelty of an unprincipled and infuriated soldiery.

Again during the same month, this time regarding Goliad, the *Telegraph* urged:

> Our volunteers still hold Goliad and are determined not to relinquish it into the hands of the enemy. We consider it necessary that this port should be maintained as well as Bexar; since if Goliad should fall into the hands of the enemy, it might materially assist him in his operations.

The Mexicans likewise looked on Bexar and Goliad as the "keys to Texas" and arduous and hazardous as an overland march of an army from Laredo to San Antonio was bound to be, Santa Anna planned to risk one in order to establish himself at this vantage point.

But notwithstanding this feeling about these posts on the part of both Texans and Mexicans, the wrangle between the Governor and the Council had so terribly weakened the Texan resistance that, by the middle of January of 1836, General Houston had decided to abandon both Bexar and Goliad outright. He felt that because of the isolation of the forts from the colonies, it would be best to concentrate his forces on the border to protect the interior by strong scouting parties. Accordingly, on January 17, he wrote Governor Smith the following letter, enclosing with it, as reason for his decision, a letter he had received from Colonel Neill, then in command at Bexar.

Headquarters, Goliad
January 17, 1836

To his Excellency Henry Smith:

Col. Bowie will leave here in a few hours for Bexar, with a detachment of from 20-50 men. Capt. Patton's company, it is believed, are now there. I have ordered the fortifications in the town of Bexar to be demolished, and if you should think fit, I will remove all the cannon and other munitions of war to Gonzales and Copano, blow up the Alamo and abandon the place, as it will be impossible to keep up the station with volunteers. The sooner I can be authorized the better it will be for the country...I have sent to Cap. Dimmitt to raise 100 or more men and march to Bexar forthwith, if it should be invested, and if not, to repair to headquarters with his company. Capt. Patton will do likewise. I would myself have marched to Bexar with a force, but the Matamoros fever rages so high, I must see Col. Ward's men...

Yr. Obt. Servt,

Sam Houston
Commander-in-Chief of the Army[35]

The letter from Colonel Neill that called forth Houston's letter and his decision to abandon Bexar was as follows:

Commandancy of Bexar - Official
January 14, 1836

Major-General Samuel Houston

Sir:

This is the third official since my command at this place, and they are all of the same nature, complaining of scarcity of Provisions, men, and money,

35 Sam Houston to Gov. Smith, January 17, 1836, *Archives of the State Department*, Book No. 3, p. 236; Brown, *History of Texas*, I, 531.

and I think we have plenty of ordinance, small arms, cannon and musket cartridges but no rifle powder.

These men all under my command have been in the field for the last four months; they are almost naked, and this day they were supposed to have received pay for the first month of their enlistment, and almost every one of them speaks of going home, and not less than 20 will leave tomorrow, and leave here only about 80 efficient men under my command; and there are at Laredo three-thousand men under the command of General Ramirez and two other generals, and as it appears by a letter received here last night, one thousand of them are destined for this place and two thousand for Matamoros. We are in a torpid defenseless situation; we have not and cannot get from all the citizens here horses enough since Johnson and Grant left, to send out a patrol or spy. Captain Salvador Flores, a Mexican, has volunteered to go with two others as spies all the way to Laredo, to learn the situation of the enemy, or meet them on the road and report to us here the movements and destination of the enemy.

I can say to you with Confidence that we can rely on great aid from the citizens of this town in case of an attack. They have no money here, but Don Jasper Flores and Louiscano Navarro have offered us all their goods, groceries and beeves for the use and support of the army. But men will not be satisfied without some money to pay their little incidental expenses which we must have.

I have sent to the command of Major Dimmitt three pieces of artillery and must have in return three loads of supplies, as per contract with owners of said wagons.

I hope we will be reinforced in 8 days here, or we will be overrun by the enemy. But if I have only One Hundred men, I will fight One Thousand as long as I can and then not surrender.

I have sent, this day, a similar letter to the Governor and Council at San Felipe, learning from Doctor Pollard that you would be in Goliad before this letter would come. I hope that you will send me one hundred men from Goliad, unless they have already been sent from some other quarter, as it is absolutely necessary for the support of this place.

Fourteen days has expired since I commenced informing my superior officers of my situation, and not even an item of news have I received from any quarter. I hope tomorrow or next day will bring something good.

There has been a Comanche Indian in here, wishing to treat with us as a nation, and has set the 20th of April for the purpose of meeting our commissioners at this place to enter into a treaty of amity, commerce and limits with us.

Private

You will learn what sneaking and gambling has been done to operate against you by J. & G. You will hear all about the Houston flag, and the Houston

House in Bexar. For fear you would be elected commander of the volunteer army, they never would let it come near an election, but shuffled it off and threw all the army into confusion several times, and the responsibility on the heads of the several captains. I am at all times ready to obey the several orders of my commander-in-chief in a respectful manner and remain with high regard

Your. Obt. Servt,

J. C. Neill
Lieut. Col. Comd-g.[36]

Two days later, on January 16, Doctor Amos Pollard, the head physician at Bexar, wrote to Governor Smith. He begged for supplies and stressed the trend of political issues at Bexar. He wrote:

Bejar
January 16, 1836

Excellent Sir:

I have but a moment to write you as I am so busy in regulating the Hospital. Things have been in the worst possible state here as you are aware. I hope and have reason to believe they will soon become much better. I ought to have written by the express but knew not when it started. I have only to say that we are much in want of money and that some could be collected on goods being brought into this place and the Commandant [would] do it [but] he is ignorant of the rate of duties established by the government. Were he in possession of that knowledge, he would avail himself of it now as there are goods here and he talks of charging but four per cent. I am interested in this, you will see, for the Hospital is in great want of a little money.

We will endeavor to elect as many of our countrymen as possible from this jurisdiction. What the prospect is I have not been able to learn. I think we have now an excellent opportunity to completely conquer our most formidable foe—our internal enemy, the Mexican Tory party of the country. I hope every friend of his country will be diligent at his post and from the righteousness of our cause we cannot but succeed.

I am your Excellency's
humble servant,

Amos Pollard[37]

This letter from Pollard as well as one from Colonel Neill on January 23, followed by the proceedings of an indignation meeting of the soldiers on January 26, all show clearly the trend of politics at Bexar. The troops here were unanimously for independence, for Smith and for Houston. The more radical ones, like Pollard, thoroughly distrusted Mexicans and were eager for a voice in the election

36 J. C. Neill to Sam Houston, January 14, 1836, *Army Papers*, 1835-1936, State Library.
37 Pollard to Smith, January 6, 1836, *Army Papers*, State Library.

of delegates to the March 1 Convention. Here, Neill asks for an election writ to give the soldiery their say in the process:

Private
Bexar
January 23, 1836

To His Excellency Henry Smith:

Dear Sir:

I ask this privilege of you to send me here at this place a writ of Election for the Volunteer Army now under my command to authorize them to elect two delegates to the Convention to be held at Washington. The reasons I request this is that not a man here under my command will or can have a voice in an Election, [except] by and through that method. They are all Volunteers. They are all in favor of Independence.

Such men should be represented in the Council of their Country and that, too, by men chosen from among themselves. The citizens have all declared for us and will on the first day of next month take the oath to support the provisional Govt. You have the highest regards of the whole Army, and you shall be sustained for your firmness and philanthropy.

Yours in haste,
Very Respectfully,

J. C. Neill
Lt. Col. Comd Bexar[38]

Conditions continue to grow from bad to worse at Bexar. Rumors swirled concerning preparations that the Mexicans were making for the invasion of Texas. In desperation, Neill sent out two more letters on January 27—one to the Council and the other to Smith. He enclosed to Smith and to the Council a copy of an address that General Sesma had made to his troops at Saltillo. These letters vividly set forth the hopelessness of Neill if he were not soon reinforced. He wrote to the Council:

Bexar
January 27, 1836

President & Members of
the Executive Council of Texas

Gents:

I have received your dispatches per express and am truly astonished to find your body in such a disorganized situation. Such interruptions in the General Council of Texas have tendencies—they create distrust and alarm, and at this critical period of our History are much to be lamented. I do hope,

---

38 Neill to Smith, January 23, 1836, *Army Papers*, State Library.

however, to hear of a reconciliation of matters. Our Govt. appears to be without a legitimate head and unanimity of action is certainly necessary to answer the ends and to effect the objects contemplated by the Consultation.

I enclose you a copy of the Proceedings of a meeting held at this place [on the] 26th which will convey to you some idea of the feeling of the Army on the subject.

I also enclose to you the address of the Commandant of the Post of Saltillo to his subalterns. Every courier from the West seems to corroborate the previous statements in relation to the preparations of the Mexicans for War.

I remain Yrs. Resp.,

J. C. Neill
Lt. Col. Comd Bexar[39]

The General-in-Chief of the 1st Division
Operating Against Texas, to his Subalterns

Companions in Arms:

We are going to open a campaign the most righteous that a Mexican Army can have before them. You have made yourselves independent of the Spanish Government, notwithstanding the right that Government had in appearance over you. How then will you now permit that your country shall become Prey of adventurous Colonists who want to make themselves our Rulers and Arbiters in exchange for the hospitality they received. No, Soldiers! I see your countenances full of indignation against those perfidious men. The Gen'l-in-Chief, the illustrious Conqueror of Tampico has distinguished us by placing us in the Van Guard. Let us prove ourselves worthy of his confidence and fly to show those men that the Mexicans are in character as mild in peace as they are dreadful in war. Let your bayonets chastise the daring of these cowards and show to the world that there is no power that can subjugate us. Soldiers, we are going to defend our Independence, our Religion, our Customs and our Homes, for everything would be lost if those infamous men were to succeed in domineering over us. Fly then to defend such precious objects, persuaded that your enemies, although Proud, are Weak. What victory will be yours and that in the midst of privations and in dangers. Your Chief and your Friend will be in the Van...

-Joaquin Romero Sesma[40]

The letter to Smith alone, written the same day, is yet another plea for money and provisions:

39 Neill to the Council, January 27, 1836, *Army Papers*, State Library.
40 Neill to the Council, January 27, 1836, *Army Papers*, State Library.

Commandancy of Bexar
January 27, 1836

To His Excellency Henry Smith, Governor of Texas

Dear Sir:

I have received a copy of resolutions enacted by the Council and approved by James W. Robinson, Acting Governor as signed, empowering me (as said therein without giving me the means) to do sundry acts to my own relief as commander of this place. In my communications to the Executive, I did not ask for pledges and resolves but for money, provisions and clothing. There has been money given or loaned by private individuals expressly for use of this army and none has been forwarded. Mr. Clay from Alabama gave or loaned $500 (in the presence of our Express and on the pledge that sum will keep the army here for the present) to the Council for the use of this garrison expressly. My Express, after having been detailed two days to receive that $500, was told by the committee that they had appropriated it otherwise. But it appears that a legitimate Executive has not had my returns by express before him. I wish to be advised. I wish to keep up a correspondence with you, public or private. Enclosed are our resolves; they speak their import. Certain intelligence in confirmation of fact that 1,400 troops of the Central Army are on the Rio Grande making every preparation to attack us was received this morning.

Enclosed is a transcript of an address of the Comd. in Chief of the Central Army to his soldiers.

I am, sir, Respectfully

J. C. Neill, Lt. Col
Comd. Bexar[41]

Indeed, things were desperate and as Neill wrote, the soldiers could not be kept at a post so poorly defended and so badly in need of money. Even the private soldiers began writing to Governor Smith of their situation. On January 24, M. Hawkins wrote a long letter telling of the conditions; he ended with these words: "Indeed we are badly off for money; this morning after applying to headquarters I could not raise a bit to pay for washing a shirt and so must go with a dirty one."[42]

Something had to be done. As we have seen, on the 17th of January, Houston ordered Bowie, then with him at Goliad, to go to Neill's assistance. Bowie left immediately with thirty men, arriving in Bexar 19th. Smith, after having received so many appeals from Bexar, to help the situation relieved Lieutenant-Colonel William B. Travis of superintending the recruiting service and ordered him to San Antonio. Colonel Travis's letter to Smith on January 28 shows something of the apathy into which the people had fallen, and states some reasons for it.

---

41 Neill to the Council, January 27, 1836, *Army Papers*, State Library.
42 M. Hawkins to Henry Smith, January 24, 1836, *Lamar Papers*, I, 308-309.

Burnam's, Colorado
January 28, 1836

To His Excellency Henry Smith

Sir:

In obedience to my orders I have done everything in my power to get ready
to march to the relief of Bexar, but owing to the difficulty of getting horses
and provisions, and owing to desertions, etc., I shall march today with only
about thirty men, all regulars except four. I shall however go on and do my
duty, if I am sacrificed, unless I receive new orders to counter march. Our
affairs are gloomy indeed. The people are cold and indifferent. They are worn
down and exhausted with war, and in consequence of dissentions between
contending and rival chieftains, they have lost all confidence in their own
government and officers. You have no idea of the exhausted state of the country. Volunteers can no longer be had or relied upon. A speedy organization,
classification and draft of the Militia is all that can save us now. A regular army
is necessary—but money and money alone can raise and equip a regular army.
Money must be raised or Texas is gone to ruin. Without it, war cannot be carried on in Texas. The patriotism of a few has done much; but that is becoming
worn down. I have strained every nerve. I have used my personal credit[43] and
have neither slept day nor night since I rec'd orders to march—and with all
this exertion, I have hardly been able to get horses and equipment for the few
men I have.

> I have honor to be
> Your Excellency's Obt. Serv't.
>
> W. Barret Travis, Lt. Col. Comdt.[44]

His discouragement seems to have become greater overnight and, on January
29, he wrote another letter to Smith urging that he be relieved from the duty
of going to Bexar in command of so few troops. A hint of personal ambition is
discernible in this letter. Travis saw no chance for military preferment at Bexar
where Neill and Bowie were already in charge, and pleads not to be sent there as
a subaltern. This circumstance throws some light on another trouble that arose at
Bexar a short time later. Travis's letter of the 29th is as follows:

---

43 *Comptroller's Military Service Papers*, No. 5936, Archives of the State Library. This document is a
claim against the Republic of Texas by Travis's administrator, John Rice Jones, for the sum of $143,
paid out by Travis from his own funds in equipping a company of soldiers at Burnam's in January
1836. The account is itemized and contains such articles as blankets, coffee, corn, bread, twine,
frying pans, tent, spurs, leggings, bridles, rope and a flag.
44 Travis to Smith, January 28, 1836, *Army Papers*, State Library; also found in Johnson & Barker,
   Texas and Texans, I, 398-399.

Burnam's, Colorado
January 29, 1836

To His Excellency Henry Smith
Governor of the State of Texas

Sir:

This will be handed to you by Capt. Jackson who will explain to you the situation of things here. I leave here with the troops under Capt. Forsythe, but shall await your orders at Gonzales or some other point on the road. I shall however keep the 30 men of Forsythe's company in motion toward Bexar, so that they might arrive there as soon as possible.

Not having been able to raise 100 volunteers agreeably to your orders, and there being so few regular troops together, I must beg that your Excellency will recall the order for me to go on to Bexar in command of so few men. I am willing, nay anxious, to go to the defense of Bexar, and I have done everything in my power to equip the enlisted men and get them off. But, Sir, I am unwilling to risk my reputation (which is ever dear to a soldier) by going off into the enemy's country with such little means, so few men and them so badly equipped—the fact that there is no necessity for my services to command these few men. The company officers will be amply sufficient. They should at all events be sent to Bexar or to the frontier of Nueces. They may now go on to San Antonio under command of Capt. Forsythe, where they can be employed if necessary, and if they are not needed there they may be sent to San Patricio or some other point.

I am now thoroughly convinced that none but defensive measures can be pursued at this inclement season. If the Executive or Major-Gen'l desire or order it, I will visit the post of San Antonio or any other for the purpose of consulting or communicating with officers in command there—or to execute any commission I may be entrusted with, but I do not feel disposed to go to command a squad of men, and without the means of carrying on a campaign. Therefore, I hope your Excellency will take my situation into consideration and relieve me from the orders which I have hithertofore received, so far as they compel me to command in person the men who are now on the way to Bexar. Otherwise I shall feel it due to myself to resign my commission. I would remark that I can be more useful at present in superintending the recruiting service.

I have honor to be
Your Excellency's
Friend & Obt. Serv't.

W. Barret Travis
Lt. Col. Comdt. of Cavalry[45]

---

45 Travis to Smith, January 29, 1836, *Army Papers*, State Library.

But Governor Smith did not grant Travis's request nor did he answer his letter. Travis did not resign his commission as he had threatened, but like the good soldier and true patriot that he was, he marched on with his troops to Bexar, reaching that place on the 2nd or 3rd of February.[46] As has already been mentioned, Colonel James Bowie and Captain Patton were already there. In his account of the events at the Alamo, Dr. Sutherland indicates that Patton arrived on January 18 with ten men, Bowie on the 19th with thirty and Travis on February 3 with twenty-five. This statement is not at odds with Travis's statement that he had 30 men, however. In a private postscript to a later letter to the Governor, Travis gives the names of five of his men who had deserted en route to Bexar.

On February 2, Bowie made his first report to Governor Smith. The letter is long but is worthy of being quoted in full, although it reiterates the same old story—need of money and supplies. There is an additional note, however that is of considerable interest. Bowie has nothing but praise for Colonel Neill and the soldiery. He commends the attitude and the behavior of the citizens of Bexar. Travis in a later letter censures them bitterly, but it must be remembered that Travis, like Smith, had absolutely no confidence or faith in any Mexican; then, too, the attitude of many of the people of Bexar evidently changed after the arrival of Santa Anna and his army. They were greatly frightened; their homes, their families, their all were at the mercy of these invaders. So even those who were in sympathy with the Texans and who were doing all they could to befriend them had to declare neutrality or feign friendship for Santa Anna.

No doubt the majority were ready to declare themselves on the side of the winner, whomever he may be. Of Neill and Bexar, Bowie wrote:

> Bejar
> 2nd February, 1836
>
> To His Excy H. Smith
>
> Dear Sir:
>
> In pursuance of your orders, I proceeded from San Felipe to La Bahia and while there employed my whole time in trying to effect the object of my mission. You are aware that General Houston came to La Bahia soon after I did; this is the reason I did not make a report to you from that post. The Comdt-in-Chg has before this communicated to you all matters in relation to our military affairs at La Bahia; this makes it wholly unnecessary for me to say anything on the subject.
>
> Whilst at La Bahia, General Houston received dispatches from Col. Comdt. Neill that good reasons were entertained that an attack would soon be made by a numerous Mexican army on our important post at Bexar. It was forth-

---

46 DeShields (ed.), "John Sutherland's Account of the Fall of the Alamo," *Dallas News*, February 5 & 12, 1911. John S. Ford, "Dr. Sutherland's Account of the Siege of the Alamo," *Memoirs* (MS.), Archives of the University of Texas.

with determined that I should go instantly to Bexar. Accordingly, I left Gen'l
Houston and with a very few efficient volunteers came to this place about
2 weeks since. I was received by Col. Neill with great cordiality, and the
men under my command enlisted at once into active service. All I can say
of the soldiers stationed here is complimentary to both their courage and
their patience. But it is the truth and your Excellency must know it, that
great and just dissatisfaction is felt for the want of a little money to pay the
small but necessary expense of our men. I cannot eulogise the conduct of
Col. Neill too highly; no other man in the army could have kept men at
this post under the neglect they have experienced. Both he and myself have
done all we could; we have industriously tried all expedients to raise funds
but hitherto it has been to no purpose. We are still laboring night and day
laying up provisions for a siege, encouraging our men, and calling on the
Government for relief.

Relief at this post in men, money and provisions is of vital importance and is
wanted instantly. So this is the real object of my letter. The salvation of Texas
depends in great measure in keeping Bexar out of the hands of the enemy. It
serves as the frontier picquet guard and, if it were in the possession of Santa
Anna, there is no stronghold from which to repel him in his march toward
the Sabine. There is no doubt that very large forces are being gathered in
several of the towns beyond the Rio Grande, and late information through
Señor Cassiana and others worthy of credit is positive in the fact that sixteen
hundred or two thousand troops with good officers, well armed and with
plenty of provisions were on the point of marching (the provisions being
cooked, etc.) A detachment of active young men from the volunteers under
my command have been sent out to Rio Frio; they returned yesterday without information, and we remain yet in doubt whether they intend an attack
on this place or go to reinforce Matamoros. It does, however, seem certain
that an attack is shortly to be made on this place, and I think it is the general
opinion that the enemy will come by land.

The citizens of Bexar have behaved well. Colonel Neill and myself have
come to the solemn resolution that we will rather die in these ditches than
give it up to the enemy. These citizens deserve our protection, and the public safety demands our lives rather than to evacuate this post to the enemy.
Again we call aloud for relief; the very weakness of our post will at any rate
bring the enemy on. Some volunteers are expected: Capt. Patton with 5 or
6 has come in. But a large reinforcement with provisions is what we need.

-James Bowie

I have information just now from a friend whom I believe, that forces at the
Rio Grande are two thousand complete; he states further that five thousand
more are a little back and marching on. Perhaps the two thousand will wait
for a junction with the five thousand. This information is corroborated by all
that we have heard. My informant says that they intend to make a descent on
this place in particular, and there is no doubt of it. Our force is very small,

the returns this day to the Comdt. show only one hundred and twenty officers and men. It would be a waste of men to put our brave little band against thousands.

We have no interesting news to communicate. The army has elected two gentleman to represent the Army and trust they will be received.

-James Bowie[47]

It must be held in mind that Houston had sent Bowie with orders to Neill to destroy the fortifications, blow up the Alamo and evacuate the town. Neill had replied that mules and horses could not be obtained with which to move the guns.[48] But here, in this letter, Bowie says that he and Neill have come to the conclusion that they'd rather die than surrender the Alamo to the enemy, even though he feels it would be a waste of men to fight a battle against 7,000 of the enemy. Bowie's letter was written as a strong plea for reinforcements, but his statements compel the reader to wonder how much the decision to die rather than surrender the fort was responsible for Neill's inability follow orders and to destroy the Alamo.

In his account of the fall of the Alamo, Dr. Sutherland said, "Every volunteer had a horse, but forage being unobtainable, these were kept in a herd on the Salado, five or six miles east of the city where grass and water were abundant." A comparison of Neill's and Dr. Sutherland's statements regarding available horses demonstrates that the belief that "Bexar was the key to Texas," and must be kept out of the enemy's grasp at all costs, was really the reason the Commander-in-Chief's order was not obeyed. The place, moreover, seemed to cast some sort of spell over the Texan leaders. However indifferent or reluctant the man might be before going to Bexar, once there, he was soon writing to the Governor, the Council, the Commander-in-Chief—anybody that had authority to give aid— saying "Bexar is the key to the situation, public safety demands our lives rather than the surrender it into the hands of the enemy." And so the decision was made to hold the post against all odds, and a small band of resolute men was assembled for its defense.

Writers of Texas history have frequently attempted to determine exactly when Travis, Bowie, Bonham and Crockett entered the Alamo. The answer, or at least a very good clue, is supplied by a letter written by Green B. Jameson on February 11. Jameson says:

We are now 150 strong, Colonel Crockett and Colonel Travis both here and Colonel Bowie in command of the volunteer forces. Colonel Neill left today on account of an express informing him of illness in his family.

47 Bowie to Smith, February 2, 1835, *Army Papers*, State Library.
48 Houston to Smith, January 17, 1836, *Army Papers*, State Library; Yoakum, *History of Texas*, II, 458.

Concerning the arrival in San Antonio of Bowie and Travis, the records are fairly definite and in accord. As has already been stated, Bowie arrived with a company of 30 soldiers from Goliad on the 19th of January, and Travis with 25 soldiers, came early into the Alamo on the morning of February 3. In a letter written January 30, 1860, Houston says that Bonham accompanied Bowie to the Alamo from Goliad with orders to blow up the Alamo.[49] This statement is, in all probability, correct, for the fragmentary records we have concerning Bonham practically verify it.

James Butler Bonham arrived in Texas on December 12, 1835. On the 20th of that month, he entered the Texan army as a lieutenant of cavalry[50] and went to San Felipe where he became associated with his friend, Travis, in the recruiting office at that place. On January 11, he was still at San Felipe but the recruiting business was dull and he was eager for action. Houston, writing to J. W. Robinson, about the same time, mentions Bonham in saying, "Bonham ought to be made a major by all means. His influence in the army is great."[51] So, on January 11, Bonham was at San Felipe, but on January 23, he was at Bexar and served as chairman of a committee on resolutions for the indignation meeting, held by the soldiers of the post against the Council, because of the impeachment of Smith.[52] It is certain that he went to Bexar sometime between the 11th and 23rd of January. No doubt he arrived there with Bowie on the 19th (having left Goliad on the 17th) as Houston states.

The date of Crockett's arrival is not so definitely clear, but records make it fairly evident that he reached San Antonio on or about the 7th of 8th of February. Green B. Jameson's letter of February 11 states that Crockett, Bowie and Travis were all in the Alamo as of that date. Dr. Sutherland states that "in a few days—less than a week after Travis arrived—Colonel David Crockett with twelve others direct from Tennessee came."[53] Travis arrived on the 3rd, and since they were all there by the 11th, Crockett's arrival was sometime between these dates, less than a week from February 3.

For a few weeks after the sturdy band of defenders assembled at Bexar, an even graver danger than the Mexican army threatened them. This danger was internal discord brought about by conflicting personalities and interests and, in no small part, by an ambiguous chain of command within the government and within the walls of the Alamo. As has been noted, Colonel Neill left San Antonio on February 11 for the colonies, owing to a family emergency, leaving Travis in command. The following letter from Travis explains conditions through his eyes:

---

49 Houston to F. M. White, January 30, 1860, *Houston Letters*, State Library.
50 *Comptroller's Military Service Records (1836)*, No. 7474, State Library.
51 Houston to J. W. Robinson, January 11, 1836, *Lamar Papers*, I, 294.
52 Neill to Smith, January 23, 1836, *Army Papers*, State Library.
53 DeShields (ed.), "Sutherland's Account of the Fall of the Alamo," *Dallas News*, Feb. 5, 1911.

Commandancy of Bexar
February 12, 1836

To His Excellency, H. Smith
Governor of Texas

Sir:

You have no doubt already received information by express from La Bahia that tremendous preparations are making on the Rio Grande and elsewhere in the Interior for the Invasion of Texas. Santa Anna by the last accounts was at Saltillo with a force of 2,500 men and General Sesma was at Rio Grande with about 2,000. He has issued his Proclamation [announcing] vengeance against the people of Texas and threatens to exterminate every white man within its limits. This being the frontier Post nearest the Rio Grande will be the first to be attacked. We are illy prepared for their reception as we have not more than 150 men here and they in a very disorganized state. Yet we are determined to sustain it as long as there is a man left, because we consider death preferable to disgrace, which would be the result of giving up a Post which has been so dearly won, and thus opening the door for the Invaders to enter the sacred Territory of the colonies. We hope our countrymen will open their eyes to the present danger and wake from their false security. I hope that all party dissentions will subside, that our fellow Citizens will unite with the Common Cause and fly to the defense of the frontiers.

I fear it is useless to waste arguments upon them. The Thunder of the Enemy Cannon and the pollution of their wives and daughters—the Cries of their famished Children and the smoke of their burning dwellings [only this] will arouse them. I regret that the Govt. has so long neglected a draft of the militia which is the only measure that will ever again bring the Citizens of Texas to the Frontiers.

Money, clothing and provisions are greatly needed at this Post for the use of the Soldiers.

I hope your Excellency will send us a portion of the money which has been received from the U. S. as it cannot be better applied; indeed we cannot get along any longer without money and with it we can do everything.

For God's sake, and the sake of our country, send us reinforcements. I hope you will send to this Post at least two companies of Regular Troops—Capt. Allen's Co—under Lt. Thornton now at Goliad, and the company of Regulars at Copano under the command of Lt. Turner might well be ordered to this Post as they could reach here in 4 days on foot.

In consequence of the sickness of his family Lt. Col. Neill has left this Post to visit home for a short time and has requested me to take command of the Post. In consequence of which I feel myself delicately and awkwardly situated. I therefore hope that your Excellency will give me some definite orders and that immediately.

The troops here to a man recognize you as their legitimate Governor and they expect your fatherly care and protection.

In conclusion, let me assure your Excellency that with 200 men, I believe this place can be maintained—and I hope they will be sent us as soon as possible, yet should we receive no reinforcements, I am determined to defend it to the last, and should Bejar fall, your friend will be buried beneath its ruins.

> I have honor to be Your Most obt.
> very humble Serv't.
>
> W. Barret Travis
> Lt. Col. Comdt.[54]

On the next day, February 13, Travis wrote to Governor Smith again.

Bexar
February 13, 1836

To His Excellency, Henry Smith

Dear Sir:

I wrote you an official letter last night as Comdt. of this post in the absence of Col. Neill and if you had taken the trouble to answer my letter from Burnam's I should not now have been under the necessity of troubling you. My situation is truly awkward and delicate. Col. Neill left me in command, but wishing to give satisfaction to the volunteers here and not wishing to assume any command over them, I issued an order for the election of an officer to command them with the exception of one company of volunteers that had previously engaged to serve under me. Bowie was elected by two small companies, and since his election has been roaring drunk all the time, has assumed all command & is proceeding in a most disorderly and irregular manner—interfering with private property, releasing prisoners sentenced by courtmartial & by the civil court & turning everything topsy turvy. If I didn't feel my honor and that of my country comprometted, I would leave here instantly for some other point with the troops under my immediate command as I am unwilling to be responsible for the drunken irregularities of any man. I hope you will order immediately some regular troops here as it is more important to occupy this post than I imagined when last I saw you. It is the key of Texas from the interior. Without a foothold here, the enemy can do nothing against us in the colonies, now that our coast is guarded by armed vessels. I do not solicit the command of this post, but Col. Neill has applied to the Commander-in-Chief to be relieved and is anxious for me to take command. I will do it, if it be your order for a time until an artillery officer can be sent here. The enemy is on the Rio Grande with 1,000 strong and is making every preparation to invade us. By the 15th of March I think Texas will be invaded and every preparation should be made to receive them.

> I have honor to be etc.
> W. Barret Travis

P. S. This is a private letter and is directed to Nibbs for fear it may fall into bad hands.

---

54 Travis to Smith, February 12, 1836, *Army Papers*, State Library.

By the same express, John J. Baugh made further explanation of the situation at Bexar. He wrote:

> Garrison of Bejar
> February 13, 1836
>
> Sir:
>
> Lt. Col. J. C. Neill being suddenly called home, in consequence of the illness of some of his family, requested Col. Travis, as the senior officer, to assume the command of the Post during his absence. Col. Travis informed the volunteers in the garrison that they could, if not satisfied with him as a commandant *Pro Tem* elect one out of their own body. The volunteers, being under a wrong impression and ever ready to catch at any popular excitement, objected to Col. Travis upon the grounds of his being a Regular officer and immediately named Col. Bowie as their choice.
>
> An election was consequently ordered by Col. Travis and Bowie was elected without opposition. None but volunteers voted, and in fact not all of them. The consequence was a split in the garrison. Col. Travis as a matter of course could not submit to the control of Bowie, and he (Bowie) availing himself of his great popularity among the volunteers seemed anxious to arrogate himself the entire control.
>
> Things passed on this way yesterday and today until at length they have become intolerable. Bowie as commander of the volunteers has gone so far as to stop carts laden with the goods of private families removing into the country. He has ordered the prison doors to be opened for the release of a Mexican convicted of theft who had been tried by a jury of 12 men, among which was Col. Travis and Col. Bowie himself. He has also ordered and effected the release of D. H. Barre, a private in the Regular Army attached to the Legion of Cavalry, who had been tried by a Court Martial and found Guilty of desertion, and actually deliberated him from prison with a Corporal's Guard with loud huzzahs. But the most extraordinary step of all and that which sets aside all law, Civil and Military, is that which follows:
>
> > *Commandancy of Bejar*
> > *Feb. 13, 1836*
> >
> > *Capts of Corps -*
> >
> > *You are hereby requested to release such prisoners as may be under your direction for labor or otherwise.*
> >
> > > *James Bowie*
> > > *Commander of Volunteer forces of Bejar*
>
> Under this order, the Mexican who had been convicted by the civil authorities and the soldiers convicted by court martials and some of whom had been placed in the Alamo on the public works were released.
>
> Antonio Fuentes, who had been released as above said, presented himself to the judge under the protection of Capt. Baker of Bowie's volunteers and

demanded his clothes, which were in the Calaboose, stating that Col. Bowie had set him at liberty; whereupon the judge [Seguin] ordered him remanded to prison, which was accordingly done. As soon as this fact was reported to Bowie, he went in a furious manner and demanded of the judge a release of the prisoner, which the judge refused saying that he "would give up his office and let the military appoint a judge." Bowie immediately sent to the Alamo for troops and paraded in the Square under arms in a tumultuously and disorderly manner; Bowie himself and many of his men being drunk which has been the case since he has been in command.

Col. Travis protested vigorously against these proceedings to the Judge and others, and as a friend to good order, and anxious to escape the stigma which must inevitably follow, he has drawn off his troops to the Medina where he believes he may be as useful as in the garrison, at all events save himself from implication in this disgraceful business.

I have ventured to give you this hasty sketch of passing events, in justice to myself and others who have had no hand in these transactions.

Your Obt. Serv't.

J. J. Baugh
Adj. of Post of Bexar[55]

These letters explain Travis's side of the difficulty. From Bowie and his friends, there is not a word of explanation to be found, although R. M. Potter in his article, "The Fall of the Alamo," writes of the affair in a way that shows Bowie in a somewhat better light.[56] He says that Travis was unwilling to remain at the Alamo as a subordinate after Neill's departure. Neill was uneasy that the volunteers would make trouble if left under the authority of a commander from the regular army. To quell that storm without interfering with Travis's rights, he prepared an order for an election of a lieutenant-colonel of volunteers. He was about to depart when his men found out what he had done, whereupon they seized him and even threatened his life unless he should comply with their wishes for the election of a full colonel. He yielded and on an amended order, James Bowie was unanimously elected a full colonel of volunteers. Furthermore, Potter shows that considerably more than half of the troops at the Alamo were volunteers. Thus, as a colonel, Bowie claimed to outrank Travis. From Jameson's letter of February 11, previously quoted, it seems that the election of the colonel for the volunteers took place before Neill's departure, as he says, "We are now 150 strong, Colonel Crockett and Colonel Travis both here and Colonel Bowie in command of the volunteer forces. Colonel Neill left today."

53 Travis to Smith, February 13, 1836, *Army Papers*, State Library; Baugh to Smith, February 13, 1836, *Ibid*.

56 R. M. Potter, "The Fall of the Alamo," *Magazine of American History*, II, Part I, p. 1.

Juan N. Seguin, many years later, said that Travis did not withdraw to the Medina, only threatened to do so. This was probably the truth, for we find that by the 14th, Travis and Bowie had patched up their difficulties sufficiently to coauthor the following letter to Governor Smith:

Commandancy of Bexar
February 14, 1836

To His Excellency, H. Smith
Governor of Texas

Sir:

We have detained Mr. Williams for the purpose of saying that this garrison is in a very destitute situation. We have but a small supply of provisions and are without a dollar. We therefore beg leave to call the attention of your Excellency to the wants of this post, as we learn that 20,000 dollars have been sent to Copano for the use of troops there. We think it but just that you should send us at least 5,000 dollars which we understand that you have at your command.

We have borrowed 500 dollars here, which has long since been expended and besides which, we are greatly in debt and our credit is growing worse daily. It is useless to talk of keeping up the garrison any longer without money as we believe that unless we receive some shortly, the men will all leave.

From all the information we have received, there is no doubt but that the enemy will surely advance upon this place, and that this will be the first point of attack. We must, therefore, urge the necessity of sending reinforcements as speedily as possible to our aid.

By an understanding of today, Col. J. Bowie has the command of the volunteers of the garrison and Col. W. B. Travis of the regulars and volunteer cavalry.

All general orders and correspondence will henceforth be signed by both until Col. Neill's return.

> We have the honor to be your
> Obedient Servants,
>
> W. Barret Travis
> Comdt. of cavalry
>
> James Bowie
> Comdt. of Volunteers[57]

But this "understanding" of the 14th appears to have been but a truce, for there are evidences of grave differences between these leaders even after the arrival of the Mexicans.

---

57 Bowie and Travis to Smith, *Archives of the State Department*, Book No. 3, p. 250.

To what extent this squabble affected the discipline of the troops and the general business of preparation is hard to determine. It is a well-known fact that discipline was exceedingly lax, and that the scout service was very poor. Potter thinks this neglect of scout service, an indication that Travis had little control over his men "who were willing to die by him, but not ready to obey him."[58] The whole situation, however, is in keeping with the attitude of the frontier solider throughout the war. The same spirit was manifest in Austin's army before the capture of Bexar, and we find it again in Fannin's army at Goliad. Dr. Sutherland seems to sum up the situation neatly. In his account of the fall of the Alamo, he says:

> Of the troops remaining at Bexar Neill was nominally in authority, but in truth, the Texan volunteer like most other volunteers, engaged in a desultory warfare such as was then being carried on, was each one pretty much his own commander, save when the near presence of conflict with the enemy compelled them, in self defense, to choose and obey a leader. There was no regular commissariat at Bexar—the men scattered in squads over the city, getting food where they could, and sleeping when and where it suited their convenience. But braver men were never assembled in a fighting band. There was not a one but was ready to fight should the enemy dare come into view, yet few believed the Mexicans would dare come—at least for some time—to suppress the revolt in Texas, for they thought the lesson taught the Mexicans by the defeat of Cos was amply sufficient to keep them away. Then, too, the expedition under Johnson and Grant gave them an additional feeling of security, for they argued even if the reports of the great invasion were true, it would be intercepted by Johnson and Grant, and that they would get the news in time to make needful preparations. So, while almost every volunteer had a horse, forage was unobtainable, and these horses were kept in a herd on the Salado, five or six miles from Bexar where grass was abundant. Consequently, no organized, sustained effort was made to keep informed as to what the Mexicans were doing.[59]

There were, however, efforts at preparation of the fortress. Green B. Jameson had been appointed chief engineer of the post, and was busy remounting guns and strengthening the defense of the Alamo to meet the invasion. He had even studied out and submitted plans to the government for remodelling the fort so as to make it stronger and more easily and securely manned with fewer soldiers. No doubt this work was carried on in a somewhat irregular way, with the officers

58 R. M. Potter, *Texas Almanac*, 1868, 33, 38.
59 DeShields (ed.), "John Sutherland's Account of the Fall of the Alamo," *Dallas News*, Feb. 5, 1911.

themselves often doing much of it. Indeed, some of the officers seem to have been keenly cognizant of the impending danger, and evidence is found that H. J. Williamson, a young Philadelphian fresh from West Point training, did his utmost to establish systematic drill among the troops. To his despair, the men refused to drill unless it pleased them to do so, but they often good-naturedly submitted.[60] No doubt there were other officers who were as earnest as was Williamson, but the fact remains that drills and other military exercises were not a matter of daily routine. In fact, the army at the Alamo had practically no organization of a strictly military nature.

There was another officer, Juan N. Seguin, a Mexican captain under Travis's command, whose father was alcalde of the city, who thoroughly realized the danger and kept on the alert. The Seguins not only sympathized with the Texans but gave active cooperation in every way. Quietly, Juan Seguin despatched his own nephew, Blaz Herrera, to Laredo, to spy on the movements of the enemy. About the middle of February, Herrera hurried back and reported that a large Mexican force was crossing the Rio Grande and was marching for the interior. Seguin reported this to Travis, vouching for the integrity of his messenger.[61] Nevertheless, few of the Texans would believe the report, decrying it as "more Mexican lies, and another false alarm." The Mexican population of Bexar, however, became greatly excited and all who could find the means of conveyance began moving their families to the country.[62] It was amid conditions such as these that the Texans allowed themselves to be "surprised" at the coming of Santa Anna's forces on February 23.

---

60 Frank Templeton, *The Fall of the Alamo*, 128-129.

61 DeShields (ed.), "John Sutherland's Account of the Fall of the Alamo," *Dallas News*, Feb. 5,1911;
   Rodrigues, *Memoirs*, 8-10.

62 *Telegraph and Texas Register*, January 30, 1836; William Corner, *San Antonio Guide and History*, 120.

CHAPTER IV
SANTA ANNA'S COSTLY MARCH TO BEXAR

When Antonio Lopez de Santa Anna was elected president of Mexico in 1833, he was a leader of the Federalist Party and was supposed to be in favor of radical reforms. But what the man really wanted was power, rank and wealth for himself. He saw that these coveted things lay in the hands of the church and of the central government and soon stripped off his mask of republicanism. By a *coup d'etat* he contrived to bring about the Plan de Cuernavaca which declared against proscriptive laws, religious reforms and toleration of Masonic sects,[1] and pronounced all laws void which were contrary to these views.[2] This plainly meant that Santa Anna wished to become dictator and that the reactionaries would help him to accomplish his ambition in order to effect their own designs. His end was accomplished by dissolving Congress and amending the constitution, overthrowing the state legislatures and dismissing cabinet members who were not subservient to his will.

Five republican states—San Luis, Jalisco, Nuevo Leon, Zacatecas and Coahuila-Texas—vigorously protested. Troops were sent under trusted generals to reduce nearer states, while Santa Anna himself led troops to subdue Zacatecas. On May 10, 1835, this was accomplished with great brutality. Francisco Garcia, the governor, was defeated and overthrown, and the soldiers of Santa Anna committed the most scandalous outrages against the citizenry. Zacatecas was completely crushed. Santa Anna himself ruthlessly seized the products of the rich mines there, as well as the funds of the state.[3] For a while, he hesitated concerning the course to pursue with regard to Texas. Vice-president Farías's plan of settling natives, subsidized by the government, on the Texan frontier had been a complete failure. Mexicans could not be hired to go as colonists either to Texas or to California.[4] Santa Anna, with his hands full of the business of subduing Zacatecas and the other revolting states, adopted a seemingly conciliatory attitude toward Texas. Consequently, as has been noted before, the objectionable Law of April 6, 1830, was partly revoked, several new municipalities were set up and other conciliatory steps were taken. But with Zacatecas crushed, and with the wealth of that state in his hands, Santa Anna was finally ready to give his attention to Texas.

---

1 Clarence R. Wharton, *El Presidente, Santa Anna*, 24-25. Wharton says, "Santa Anna himself was a Yorkish Rite Mason, although he disavowed affiliation with any secret order. It is known, however, that he gave the distress signal of the Masonic order when he was brought in as a prisoner at San Jacinto in 1836, and it is a tradition in Texas that this signal, given to John A. Wharton, founder of the first Masonic lodge in Texas, saved Santa Anna's life.

2 Rives, *The United States and Mexico*, I, 228.

3 Bancroft, *History of Mexico*, V, 140.

4 Filisola, *Guerra de Tejas*, II, 39-43.

Accordingly, on August 31, 1835, in order to stir up the Mexican people and to begin preparations for his campaign, he issued through the Minister of Relations, to all governors and local officials, the following pronouncement.

> The colonists established in Texas have recently given the most unequivocal evidence of the extremity to which perfidy, ingratitude and the restless spirit that animates them can go, since—forgetting what they owe to the supreme government of the nation which so generously admitted them to its bosom, gave them fertile lands to cultivate, and allowed them all the means to live in comfort and abundance—they have risen against that same government, taking up arms against it under the pretense of sustaining a system which an immense majority of Mexicans have asked to have changed, thus concealing their criminal purpose of dismembering the territory of the Republic.
>
> His Excellency, the President ad interim, justly irritated by a conduct so perfidious, has fixed his entire attention upon this subject; and in order to suppress and punish that band of ungrateful foreigners, has directed that the most active measures be taken, measures required by the very nature of what is in reality a crime against the whole nation. The troops, destined to sustain the honor of the country and the government, will perform their duty and will cover themselves with glory.[5]

It was Santa Anna's plan to quietly and gradually gather at Bexar, where he had already stationed his brother-in-law and favorite general, Cos, an adequate force with which to begin his campaign in the spring.[6] Therefore, when Cos reported in October of 1835 that all the Texan colonists—even Austin's, heretofore submissive—had risen, Santa Anna ordered General Sesma, the military ex-governor of Zacatecas, to march to Bexar with four battalions and a battery of light artillery. A little later, this order was despatched to Sesma:

> The foreigners who are making war on the Mexican nation in violation of every rule of law, are entitled to no consideration whatsoever; and consequently, no quarter shall be given them, of which order you will give notice to your troops. These foreigners have with audacity declared war to the death on Mexicans and ought to have it given to them in the same manner.[7]

5 Dublan y Lozano, *Legislacion Mexicano*, III, 64-65.
6 Santa Anna to the Minister of War, January 15, 1835, *University of Texas Manuscripts*, Guerra, Frac. 1, Leg. 1, Op. Mil. 1835, Texas.
7 Filisola, *Guerras de Tejas*, II, 245.

Many difficulties confronted Santa Anna in his preparation for the Texas campaign, and in surmounting them he showed great energy and ingenuity. Mexico was bled white by revolutions, changes of government and constant graft on the part of high officials. Although more than $7,500,000 had already been spent on the Mexican army in 1835, it was now necessary to raise more money and this the government was unable to do by ordinary means.[8] Finally, funds were secured, chiefly from private money lenders, with interest averaging about 4% per month.[9] And even at this ruinous rate, most of the loan of $400,000, which was finally floated, was to be paid chiefly in supplies laid down at Matamoros.[10] Indeed the scarcity of money among the Mexican troops was as serious a matter as it was among the Texan soldiery. Although the Mexican soldiers were expected to live upon the country through which they passed, they often were hungry and in distress for the most trivial sums of money.[11]

Furthermore, the Mexican officials underrated the difficulties of the undertaking. In the first place, they felt confident that the colonists would have little chance when pitted against the Mexican army and would, therefore, make only slight resistance. Little did they expect to find at Bexar an army that would make stubborn resistance, and which, to the last man, would die fighting. They further took little accounting of the great distances their armies must march to fight against a foe in his own land defending his own fireside. Had they considered all of these factors, however, the manner of their attack likely would not have changed—Mexico had no navy with which to transport troops, no merchant marine and little money to buy or charter ships.

Santa Anna's difficulties were not all a function of poor finances. He found it just as hard to raise troops as to raise money, and all his histrionic powers— which were by no means small—were called into service. He made bombastic, flowery speeches to stir up the patriotic passions and the zeal of the common people; he invented catchy slogans, dear to the Latin's heart, and created new military orders and decorations. One of the most notable and interesting of these is described in *El Mosquito Mexicano* of January 22, 1836. It was in the form of a decree from José María Tornel, the Secretary of War. This decree reads:

> Attention! Civil wars are always bloody; Our soldiers ever aspire to shed the blood of foreigners who seek to take away from us our rights and menace our independence. This war is righteous, and should be without remorse; and this nation will adorn with flowers the tombs of its defenders. Remember soldiers, in civil war, triumphant victories must always be accompanied by the mourning and by the tears of widows

---

8 Santa Anna, *Manifiesto Que de Sus Operaciones en la Campaña de Tejas*, 6.
9 Nicito de Zamacois, *Historia de Mejico*, XII, 68, 69; *El Mosquito Mexicano*, December 8, 1835.
10 Ramón Caro, *Verdadera Idea*, 2-4, 148-168.
11 Zamçois, XII, 69.

and orphans. It is in the face of such reflections that our brave troops start out on a campaign, so full of privation, to retrieve the disasters at Bexar. So many misfortunes have already been suffered, and so many more may come that the Supreme Government is supremely indignant and ardently desires vengeance. It therefore esteems it very fitting that it should enact the following law:

> Art. I. The war against Texas is national;

> Art. II. To reward services that the army will make in this campaign and in wars of like nature, there is established a military order to be called the Legion of Honor;

> Art. III. In order to be admitted to this order it is necessary to have made the Texas campaign or to serve in Tampico, or other points of foreign aggression. The general-in-chief of the army himself will record the merits of each one. [There continue, at this point, eight articles of details concerning the ceremony of decoration.]

> Art. IV. The candidate for the honor must kneel and swear: "I swear to be faithful to the country, the Government and to honor and do all that constitutes the duty of a reliant loyal gentleman of the Legion of Honor!" The soldiers and the sergeants then swear together to fight with extraordinary valor on the day of battle.

The insignia of the Legion shall be a cross, or star with five double radiants. The center shall be surrounded by a crown of laurel; at one side shall be the national arms, on the other the motto, Honor, Valor, and Country. On the reverse side of the medal in the center shall be the campaign or action for which the decoration is awarded with the words Republica Mexicana. This cross shall be of silver for the cavalrymen, but of gold for all officers. The Grand Crosses will wear a band with red border on each edge across the right and left shoulder. This is a purely military order and shall be considered the highest honor a Mexican soldier can merit. None besides soldiers ought to obtain it.[12]

Smarting under the humiliation of the defeat of Cos at Bexar in late 1835, Santa Anna had a law passed in Mexico which he thought would check immigration from the United States to Texas. It stated that the Mexican government had positive information that meetings were being held in the United States with the undisguised intent of equipping armed expeditions against the Mexican nation. The United States had repeatedly replied to protests concerning the matter stating that her authorities disapproved of such meetings and had done all possible to prevent them. Nevertheless, some speculators and adventurers continued in

---

12 *El Mosquito Mexicano*, January 22, 1836

this manner to break the neutrality laws of their own nation, and were successful in evading punishment at her hands. Therefore, the President of Mexico directed that all armed foreigners who entered the territory of the Mexican Republic should be regarded as pirates and be punished as such; also that all persons who exported arms or munitions of war to such adventurers should be regarded as hostile to the Supreme Government.[13] Ramón Caro, secretary to Santa Anna, states that this law was drafted in Santa Anna's private residence.[14]

By December of 1835, Santa Anna had determined to lead the invading army in person,[15] and with his native energy began the mobilization of troops at Saltillo. But with all his powers of organization, early in January 1836, he had collected an army of only some 6,000 to 8,000 men,[16] although, on paper, the Mexican army amounted to 27,000 regulars, and with the more or less permanently organized militia totaled 48,600.[17] Supplies and transportation facilities were equally difficult to secure. Most of the supplies came from Coahuila and other north Mexican states, and it must be held in mind that the "population of these states was not entirely unsympathetic with the Texans."[18]

When General Sesma received his orders in October of 1835 to march to Bexar with four battalions of infantry and one battery of artillery, he began immediately to equip his men for the march. But in November, he was obliged to start for Laredo with only about 1,500 men, and with insufficient supplies. Consequently, he was forced to requisition such supplies as he needed, giving script on the government as payment. His march through Nuevo León left the people outraged and resentful.[19] Sesma pressed on, but the distance from Zacatecas to Laredo is about 500 miles and it was December 27 before he arrived there to find General Cos with his defeated army of 800 men together with a large number of women and children who had arrived on Christmas Day. When Santa Anna heard of Cos's retreat, he ordered him on to Monclova to rest and recruit his men, and after Cos put his army in as good a condition as the scarcity of money and supplies would permit, he was to "return to his post to redeem, if he could, his wavering reputation."[20]

13 Filisola, *Guerra de Tejas*, II, 241-253; Dublan y Lonzano, *Legislacion Mexicano*, III, 114.

14 Caro, *Verdadera Idea*, 155.

15 Santa Anna, *Memoirs* (transl. by Willye Ward Watkins), 91, University of Texas Archives.

16 Filisola, *Guerra de Tejas*, II, 337; Santa Anna, *Memoirs* (transl. by Willye Ward Watkins), 91, University of Texas Archives.

17 Rives, *The United States and Mexico*, I, 322.

18 Governor of Coahuila and Texas to José María Monasterio, October 29, 1835, *University of Texas Transcripts*, Guerra, Frac. 1, Leg. 1, Op. Mil. 1835, Texas.

19 Juan N. de la Garza y Evia to the Minister of War, December 30, 1835, *University of Texas Transcripts*, Guerra, Frac. 1, Leg. 1, Op. Mil. 1836, Texas.

20 Cos to the Minister of War, February 1, 1836, *University of Texas Manuscripts*, Guerra, Frac. 1, Leg. 1, Op. Mil. 1836, Texas.

Sesma was ordered to San Juan Bautista for the purpose of getting his troops in condition for the long march to Texas. Already Santa Anna had sent General Fernández with a small force to reinforce Matamoros. By February 1, in spite of all the tremendous difficulties with which he had been confronted, Santa Anna was ready to set out from Saltillo. He reached Laredo by the 12th and rested there for four days, waiting for all the troops to assemble.

While waiting at Laredo, Santa Anna matured the policy to be pursued in Texas once he had conquered it. His plans were developed under ten heads, a summary of the key points is as follows:

(1) All leaders and principal promoters of the revolution should be executed.

(2) All expense of putting down the insurrection, and all losses incurred, including past due custom duties not collected, should be paid by confiscation of the property of the Texans.

(3) All who had taken part in the insurrection should be driven from the province.

(4) All foreigners who had not participated in the war who were living on the sea coast or on the borders of the United States should be removed far into the interior.

(5) All foreigners who had come since 1828 as part of an armed force should be regarded as pirates and punished as such.

(6) All grants and sales of land to non-residents should be vacated, the best of the land to be divided among the Mexican soldiers if they wished to occupy them, and no Anglo-American was to be permitted to settle in Texas. Otherwise, vacant lands should be sold at one dollar per acre, allowing the French and English each 5,000,000 acres, to the Germans somewhat more, and to the Spanish without limit.

(7) All negroes should be liberated and declared free.[21]

Although General Cos and his army had been paroled on the specific terms that they should not again take up arms against Texas, Cos is now found to be recruiting and equipping that same army in order to break that parole.[22] Cos was determined to keep his word of honor and to carry out the terms of his capitulation, but ultimately yielded to the stronger will of Santa Anna. Urrea, late governor of Durango, was ordered to go with a small force—323 infantry and 300 cavalry[23]—to unite with the force under Fernández at Matamoros. Urrea was also to be joined by an additional 300 men from Yucatán. He was then

21 Filisola, *Guerra de Tejas*, II, 370-376; Santa Anna to Minister of War, February 16, 1836, *University of Texas Transcripts*, Guerra, Frac. 1, Leg. 3, Op. Mil. 1836, Texas, Exp. de February.

22 Arie Claiborne, *The Story of the Alamo*, 10-12.

23 Urrea, *Diario*, 7-10; Yoakum, *History of Texas*, II, 65.

to cross the Rio Grande and guard the right flank of the main army. It was these troops under Urrea who, having crossed the Rio Grande on February 17, met and destroyed the remnant of the Matamoros expedition, led by Grant and Johnson, on February 27 and March 2, 1836.

It was now clear to his generals that Santa Anna meant to march overland to Bexar, and they all strongly disapproved of the plan. The second in command to Santa Anna was General Vicente Filisola, an Italian by birth, but for many years a citizen of Mexico. There were also Generals Sesma, Gaona, Tolsa, Andrade, Woll and Cos, all of whom were now ordered to concentrate their commands before Bexar.

Filisola urged to the last that the base of operations on the Rio Grande should be established at Mier. He founded his argument on the facts that this more southerly route was much shorter, that it was closer to other towns which might furnish supplies, and that an advance made by San Patricio and Goliad to San Felipe would cut Bexar off from the rest of Texas and, thus, make the taking of it easy. Indeed, the enemy might even be forced to abandon it without a battle. By this plan, also, the Mexican army would have a chance of being supported, in part, with supplies by sea. But this advice was stubbornly rejected,[24] and the troops set out on their long march of over 500 miles. The following is Filisola's account of the army, divided into five sections:

    (1) Vanguard under Sesma............1,541 men, 6 guns
    (2) First Brigade under Gaona........1,600 men, 6 guns
    (3) Second Infantry under Tolsa...... 1,838 men, 6 guns
        (this brigade included Cos's troops)
    (4) Cavalry under Andrade........... 437 men
    (5) Detachment under Urrea ....300 infantry, 301 cavalry, 1 gun

Altogether they totaled 6,019 men and 21 guns. But on Tuesday, March 4, 1836, *El Mosquito Mexicano* published the following enumeration in its account of the invading army. According to this account, the army was formed into the following brigades:

    (1) 1st composed of 1,500 men under Ramirez y Sesma
    (2) 2nd composed of 2,000 men under General Gaona
    (3) 3rd composed of 2,000 men under General Tolsa
    (4) 4th composed of 1,000 cavalry under General Andrade
    Meanwhile, General Urrea at the head of 1,000 infantry and 500 horse operates between Matamoros and Goliad.

The march from Monclova began on February 8, the brigades leaving singly at intervals of two days, each carrying one month's supplies. Santa Anna with a picked

24 Filisola, *Guerra de Tejas*, II, 255-269.

detachment pushed forward by rapid marches, passed the various brigades and
reach San Juan Bautista on February 12. On the same day, Sesma crossed the
Rio Grande at Laredo. Soon these advance forces were joined, making an army
more than 2,500 strong, and one of the most toilsome and bitter marches in
North American history began. The number of mules and horses necessary for
the transportation of supplies and baggage was extraordinary. Filisola's account
of the march describes the more than 1,800 pack mules and nearly 250 wagons
and carts that still proved insufficient to carry all of the army's provisions. A
considerable quantity had to be left behind at Monclova to be sent on as soon as
more transportation could be arranged. Following the troops were great numbers of peddlers of liquor and provisions. Said Filisola, "...the brigades more
nearly resembled great convoys of freight than an army on the march."[25]

The country through which this army had to march was a semi-desert, almost
destitute of water and food for beast or man. It was winter and the weather,
which had been mild, became suddenly very cold. Andrade's cavalry got lost in a
snow storm, in the midst of a mesquite thicket, on the first night of the march.
Many of the animals froze to death; fifty yokes of oxen were lost in this way.
Alternate cold northers and driving sheets of rain and sleet, followed by days of
scorching sun added extreme cold and heat to the thirst, hunger and fatigue of
this army marching on little more than half rations. A great number of women
were going along as camp-followers and they put additional strain on the limited rations. Sickness and exhaustion struck down both man and beast; the gun
carriages and artillery wagons became loaded with sick soldiers. The medical
service of the Mexican army, at best, was scant and poorly organized,[26] and there
were many deaths due to lack of medical attention.

Despite death and desertion, they pushed on and, at noon on February 23,
1836, the Mexican army reached the heights north of the Alazan.

They had arrived at Bexar.

25 Filisola, *Guerra de Tejas*, II, 338-339.

26 José María Tornel, *Tejas y los Estados Unidos de America en sus Relaciones con la Republica Mexicana*,
    29-30; Filisola, *Guerra de Tejas*, II, 148, 302, 311, 315.

CHAPTER V
THE ALAMO AS A FORTRESS

At this point in the narrative, a brief description of the Alamo, as it may have been seen by the arriving Mexican army, seems to be warranted. It is to be re-membered that these old buildings had been construction to serve as a mission, not a fortress and, while strong enough for defense except against siege guns, the thick walls were without redoubts or bastions. Fronting westward toward the city, which was about a half mile away, stood the old chapel, a ruin filled with the debris from its two towers, its dome, and its arched roof which had fallen in 1762. The walls of the chapel were 75 feet long, 62, wide, 22½, high, and four feet thick. From the northwest corner of this structure, a wall 12 feet high extended fifty feet westward to join the south wall of the main building, or "long barracks." This was a two-story building 186 feet long, 18 feet wide and 18 feet high. Its walls were thick and strong. At the time of the siege, the entire upper story was used as a hospital; the lower floor served as an armory and for soldiers' quarters. From the northeast corner of the chapel a wall extended 186 feet toward the north, thence 102 feet west to join the north wall of the long barracks, thus enclosing a patio, or inner court about 54 yards square. From the southwest corner of the chapel, a strongly built stockade extended 75 feet to a building called "the low barracks." This was a one-story building 114 feet long by 17 feet wide, with a *porte-cochere* in the center which passed through it and divided it into two separate parts. One part was used as the fort prison, the other for soldiers' quarters. This building formed a part of the south wall of the main area, of which the long barracks formed a part of the east wall, and some other low buildings, also used as barracks, formed a part of the west wall. The main area, enclosed by these buildings and walls, was a plot of ground 154 by 54 yards. It was not a perfect parallelogram, however, for the north end was considerably longer than the one on the south. These various enclosures covered more than two acres of ground, a space that would have required more than a thousand men to defend with the kind of fortifications the Texans had.

Although Green B. Jameson, the engineer of the fort, had done what he could to put the Alamo in better repair, it remained at the time the siege began in March of 1836, in about the same condition as General Cos had left it in De-cember of 1835. Altogether there were 18 or more guns mounted.[1] There were three 12-pounders on a scaffold in the church; four 4-pounders were on the stockade of the entrenchment in front of the church; the *porte-cochere* on the out-side was covered by a lunette of stockades and earth, mounted with two guns; an

1 Potter, *The Fall of the Alamo*, 3.; Yoakum, *History of Texas*, II, 76; Fortier & Ficklen, *Central America and Mexico*, 311.

18-pounder was located at the southwest corner of the large area; in the center
of the west barrier wall were two more 8-pounders. Near the northeast angle
of the main area, a breach had been made in the wall; another 8-pounder was
placed there to protect that weakness. After the siege was ended, Travis's lifeless
body was found on this gun. Jameson, in his plats, located a small gun in a kind
of tower room on the southwest corner of the long barracks. Some writers claim
that the flag, the Mexican tricolor (the federal flag of 1824,) floated from the
corner of this tower room; others say that it waved over the chapel. Two other
guns were mounted on a platform near the south end of the main area. All the
guns in this area were mounted on high scaffolds of stockades and earth so that
they could be fired over the walls.

The Alamo fortress was well watered by two aqueducts, one touching the
northwest corner of the main area, the other running close to the eastern wall
of the chapel. A ditch connected with the aqueduct on the west and carried
water throughout the length of the main area. Most authorities claim that the
water supply of the Alamo during the siege came from these aqueducts. This, in
all probability, is true, especially for water for the livestock within the fort and
for cleansing purposes; but the Texans had foreseen the probability of the ditches
being cut by the enemy, and had dug a well within the large area[2], thereby making
their water supply secure. The Mexicans did attempt to cut off the water from
the ditches, but seem never to have been successful in doing it.[3]

---

2 Green B. Jameson to Henry Smith, February 16, 1836, *Army Papers*, State Library.

3 Yoakum, *History of Texas*, II, 76; Bancroft, *North Mexican States and Texas*, II, 205; Thrall, *History of
Texas*, 240; Rives, *The United States and Mexico*, I, 327.

CHAPTER V
CHRONOLOGY OF AN INFAMOUS ASSAULT

Although few of the Texans at the Alamo believed the report that Blaz Herrera delivered on February 18 that a large Mexican force had crossed the Rio Grande and was advancing upon Bexar, the excitement manifested by the Mexican population of the city began to cause Travis and his men considerable uneasiness. By the morning of February 23, it was clear to all that this restlessness had developed into a well defined exodus from the town.[1] The people hurried to and fro in the streets and plazas; carts, loaded with household and kitchen goods, moved out along the various roads leading from the town. There was much subdued excitement. If questioned, these movers would declare that they were simply going into the country to commence farming operations. Nevertheless, the Texans became apprehensive and decided to place a sentry in the tower of the San Fernando church with instructions to keep vigilant watch to the west, and at first sight of Mexican troops to ring the bell. About noon of that same day the sentry sighted moving figures beyond the Alazan. Glittering lances seemed to indicate that they were cavalry troops. But at the ringing of the church bell, the troops disappeared over the hills. Since no enemy could be seen by the crowd that had assembled at the alarm, the sentry was accused of falsehood.

But the sentry's report, of course, was true, for Santa Anna's army had indeed arrived. In fact, Santa Anna had arrived at the Medina River during the night of February 20. There he halted and intended to go into camp, partly to rest his weary troops, partly to await the coming of his slower brigades. But upon learning from his scouts that the Texans were to join with the Mexicans in a fandango on the night of the 21st, he planned to push on and make an attack before daybreak of the morning of the 22nd. But before he had received this information from his scouts, his army had already pitched camp on both sides of the Medina, with the munitions wagons located on the west bank. A cold norther, accompanied by a heavy rain, had blown in causing a rapid rise in the river. Finding it impossible to make a crossing in the storm, he gave up his plan for the surprise attack. During the night of the 22nd, however, the cavalry, as the vanguard of the of the invaders, had been stationed on the heights to the west overlooking the city.[2] These cavalry troops had triggered the sentry's alarm.

In order to ascertain the truth about what the sentry had seen, Travis called for volunteer scouts to ride out and reconnoiter. Dr. John Sutherland and John W. Smith, both of whom had horses in town, offered their services. After agreeing

---

1 Rodrigues, *Memoirs*, 8-9.
2 Santa Anna to the Minister of War, February 27, 1836, *University of Texas Manuscripts*, Guerra, Frac. 1, Leg. 3, Op. Mil. 1836, Texas, Exp. de Febrero; Filisola, *Guerra de Tejas*, II, 379-380.

that the sentry should give the alarm if he saw them returning at a run, they set out on the Laredo road. Upon reaching the crest of a hill about a mile and a half out of town, the two scouts came in full view of the Mexican cavalry, formed in a battle line, the commander riding up on and down in front of it, waving his sword and apparently giving orders. Halting only long enough to estimate that the forces before them numbered from 1,200 to 1,500, they wheeled their horses and dashed back toward the city. The sentry rang the church bell. Travis, now with full realization that the enemy was indeed upon him, ordered the Texan soldiers, who were then congregated on the Main Plaza, to retire to the fortress of the Alamo.

It had rained on the morning of the 23rd, making the ground wet and slippery. Dr. Sutherland's horse was unshod and, when spurred into a run, had slipped and fallen, pinning Sutherland's leg under his body. Smith helped horse and rider to their feet, but Sutherland's knee was badly lamed. Upon reaching the city, they learned that the soldiers had all withdrawn to the Alamo, and thither they also went.

Within the fortress all was busy confusion. The men were now active and eager for orders. Already most of them were engaged in planting cannon and in other work preparing for defense. As Sutherland and Smith rode into the enclosure, they met Colonel Crockett, who accompanied them to Travis. Sutherland reported the news that the Mexican cavalry was almost within the city. Upon attempting to dismount, he found that he could not stand on his crippled leg. Nevertheless, he offered his services in the now inevitable fight.

Travis, upon learning of Sutherland's injury, asked if he could stand a ride to Gonzales, saying, "I must send a message to Gonzales as quickly as possible so as to rally the people to my support." Sutherland was willing to attempt the mission, and Smith volunteered to accompany his injured comrade. Crockett, still standing by, said to Travis, "And here am I, Colonel, assign me to some place, and I and my Tennessee boys will defend it all right." Travis then replied that he wished Crockett to defend the picket wall extending from the end of the barracks on the south side to the corner of the church. After a few hasty preparations and brief farewells to friends, Smith and Sutherland set out eastward. To avoid being seen and pursued by the Mexican cavalry which was just then entering the city on the west, they took the Goliad road. After half a mile, though, they turned due east and struck into the Gonzales road about a mile and a half east of the city. By that time it was three o'clock on the afternoon of the February 23rd.[3]

3 DeShields (ed.), "John Sutherland's Account of the Fall of the Alamo," *Dallas News*, February 5 & 12, 1911; or John Sutherland, "Memoirs," 50-55, *University of Texas Archives*; John Ford, *Origin and Fall of the Alamo*, 21-26; William Corner, *San Antonio de Bejar*, 120-121; Brown, *History of Texas*, I, 565

The hasty note that Travis sent by these couriers to Andrew Ponton, alcalde of Gonzales read:

Commandancy of Bexar
February 23rd, 3 o'clock PM, 1836

To Andrew Ponton, Judge and Citizens of Gonzales:

The enemy in large force is in sight. We want men and provisions. Send them to us. We have 150 men and are determined to defend the Alamo to the last. Give us assistance.

W. B. Travis
Col. Commanding
P. S. Send an express to San Felipe with news night and day. -Travis[4]

On the next day, he sent out another letter which has been called the most heroic document in American history. It briefly but graphically describes conditions at the Alamo:

Commandancy of the Alamo, Bexar
February 24, 1836

To the People of Texas and All Americans in the world

Fellow Citizens and Compatriots:

I am besieged with a thousand or more Mexicans under Santa Anna. I have sustained a continual bombardment and cannonade for 24 hours and have not lost a man. The enemy has demanded a surrender at discretion, otherwise, the garrison are to be put to the sword, if the fort is taken. I have answered the demand with a cannon shot, and our flag still waves proudly from the walls. I shall never surrender or retreat. Then, I call upon you in the name of Liberty, of patriotism, and everything dear to the American character, to come to our aid with all dispatch. The enemy is receiving reinforcements daily and will no doubt increase to three or four thousand in four or five days. If this call is neglected, I am determined to sustain myself as long as possible and die like a soldier who never forgets what is due his own honor and that of his country. VICTORY or DEATH.

William Barret Travis
Lt. Col. Comdt.

P.S. The Lord is on our side. When the enemy appeared in sight, we had not three bushels of corn. We have since found in deserted houses 80 to 90 bushels and got into the walls 20 or 30 head of Beeves. -Travis[5]

But the information to be gleaned from this letter reaches somewhat beyond the point that has been arrived at in the narrative. As has been said, by 3 p.m.

4 Brown, *History of Texas*, I, 550.
5 Travis to the Citizens of Texas, *Army Papers*, State Library; Garrison, *Texas*, 207.

on February 23, Travis and his soldiers were entrenched within the walls of the Alamo, while Santa Anna's army had possession of the town of Bexar and were establishing their batteries. Upon entering the town, Santa Anna had ordered a red flag be raised over the tower of San Fernando church. Concerning this first demand for surrender, there are differing accounts. Santa Anna's official report records that when he raised the red flag over the tower of the church, it was answered from the fort of the Alamo by a cannon shot which was immediately followed by a white flag, sent out by the garrison with an offer to evacuate the fort, provided the Texans should be allowed to retire unmolested and in arms. To this, Santa Anna replied that there would be no terms short of unconditional surrender.[6]

From letters found in Mexican archives, it appears that Juan Seguin gave a more accurate account of what actually happened. Seguin said that when the Mexicans raised the red flag, Travis immediately ordered it answered by a shot from the 18-pounder of the fort, but that just about the time the shot was fired, the Mexicans sounded a parley and raised a white flag. Travis wished to ignore this flag and the call to parley, but Bowie without consulting Travis, sent out a flag of truce to demand what the enemy wanted. Santa Anna denied having raised a white flag, and informed the messenger that the men would be recognized only as rebels, and could be allowed no other terms than a surrender at discretion. When this information was given to Travis he is said to have become very angry. He ordered his men to assemble; he harangued them and administered to them the oath of "never surrender."[7] The documents which prove Seguin's account to be correct are as follows:

> Commander of the Volunteers of Bejar to the
> Commander of the invading forces below Bejar:
>
> Because a shot was fired from the cannon of this fort at the time that a red flag was raised over the tower, and a little afterward they told me that a part of your army had sounded a parley, which however, was not heard before the firing of the said shot. I wish, Sir, to ascertain if it be true that a parley was called, for which reason I send my second aid, Benito Jameson, under guarantee of a white flag which I believe will be respected by you and your forces. God and Texas!
>
> Fortress of the Alamo, February 23, 1836,
-James Bowie (Rubric)[8]

---

6 Santa Anna to Minister of War, February 27, 1836, *University of Texas Transcripts*, Guerra, Frac. 1, Leg. 3, Op. Mil 1836, Texas.

7 Potter, "The Fall of the Alamo," 5, a reprint from *American History Magazine*, January, 1878.

8 Bowie to the Commander of Invading Forces, February 23, 1836, *Archives General de Mexico*, Frac. 1, Leg. 1, 1836, University of Texas Transcripts, p. 47.

Santa Anna did not grant Jameson an audience. Rather, he sent his response via his aid, Colonel Batres:

José Batres to James Bowie
General Headquarters of San Antonio de Bejar
February 23, 1836

As the Aide-de-Camp of his Excellency, the President of the Republic, I reply to you, according to the order of his Excellency, that the Mexican army cannot come to terms under any conditions with rebellious foreigners to whom there is no recourse left. If they wish to save their lives [they must] place themselves immediately at the disposal of the Supreme Government from whom alone they may expect clemency after some considerations [are taken up.] God and Liberty!

(This is a copy)
José Batres
(Rubric)

One will recall that the quarrel resulting from the rivalry between Travis and Bowie had merely been assuaged by the agreement for a dual command at the Alamo. It seems to have waxed hot once again on the first day of the siege, over the matter of a parley with the Mexicans. Whether these leaders again made a compromise, or conciliatory agreement, is not known, but the question of the command was definitively answered the next day when Col. Bowie was stricken down with typhoid pneumonia. The notion that Bowie's malady was typhoid pneumonia finds its origins in the words of ten respected authorities on the topic. Mrs. Juana Navarro Alsbury's account, as found in John Salmon Ford's *Journal*, says that when Bowie realized that he had typhoid fever, he had his cot carried to a small room in the low barracks on the south side of the fort, hoping to prevent the spread of the disease. She also states that, at lucid moments when the fever was somewhat abated, his soldiers would bring his cot to the main building where he would talk with them and urge that they remember that Travis was their new commander. After February 24, Bowie was too ill for service and Travis had sole command at the Alamo.

In reply to Travis's note of the 23rd to Andrew Ponton, thirty-two men rode from Gonzales, passed through the enemy's lines and entered the Alamo. Per Travis's request, Ponton sent on to San Felipe the call for help, and on February 27, Governor Smith published it as a handbill, urging all Texans to arouse themselves to the cause so that proper reinforcements might finally be sent to the besieged fort. The fiery text of Smith's plea can be found in the *Governor and Council Papers* of the State Library, as well as in Brown's *History of Texas*, but it is fitting to include it here. It reproduced Travis's plea for assistance and continued:

Fellow Citizens and Countrymen:

The foregoing communication from Colonel Travis, now in command at Bexar, needs no comment. The garrison composed of only 150 Americans, engaged in a deadly conflict with 1,000 of the mercenary troops of the Dictator, who are daily receiving reinforcements, should be a sufficient call upon you without saying more. However secure, however fortunate our garrison may be, they have not the provisions, nor the ammunition to stand more than a thirty days' siege at the farthest.

I call upon you as an officer, I implore you as a man, to fly to the aid of your besieged countrymen and not permit them to be massacred by a mercenary foe. I slight none! The call is upon <u>ALL</u> who are able to bear arms, to rally without a moment's delay, or in fifteen days the heart of Texas will be the seat of war. This is not imaginary. The enemy from 6,000 to 8,000 strong are on our border and rapidly moving by forced marches for the colonies. The campaign has commenced. We must promptly meet the enemy or all will be lost

Do you possess *honor*? Suffer it not to be insulted or tarnished!

Do you possess *patriotism*? Evince it by your bold, prompt and manly action!

If you possess even *humanity*, you will rally without a moment's delay to the aid of your besieged countrymen!

But this heartfelt appeal came too late. Troops could hardly have been mustered to save the Alamo, even if the apathy of the people had been less. The only real hope for assistance lay in the chance of a union of the troops at Goliad with those at Bexar.

Nor did Travis neglect to request help from Goliad. At the same time that he sent his message to Andrew Ponton, he also sent a courier to Fannin, asking for help. At this time Fannin had under his command at Goliad some 420 men. The first message from the Alamo reached him on February 25. He set out for Bexar on the 28th with three hundred men and four guns, leaving Captain Ira Westover in command at Goliad; but he had gone only a few hundred yards when one of his wagons broke down, and being short of draft animals, as well as of provisions for his soldiers, he decided to hold a council of war to discuss the propriety of attempting to go to the relief of Travis. This council of war voted to return to Goliad.[9]

9 Yoakum, *History of Texas*, II, 28; General John E. Holler, "Capt. John Sowers Brooks," *Texas Historical Quarterly*, IX, 257.

The faithful scout, John W. Smith, bore Travis's last message through the Mexican lines on the night of March 3.[10] The soldiers at the Alamo knew that the convention was in session at Washington, although they had no news of its proceedings, so it was to the President of the Convention that Travis addressed his last appeal. As we have already seen, Governor Smith had no power, the Council never had a quorum after January 18, and Houston, the commander-in-chief of the Texas army, was in east Texas on a furlough.

After Houston's return from Refugio, where he attempted to quell the Matamoros fever, he made to Governor Smith a full report concerning the command of the troops, and of his reasons for being unwilling to be made "a scape-goat for the errors of others that would surely bring disaster upon the country;" whereupon Smith, on January 28, issued to Houston a furlough till March 1. In granting the furlough the order stated: "Your absence is permitted in part by the illegal acts of the Council in suppressing you by the unauthorized appointment of agents to organize and control the army, contrary to organic law and the ordinance of their own body. In the meantime, you will conform to your instructions and treat with the Indians." In pursuance of these instructions, Houston and John Forbes went to Chief Bowl's village, and on February 23, effected a treaty with the Cherokee Indians. Thus, Houston, jealous of his reputation and honors as a military man, dropped, for the time being, even his claim to be commander-in-chief of the army, and Fannin who actually held under his command the bulk of the Texas forces, did nothing to relieve the hard-pressed men at the Alamo.[11]

Travis's last letter, addressed to the President of the Convention, reads as follows:

> Commandancy of the Alamo, Bexar
> March 3, 1836
>
> To the President of the Convention:
>
> Sir:
>
> In the present confusion of the political authorities of the country, and in the absence of the commander-in-chief, I beg leave to communicate to you the situation of this garrison. You have doubtless already seen my official report of the action of the twenty-fifth ult. made that day to General Sam Houston, together with the various communications heretofore sent by express, I shall, therefore, confine myself to what has transpired since that date.
>
> From the twenty-fifth to the present date, the enemy have kept up a bombardment from two howitzers, one a five and a half inch, and the other an

10 Gould, *Alamo Guide*, 18.
11 Yoakum, *History of Texas*, II, 63.

eight inch, and a heavy cannonade from two long nine-pounders, mounted on a battery on the opposite side of the river, at a distance of four hundred yards from our wall. During this period the enemy have been busily employed in encircling us in with entrenched encampments on all sides, at the following distances, to wit: In Bexar, four hundred yards west; in Lavillita, three hundred yards south; at the powder-house, one thousand yards east of south; on the ditch, eight hundred yards northeast, and at the old mill, eight hundred yards north. Notwithstanding all this, a company of thirty-two men from Gonzales, made their way in to us on the morning of the first inst. at three o'clock, and Colonel J. B. Bonham (a courier from Gonzales) got in this morning at eleven o'clock without molestation. I have fortified this place, so that the walls are generally proof against cannon balls; and I shall continue to entrench on the inside, and strengthen the walls by throwing up dirt. At least two hundred shells have fallen inside of our works without having injured a single man; indeed, we have been so fortunate as not to lose a man from any cause, and we have killed many of the enemy. The spirits of my men are still high although they have had much to depress them. We have contended for ten days against an enemy whose numbers are variously estimated from fifteen hundred to six thousand men, with General Ramirez-Sesma and Colonel Batres, the aid-de-camp of Santa Anna, at their head. A report was circulated that Santa Anna himself was with the enemy, but I think it was false. A reinforcement of about one thousand men is now entering Bexar from the west, and I think it more than probable that Santa Anna is now in town, from the rejoicing we hear.

Col. Fannin is said to be on the march to this place with reinforcements, but I fear it is not true, as I have repeatedly sent to him for aid without receiving any. Colonel Bonham, my special messenger, arrived at La Bahia fourteen days ago, with a request for aid, and on the arrival of the enemy in Bexar, ten days ago, I sent an express to Colonel F., which arrived at Goliad on the next day urging him to send us reinforcements; none have yet arrived. I look to the colonies alone for aid; unless it arrives soon, I shall have to fight the enemy on his own terms. I will, however, do the best I can under the circumstances; and I feel confident that the determined valor and desperate courage, heretofore exhibited by my men, will not fail them in the last struggle; and although they may be sacrificed to the vengeance of a Gothic enemy, the victory will cost the enemy so dear, that it will be worse for him than defeat. I hope your honorable body will hasten on reinforcements, ammunitions and provisions to our aid so soon as possible. We have provisions for twenty days for the men we have. Our supply of ammunition is limited. At least five hundred pounds of cannon powder, and two hundred rounds of six, nine, twelve, and eighteen pound balls, ten kegs of rifle powder and a supply of lead should be sent to this place without delay, under a sufficient guard.

If these things are promptly sent and large reinforcements are hastened to this frontier, this neighborhood will be the great and decisive ground.

The power of Santa Anna is to be met here or in the colonies; we had better meet them here than to suffer a wave of devastation to rage in our settlements. A blood red banner waves from the church of Bejar, and in the camp above us in token that the war is one of vengeance against rebels; they have declared us as such; demanded that we should surrender at discretion, or that this garrison should be put to the sword. Their threats have no influence on me or my men, but to make all fight with desperation and that high-souled courage that characterizes the patriot, who is willing to die in defence of his country's liberty and his own honor.

The citizens of this municipality are all our enemies, except those who have joined us heretofore. We have three Mexicans now in the fort; those who have not joined us in this extremity, should be declared public enemies, and their property should aid in paying the expenses of the war.

The bearer of this will give your honorable body a statement more in detail, should he escape through the enemy's lines.

God and Texas — Victory or Death

Your Obedient Servant,

W. Barret Travis
Lieut-Col. Com.

P. S. The enemy's troops are still arriving, and the reinforcements will probably amount to two or three thousand.

By the same messenger who bore this appeal, Travis sent out several private letters. To a friend, he wrote:

Take care of my little boy. If the country should be saved, I may make him a splendid fortune; but if the country should be lost and I should perish, he will have nothing but the proud recollection that he is the son of a man who died for his country.[12]

Along with these letters from Travis, John W. Smith carried many others from men in the ranks to their friends and relatives. It was on this day, March 3, at eleven o'clock in the morning, that Bonham for the last time reentered the fort. Travis's letter of this date contains the last information from official Texan sources concerning the progress of the siege. For the rest of the drama, therefore, we must look to Mexican sources, supplemented or modified by what little the women and the negro servants of the fort could tell. The reports made by the women are fragmentary at best. Since they were secluded in the old chapel during the siege and final assault, they saw little of the fighting. They heard the guns and the shouts and cries of the men, but until the final moments, they saw almost nothing of the battle. Before turning to the last tragic scene, it

12 DeShields (ed.), "John Sutherland's Account of the Fall..." *Dallas News*, Feb. 12,1911.

will be beneficial to recapitulate and supplement from both Texan and Mexican sources, the events that lead to it. The following brief chronology is compiled from all available sources:

First Day, Tuesday, February 23 — The Texans discovered the arrival of the first division of the Mexican army. Travis ordered his troops into the Alamo, and they retired to the fort in good order. Although preparations for a siege were insufficient and food was scarce, the Texans were fortunate enough to drive off the streets of Bexar into the stock pens of the fort some thirty head of cattle, and to find, in deserted Mexican *jacals* near the Alamo, ninety bushels of corn.[13] Santa Anna demanded a surrender at discretion, to which the Texans replied with a single shot from an 18-pounder cannon. They hoisted their flag and raised their battle cry—"Victory or Death." Travis sent out messengers to Gonzales and to Goliad, seeking help. James Butler Bonham, whom Travis had sent on February 16 as a private messenger to Fannin, returned and entered the Alamo after the investment had begun. Santa Anna's troops occupied the town and displayed, from the tower of the San Fernando church, a blood red flag which signified "no quarter." The siege had begun but the investment was yet to come.

Second Day, Wednesday, February 24 — Travis sent out couriers to Goliad and to Washington. The Mexicans bombarded the fort vigorously, but did no harm. After midnight the Texans sallied forth and destroyed some wooden *jacals* just beyond the Alamo's walls, and brought the wood into the fort for cooking purposes. No Texans were killed or wounded.

Third Day, Thursday, February 25 — Santa Anna moved his headquarters across the river and with the battalion of Cazadores of Matamoros, tried to erect a battery in front of the gate of the Alamo. The Texans opened their batteries; the Mexicans were reinforced by the batteries of Ximenes, but according to their own account, they suffered two killed and six wounded. Temporarily they gave up the attempt to set up their guns; but during the night, protected by some old houses between the Alamo and the bridge, they succeeded in erecting a battery 300 yards south of the Alamo gate. They also erected another battery near the old powderhouse, about 1,000 yards to the southeast, and they posted their cavalry at the old Casa Mata on the Gonzales road to the east. During the night the Texans sallied out and burned the straw and wooden houses in the vicinity of the fort that had furnished cover to the enemy. A strong norther had blown in about nine o'clock and the temperature fell rapidly.

13 State Department, Memorial No. 39, File Box 60 shows an application by one Gabriel Martinez on June 1, 1850, for pay for one house (*jacal*) destroyed March 1836 by Texans. Martinez said that the house was situated on the east side, close to the Alamo, and that it contained clothes and 36 *fanegas* of corn. Its appraised value was $170.

Fourth Day, Friday, February 26 — There was a skirmish at daylight between a detachment of the Texans and Mexican cavalry which was stationed east of the fortress. Santa Anna received reinforcements and doubled his guard, placing sentinels nearer the Alamo, but the Texans sallied forth for wood without loss. All day the Mexicans kept up a continual firing of their cannon. Being short of ammunition, the Texans answered only occasionally. An unsuccessful attempt was made by the Mexicans to cut the garrison off from water. After nightfall the Texans burned some old houses northeast of the fort and near a battery which the Mexicans had erected on the Alamo ditch about 800 yards distant.

Fifth Day, Saturday, February 27 — Bonham left for Goliad and Gonzales to hasten reinforcements. The Mexicans kept up a desultory fire without damage to the Texans, but frequent night alarms, necessity for unending watchfulness and ceaseless expectation of assault were beginning to wear on them. The Mexicans sent out foraging squads to the farms of Seguin and Flores. They decided to make another attempt to cut off the water from the Texan garrison, this time on the side next to the old mill. They did not succeed but they watched with interest the activity of the Texans in repairing entrenchments and in throwing up mounds of dirt against their enclosing walls. A courier was despatched to Mexico to inform the government of the successful occupation of Bexar.

Sixth Day, Sunday, February 28 — A vigorous bombardment was kept up all day; the investment drew closer because the Mexicans had received news that a reinforcement of 200 men was coming to the Alamo from La Bahia.

Seventh Day, Monday, February 29 — The Texans looked in vain for reinforcements from Fannin. The bombardment continued fiercely, but still without damage to the Texans. Santa Anna reconnoitered, and in the afternoon posted the battalion of Allende at the east of the Alamo. At midnight, Sesma left camp with the cavalry of Dolores and the infantry of Allende to meet the reinforcements of the Texans which were supposed to be coming from Goliad. Late in the night, Travis sent Juan N. Seguin and his nephew out to hurry along reinforcements, should they arrive, and to bring in supplies to the fort if they were able.

Eighth Day, Tuesday, March 1 — Early in the morning General Sesma wrote from the Mission of Espada that there was no enemy, nor trace of one to be found on the road. The cavalry and the infantry under his command returned to camp, but Santa Anna himself went out to reconnoiter the mill site to the northeast of the Alamo. He ordered Colonel Ampudia to construct more trenches. In the afternoon the Texans fired two twelve-pound shots at Santa Anna's headquarters, one struck the house in which he lived. After nightfall, thirty-two soldiers from Gonzales were piloted into the fort by John W. Smith.

Ninth Day, Wednesday, March 2 — The bombardment was vigorous. The Texans were very weary, but continued to fight as their means and their strength permitted. They still hoped for reinforcements from Goliad. In the afternoon Santa Anna discovered a road within pistol shot of the Alamo; he ordered the battalion of Ximenes to guard it to prevent the exit of Texan couriers.

Tenth Day, Thursday, March 3 — The Mexicans tightened the investment, and erected a battery on the north of the Alamo within pistol shot. They were reinforced by the arrival of the Zapadores of the battalions of Aldama and Toluca; and were rejoiced by a despatch from Urrea, announcing that he had routed the colonists of San Patricio, killing sixteen, and taking twenty-one prisoners. James Butler Bonham, whom Travis had sent to Goliad and Gonzales for reinforcements, arrived at eleven o'clock A. M., and reentered the Alamo without molestation. Travis sent out his last courier (John W. Smith) with a letter to the President of the Convention, and after midnight, the Texans made a sally and had a skirmish with the Mexican advance. Indeed, according to the quasi-legendary accounts, this was, as Sidney Lanier expressed it, "one of the most pathetic days of time."

Eleventh Day, Friday, March 4 — Beginning with the eleventh day we must turn exclusively to the Mexican sources and to the reports of the non-combatant survivors of the massacre. The Mexicans began firing early and kept up a heavy bombardment all day, but few shots were returned from the Alamo. Santa Anna called a meeting of his generals and colonels. After a long conference, Generals Cos, Castrillon and others were of the opinion that the Alamo should not be assaulted before the arrival of the two 12-pounders which were expected on the 7th. Santa Anna, Sesma, and Almonte thought it unnecessary to wait for the guns. No public decision was announced. Filisola says that on this day, late in the evening, Travis sent Santa Anna, by a woman messenger, a proposal to surrender the fort with all the munitions and arms, making only one condition—that his own life and the lives of his men be spared. Santa Anna's answer was that the only surrender that he would accept would be one at discretion, without guaranty even of life, which traitors did not deserve. Granting that such a reply was made, the Texans knew that they could only sell their lives as dearly as possible.[14]

Twelfth Day, Saturday, March 5 — The bombardment was desultory, but Travis probably realized that it was but the lull before the final assault. During the afternoon a few shots from the enemy's guns fell within the fort. By ten o'clock in the evening all firing had ceased, the besieging forces were with-

---

14 Filisola, *Guerra de Tejas*, II, 9-14. Here Filisola does not record Travis's proposal to surrender as an official report, but rather as a rumor.

drawn; the batteries were all hushed. All was quiet. And this Mexican ruse had
its intended effect. In a short time the exhausted Texans were fast asleep. For
more than eleven days and nights they had been constantly at their posts. They
had not even left their posts of duty to eat, for a few had cooked the beef and
cornbread for their comrades, who ate it at the walls. Coffee would have been
a boon, but their scant supply had been exhausted long before this day. It is no
wonder that a moment's respite found these worn-out men asleep. Yet they did
not leave their posts of duty, but lay near the walls with their weapons in hand.[15]

By two o'clock on the afternoon of Saturday, March 5, Santa Anna had decided to ignore the advice to await the arrival of the 12-pounders and act on his
own opinion. He issued secret orders to prepare for the storming of the Alamo
at four o'clock on the following morning. The orders were carefully prepared in
great detail. On March 4, companies of Santa Anna's third brigade had arrived
by forced marches, and the Alamo was now surrounded by more than 5,000
men.[16]

The infantry of all the battalions were directed to form in four columns of
attack to be led by the most experienced commanders of the army: the first
column was commanded by General Cos who had dishonorably broken his parole with the Texans; the second, by Colonel Francisco Duque, with General
Castrillon as his successor in case of death or disability; the third, by Colonel
José María Romero, with Colonel Mariana Salas as his alternate; the fourth,
by Juan Morales with Colonel José Miñón to take his place in case of casualty.
Each column was supplied with axes, crowbars, and scaling ladders. The light
companies of all battalions were joined with the battalion of engineers to form
the reserve. The reserve was commanded by Santa Anna in person but was
under the direct orders of Colonel Agustín Amat. The cavalry commanded by
Sesma was to be stationed in the rear, at different points about the fortress, so as
to prevent desertion of their own troops and to intercept any Texan who might
attempt to escape.[17]

Probably the best account of the final assault and fall of the Alamo was published by Vicente Filisola in 1849. His narrative, beginning with the evening of
March 4, says:

15 In addition to the sources already cited, the following works were used in compiling the forego-
    ing chronology: Kennedy, *Texas*, II, 176-180; Yoakum, *History of Texas*, II, 76-80; Bancroft, *North
    American States and Texas*, II, 205-210; C. W. Raines, "Life of Santa Anna," *Texas Monthly Magazine*,
    May 1897-May 1898; Linn, *Reminiscences of Fifty Years in Texas*, 130-136; Potter, "The Siege of the
    Alamo," reprint from *American Magazine*; Foote, *Texas and Texans*, II, 220; Gould, *Alamo Guide*,
    17-20; Johnson & Barker, *Texas and Texans*, I, 404-406.
16 Kennedy, *Texas*, II, 183 (Almonte's Diary.)
17 Filisola, *Guerra de Tejas*, 7-9; *Texas Almanac*, 1870, 37; Johnson & Barker, *Texas and Texans*, I, 406-
    407. These orders were signed by Juan Valentine Amador, and certified by Santa Anna's secre-
    tary, Ramón Martinez Caro.

On this same evening, a little before nightfall, it is said that Barret Travis, commander of the enemy, had offered to the general-in-chief, by a woman messenger, to surrender his arms and the fort with all the materials upon the sole condition that his own life and the lives of his men be spared. But the answer was that they must surrender at discretion, without any guarantee, even of life, which traitors did not deserve. It is evident, that after such an answer, they all prepared to sell their lives as dearly as possible. Consequently, they exercised the greatest vigilance day and night to avoid surprise.

On the morning of March 6, the Mexican troops were stationed at 4 o'clock, in accord with Santa Anna's instructions. The artillery, as appears from these same instructions, was to remain inactive, as it received no orders; and furthermore, darkness and the disposition made of the troops which were to attack the four fronts at the same time, prevented its firing without mowing down our own ranks. Thus the enemy was not to suffer from our artillery during the attack. Their own artillery was in readiness. At the sound of the bugle they could no longer doubt that the time had come for them to conquer or to die. Had they still doubted, the imprudent shouts for Santa Anna given by our columns of attack[18] must have opened their eyes. As soon as our troops were in sight, a shower of grape and musket balls was poured upon them from the fort, the garrison of which at the sound of the bugle, had rushed to arms and to their posts. The three columns that attacked the west, the north, and the east fronts, fell back, or rather, wavered at the first discharge from the enemy, but the example and the efforts of the officers soon caused them to return to the attack. The columns of the western and eastern attacks, meeting with some difficulties in reaching the tops of the small houses which formed the walls of the fort, did, by a simultaneous movement to the right and to left, swing northward till the three columns formed one dense mass, which under the guidance of their officers, endeavored to climb the parapet on that side.

This obstacle was at length overcome, the gallant General Juan V. Amador being among the foremost. Meantime the column attacking the southern front under Colonels José Vicente Miñon and José Morales, availing themselves of a shelter formed by some stone houses near the western salient of that front, boldly took the guns defending it, and penetrated through the embrasures into the square formed by the barracks. There they assisted General Amador who, having cap-

---

18 Santa Anna, *Manifesto* (Transl. by C. E. Castañeda), p. 14, claims that he would have surprised the garrison but for the imprudent shouts raised by one of the columns when the signal for attack was given.

tured the enemy's pieces, turned them against the doors of the interior houses where the rebels had sought shelter, and from which they fired upon our men in the act of jumping down onto the square or court of the fort. At last they were all destroyed by grape, musket shot and the bayonet.

Our loss was very heavy. Colonel Francisco Duque was mortally wounded at the very beginning; as he lay dying on the ground where he was being trampled down by his own men, he still ordered them on to the slaughter. This attack was extremely injudicious and in opposition to military rules, for our own men were exposed not only to the fire of the enemy but also to that of our own columns attacking the other fronts; and our soldiers being formed in close columns, all shots that were aimed too low, struck the backs of our foremost men. The greatest number of our casualties took place in that manner; it may even be affirmed that not one-fourth of our wounded were struck by the enemy's fire, because their cannon, owing to their elevated position, could not be sufficiently lowered to injure our troops after they had reached the foot of the walls. Nor could the defenders use their muskets with accuracy. Because the wall [had] no inner banquette, they had, in order to deliver their fire, to stand on top where they could not live one second.

The official list of casualties, made by General Juan de Andrade, shows: officers 8 killed, 18 wounded; enlisted men 52 killed, 233 wounded. Total 311 killed and wounded.[19] A great many of the

---

19 The question of Mexican losses is discussed at length later in this text, but it seems appropriate to mention here a letter written on March 6 and published by *El Mosquito Mexicano* on April 5, 1836. Penned by a Mexican private to his brother, it is worthy of being quoted in full but its length forbids. After reciting the orders for the attack and the plan of the battle, very much as official accounts give them, the letter goes on: "The attack was made by four columns...I marched under the immediate command of General Cos, and will tell you what I saw. After a long wait, we took our places at 3 o'clock a.m. on the south side, 300 feet from the fort of the enemy. Here we remained flat on our stomachs until 5:30 (whew! it was cold), when the signal to march was given by the President from a battery between the north and east. Immediately, General Cos cried, "Forward!" and [with him] at the head of the attack, we ran to the assault, carrying scaling ladders, picks and spikes. Although this distance was short, the fire from the enemy's cannon was fearful; we fell back; more than forty men fell around me. One can but admire the stubborn resistance of our enemy, and the constant bravery of all our troops. It seemed that every cannon ball or pistol shot of the enemy embedded itself in the breasts of our men who, without stopping, cried: "Long live the Mexican Republic! Long live General Santa Anna!" I can tell you the whole scene was one of extreme terror...After some three quarters of an hour of the most horrible fire, there followed the most awful attack with hand arms. Poor things—no longer do they live—all, all of them died, and even now I am watching them burn—to free us from their putrification—257 corpses without counting those who fell in the previous thirteen days, or those who vainly sought safety in flight. Their leader, Travis, died like a brave man with his rifle in his hand at the back of a cannon, but the perverse and haughty Bowie died like a woman, in bed almost hidden by the covers. Our loss was terrible in both officers and men."

wounded died for want of medical attention, beds, shelter, and surgical instruments.

The whole garrison were killed except an old woman and a negro slave for whom the soldiers felt compassion, knowing that they had remained from compulsion alone.[20] There were 150 volunteers, 32 citizens of Gonzales who had introduced themselves into the fort the night previous to the storming,[21] and about 20 citizens or merchants of Bexar.

Considering the disposition made for attack, our loss should have been still greater if all the cannon in the fort could have been placed on the walls, but the houses inside prevented it, and from their situation they could only fire in front. Furthermore, they had not a sufficient number of gunners. Indeed, artillery cannot be improvised as readily as rebellions. Also our movement from the right and the left upon the north front, and the movement executed by Miñón and Morales with their column on the western salient, changing the direction from the southern front as instructed, rendered unavailable the pieces of artillery which the enemy had established on the three other fronts.

Finally, the place remained in the power of the Mexicans, and all the defenders were killed. It is a source of deep regret, that after the excitement of the combat, many acts of atrocity were allowed which are unworthy of the gallantry and resolution with which this operation had been executed, and stamp it with an indelible stain in the annals of history. These acts were reproved at the time by those who had the sorrow to witness them, and subsequently by the whole army, who certainly were not habitually animated by such feelings, and who heard with disgust and horror, as becomes brave and generous Mexicans who feel none but noble and lofty sentiments, of certain facts which I forebear to mention, and wish for the honor of the Mexican Republic had never taken place.

In our opinion the blood of our soldiers as well as that of the enemy was shed in vain, for the mere gratification of the inconsiderate, puerile, and guilty vanity of reconquering Bexar by force of arms, and through a bloody contest. As we have said, the defenders of the Alamo, were disposed to surrender, upon the sole condition that their lives should be spared. Let us even grant that they were not so disposed—what could the wretches do, being surrounded by 5,000 men, without proper means of resistance, no possibility of retreating, nor any hope of receiving proper and sufficient reinforcements to compel the Mexicans to

---

20 Caro, *Verdadera Idea*, II. Caro gives the number of Texans killed as 183.
21 Filisola makes an error here. The Gonzales men, as we know, went into the Alamo on the night of March 1.

raise the siege? Had they been supplied with all the resources needed, that weak enclosure could not have withstood for one hour the fire of our twenty pieces of artillery which if properly directed would have crushed it to atoms and levelled down the inner buildings...

The massacres of the Alamo, of Goliad, of Refugio, convinced the rebels that no peaceable settlement could be expected, and that they must conquer, or die, or abandon the fruits of ten years of sweat and labor, together with their fondest hopes for the future.[22]

Here, Filisola expressed in a few eloquent words the chief reason why the men of the Alamo fought till the last drop of lifeblood was spent. "They knew they must conquer, or die, or abandon the fruits of ten years of sweat and labor, together with their fondest hopes for the future."

Then there is Santa Anna's report to the Mexican war department which, although false in many respects, delineates, unwittingly, an engagement of thrilling heroism on the part of the Texans:

Most Excellent Sir:

Victory belongs to the army which at this very moment, 8 o'clock a.m., achieved a complete and glorious triumph that will render its memory imperishable.

As I stated in my report to your Excellency on the 27th of last month, concerning the taking of this city, I awaited the arrival of the First Brigade of Infantry to commence active operations against the Fortress of the Alamo. However, the whole brigade having been delayed beyond expectations, I ordered that three of its battalions, namely, the Engineers, Aldama, and Toluca, should force their march to join me. These troops together with the battalions of Matamoros, Jiminez, and San Luis Potosi, brought the force at my disposal, recruits excluded, up to 1,400 Infantry. This force divided into four columns of attack, and a reserve, commenced the attack at 5 o'clock, a.m. They met with stubborn resistance, the combat lasting more than one hour and a half and the reserve having to be brought into action.[23]

The scene offered by this engagement was extraordinary. The men fought individually, vying with each other in heroism. Twenty-one[24] pieces of artillery used by the enemy with the most perfect accuracy, the brisk fire of the musketry which illumed the interior of the Fortress and its walls

22 Filisola, *Guerra de Tejas*, 4-19.

23 *Memoirs of General Antonio Lopez de Santa Anna* (transl. by Willye Ward Watkins,) 92, University of Texas Archives. In his memoirs, Santa Anna describes the final assault as a "struggle so stubbornly maintained for four hours." According to other sources, his official report was more likely true concerning the length of the final battle.

24 In his memoirs, Santa Anna says there were 18 pieces of artillery.

and ditches, could not check our dauntless soldiers, who are entitled to
the consideration of the Supreme Government and to the gratitude of the
nation.

The fortress is now in our power with its artillery stores, etc. More than
600[25] corpses of foreigners were buried in the ditches and entrenchments,
and a good many, who had escaped the bayonet of the infantry, fell in the
vicinity under the sabres of the cavalry. I can assure your Excellency that
few are those who bore to their associates the tidings of their disaster.

Among the corpses are those of Bowie and Travis who styled themselves
colonels, and also that of Crockett, and several leading men, who had entered the Fortress with dispatches from their Convention. We lost about
70 men killed and 300 wounded, among whom 25 are officers.

The following report written by Francisco Ruiz, the alcalde of San Antonio,
is also of interest and value. Ruiz or "Don Pancho," as he was frequently called,
was a staunch Texas supporter but, as alcalde of Bexar, he thought he should
appear outwardly neutral. His father was a delegate to the Convention and one
of the first to sign the Texan Declaration of Independence. Santa Anna, who
knew these facts, doubted the neutrality of the alcalde and kept him under
surveillance. In José María Rodrigues's *Memoirs of Early Texas,* he suggests that
the reason Santa Anna ordered Ruiz to perform the gruesome task of preparing
the funeral pyres for the Texans and burying the Mexican dead, was to retaliate
for the disloyalty of the Ruiz family to Mexican centralism, and because of their
sympathy for the Texans.[26] Alcalde Ruiz's statement follows:

On the 6th of March 1836, at 3 a.m., General Santa Anna at the head of
4,000 men advanced against the Alamo. The infantry, artillery and cavalry
had formed about 1,000 varas from the walls of the same fortress. The
Mexican army charged and were twice repulsed by the deadly fire of Travis's artillery, which resembled a constant thunder. At the third charge the
Toluca battalion commenced to scale the walls and suffered severely. Out
of 830 men only 130 of the battalion were left alive.

...I, with the political chief Don Ramon Musquiz and other members of
the corporation [and] the curate Don Refugio de la Garza...had assembled
during the night at a temporary fortification on Protero Street, with the
object of attending the wounded, etc. As soon as the storming commenced
we crossed the bridge on Commerce Street with this object in view and,
about 100 yards from the same, a party of Mexican dragoons fired upon us
and compelled us to fall back on the river to the place that we had occupied

25 Caro (*Verdadera Idea,* 11), writing in 1837 says, "Although in the past (March 6, 1836) Santa
Anna gave to the Supreme Government more than 600 enemy killed, I wish to say that I myself
wrote it, putting the number as his Excellency ordered; but now that I speak the truth, I say
not more than 183."
26 Rodrigues, *Memoirs,* 10-14.

before. Half an hour had elapsed when Santa Anna sent one of his aides-de-camp with an order for us to come before him. He directed me to call on some of the neighbors to come with carts to carry the [Mexican] dead to the cemetery and to accompany him, as he desired to have Colonels Travis, Bowie, and Crockett shown to him.

On the north battery of the fortress convent, lay the lifeless body of Col. Travis on the gun carriage, shot only through the forehead. Toward the west and in a small fort opposite the city, we found the body of Colonel Crockett. Col. Bowie was found dead in his bed in one of the rooms on the south side.

Santa Anna, after all the Mexican bodies had been taken out, ordered wood to be brought to burn the bodies of the Texans. He sent a company of dragoons with me to bring wood and dry branches from the neighboring forests. About three o'clock in the afternoon of March 6, we laid the wood and dry branches upon which a pile of dead bodies was placed, more wood was piled on them, then another pile of bodies was brought, and in this manner they were all arranged in layers. Kindling wood was distributed through the pile and about 5 o'clock in the evening it was lighted.

The dead Mexicans of Santa Anna were taken to the graveyard but not having sufficient room for them, I ordered some to be thrown into the river, which was done on the same day.

The gallantry of the few Texans who defended the Alamo was really wondered at by the Mexican army. Even the generals were astonished at their vigorous resistance, and how dearly victory was bought.

The generals under Santa Anna who participated in the storming of the Alamo were Juan Amador, Castrillon, Ramirez y Sesma, and Andrade.

The men [Texans] burnt were one hundred and eighty-two. I was an eye-witness, for as alcalde of San Antonio, I was with some of the neighbors, collecting the dead bodies and placing them on the funeral pyre.

-Francisco Antonio Ruiz[27]

As might be expected, we have from the survivors of the garrison meager and conflicting accounts. These survivors were women and children and negro servant boys. Most of the women and children were in the church and saw little of the fighting until the last few minutes of the assault. The negro servants were greatly frightened. Joe, Travis's boy, stated that after his master fell, he ran to the long barracks and hid himself.[28] The scouts who were in and out of the fortress during the siege were valuable eyewitnesses of conditions prior to the final assault, but John Sutherland is the only one of them who has left a written account. John W. Smith, so far as can be ascertained, left no record of the part

27 Translated by J. H. Quintero, *Texas Almanac*, 1860, 80-81.
28 Gray, *From Virginia to Texas*, 137.

he played in this episode except oral statements, and such reports are prone to run to legend as they pass strictly via word-of-mouth. Gleaned from these accounts, however, the main facts as handed down agree on the whole with the Mexican accounts.

By the night of March 5, the garrison was exhausted by their vigilant watch and hard labor, yet they toiled on until nearly midnight. They knew well that the worst of the fight lay still ahead of them and the officers, at least, understood that the cessation of the enemy's fire was but the lull before the storm. Notwithstanding this realization of conditions, exhausted bodies demanded their tolls and, when the Mexicans ceased fire and retired from their batteries, the men of the Alamo lay down at their posts, arms in hand, to steal a bit of rest. Sentinels were set, and three picket guards were stationed beyond the walls.[29] These guards, too, must have fallen asleep—or perhaps they were run upon and bayoneted—for they gave no alarm. In fact, there seems to have been but one man awake, a captain, who gave the alarm.[30]

Up to the moment of the attack, the Mexicans maintained the strictest silence. But when the hour for the assault had arrived, a shout went up; then a single bugle note, followed by silence again except for the rush and tramp of the soldiers.[31] Instantly, Travis was on his feet. He seized his rifle and sword and, calling to Joe, his slave boy, to follow, he ran across the large area to a cannon on the wall at the northwest corner of the large area. As he went, he called out to his men, "Come on boys! The Mexicans are upon us!"[32] By this time the Mexican bands at the southwest battery had struck up notes of the dreadful *El Degüello,* and then all was confusion, for the Texans were up and at their posts, ready for their last desperate fight. The guns on the walls and the rifles both opened on the Mexicans with such severity that they were forced to fall back. Twice the attacking forces applied their scaling ladders to the walls, but twice were beaten back.[33] Their third attempt to scale the walls was successful. This came at daybreak; and just as the Mexicans broke over the walls, Travis fell, shot through the forehead as he stood behind his cannon and made ready to fire his rifle.

There were reports, both Mexican and American, that the single gunshot wound to Travis's head was self-inflicted. Both Anselmo Borgarra, the messenger from the Mexicans at San Antonio to Seguin at Gonzales, and Antonio Perez, their messenger to Navarro and Ruiz at San Felipe, reported that Travis

29 Gray, *From Virginia to Texas*, 135.
30 *Ibid.*, 135.
31 Letter of a Mexican soldier to his brother, March 6, 1836, published in *El Mosquito Mexicano,* April 5, 1836.
32 Gray, *From Virginia to Texas*, 137.
33 *El Mosquito Mexicano,* April 5, 1836; *Telegraph and Texas Register,* March 24, 1836.

shot himself when he saw the Mexicans pouring over the walls of the Alamo and realized that all hope of saving his men was gone. Then, too, the alcalde, Francis Ruiz, in his report, significantly states that Travis lay on the gun carriage, shot only through the forehead. These reports have been largely ignored or discredited by all writers of Texas history, but there is evidence that some of Travis's closest friends believed them in 1836. On March 28, 1836, Andrew Briscoe gave an account of the fall of the Alamo to the editor of the *New Orleans Post and Union* in which he said, "The brave and gallant Travis, to prevent his falling into the hands of the enemy, shot himself."

But William F. Gray in his diary, *From Virginia to Texas*, gives another account of Travis's death. He says that after the fall of the Alamo, Travis's negro slave boy, Joe, was called before the Convention at Washington and encouraged to tell what he knew of the battle. Gray was at the meeting of the Convention, saw the negro and heard him tell his story. He says that "Joe related the affair with much modesty, apparent truth, and remarkably distinctly for one of his class." A few hours after hearing Joe tell his story, Gray wrote it down in his diary. Joe said that when his master was shot, he fell within the walls on sloping ground and sat up, and that about that time a Mexican officer (Colonel Mora) came along and attempted to bayonet Travis, who, making a supreme effort, ran the Mexican through with his sword, and that both died together. But Joe also stated that he did not understand much that went on after that, for after he saw his master die, he ran and hid in one of the rooms of the long barracks, from where he said that he fired several shots.

It is not difficult to imagine that Joe's story is too circumstantial and that Ruiz's statement is more nearly accurate. The fact that Travis's only wound was a pistol shot through the forehead, together with all the attending circumstances, makes the reports carried by Borgarra and Perez seem not implausible.

When the Mexicans had finally gained the walls, they began coming into the large area of the fort in great numbers—Joe said, "they poured over like sheep." But the Texans met them with rifle and sword, and many of them were killed as they leaped from the walls to the ground within. But their overwhelming numbers prevailed. Within the walls the battle became a melee. Every man fought for himself as best he could with any weapon he could lay hands on. When rifles and pistols could no longer be fired they were used as clubs, and lacking even those, men fought with their bare hands.[34] After a short period of hand-to-hand fighting near the walls of the western barracks, the Texans took cover in the long barracks and in the church. On the western front of the long barracks the hottest fighting is said to have taken place. Here the enemy fell in heaps; but finally when the Texans had been greatly reduced, the Mexicans swarmed

---

34 *El Mosquito Mexicano*, April 5, 1836; Morphis, *History of Texas*, 176-177; Bastrop 263, G.L.O.

within that stronghold and the battle was hand-to-hand within the rooms of the long barracks until not a defender there remained alive.

The church was the last point taken. Here, as has been said, the women and children had been placed. Here, too, was the magazine. The Texans had previously agreed that the last survivor should fire a large quantity of damaged powder that they had in the magazine, but Major Robert Evans was shot as he attempted to do this.

The accounts concerning the spot where Bowie died are conflicting. Some state that he was killed on his cot in the hospital, the southwest room in the second story of the long barracks.[35] Mrs. Alsbury's account indicates that he died in a small room of the low barracks on the south side. A number of others say that on March 4 or 5, he grew so very ill that he was brought down to the church where the women and children were, both that he might be in a safer place and that he might have better care.[36] All these accounts agree that with his last strength he killed several of his assailants. They all likewise agree that his body was mutilated by the enemy.

Crockett is said to have fallen near the gate in the 50-foot wall that joined the church to the long barracks. Mrs. Dickenson, in her eyewitness account, says that she spied Crockett "lying dead and mutilated between the church and the two-story barracks. I even remember seeing his peculiar cap by his side," she noted. Nearly all accounts report that his "Tennessee boys" died near him, and that they had piled up many of the enemy about them. As Crockett had promised Travis, they had done their best to defend that portion of the fort that had been assigned to them.[37]

The last man to fall in the battle was Jacob Walker, a gunner from Nacogdoches. After his cannon had become useless and he had been severely wounded, he fled from his position on the wall of the church to the room below where the women and children were. There he was killed at Mrs. Dickenson's side, pleading for his life...but in vain. "The Mexicans tossed his body on their bayonets as a farmer would toss a bundle of hay."[38]

After the greater carnage was over, the Mexicans found five Texans hidden beneath a mattress in the long barracks. Ramón Martinez Caro describes their fate:

35 H. A. McArdle, *San Antonio Express*, December 17, 1905; DeShields (ed.), "John Sutherland's Account of the Fall of the Alamo," *Dallas News*, February 12, 1911; Brown, *History of Texas*, I, 576; Potter, *The Fall of the Alamo*, 5.

36 Morphis, *History of Texas*, 176, Mrs. Dickenson's account; Corner, *San Antonio de Bejar*, 117, Madam Candalaria's account; *San Antonio Express*, May 12, 1907, Enrique Esparza's Account. These are all eyewitness accounts.

37 Kennedy, *Texas*, 187-189; *Texas Telegraph and Register*, March 24, 1836; Gray, *From Virginia to Texas*, 137-138.

38 Morphis, *History of Texas*, 176, Mrs. Dickenson's account.

...there were 5 who hid themselves, and when the action was over, General Castrillon found them and brought them into the presence of Santa Anna who, for the moment angrily reprimanded the said general, then turned his back, at which act the soldiers, already formed in a line, charged the prisoners and killed them...All of us saw this cruelty, which is revolting to humanity; but it is the sacred truth, and I can prove it on the testimony of the whole army.

Thus fell the Alamo.
Thus died its brave defenders.

CHAPTER VI
CURRICULA VITAE OF THE PRINCIPALS

WILLIAM BARRET TRAVIS

William Barret Travis was born in Edgefield District, South Carolina, August 9, 1809. He was the son of Mark Travis and Jemima Stallworth Travis and was the oldest of their ten children, six boys and four girls. The father, Mark Travis, had a son out of wedlock, Tolliferro Travis, who was taken into the home and reared with the legitimate children.

The Travis family left South Carolina in 1818 (some writers claim 1820), and emigrated to Alabama, settling in Conecuh County. The Travises believed in education, and William Barret was given the best schooling that the times and the frontier state afforded. Before leaving South Carolina he had attended "an old field school" at Red Banks, Edgefield District.[1] There he met and became fast friends with James Butler Bonham, a boy two years older than himself. This friendship held true through life. After settling in Alabama, the Travis children were sent to Evergreen Academy, a school that was to have a long life later as Evergreen College. Alexander Travis, an uncle of young William Barret, and a Baptist preacher of statewide reputation, was for many years a director of this institution, which was always a Baptist stronghold in the state. In fact, the Travises were all staunch Baptists, and while still a young boy, William Barret joined that church.[2] In later life he was not regarded as particularly religious, but he did much to circulate Sunday school literature among the colonists in Texas, a service that was highly appreciated by the women and children of the colonies.[3]

He studied law in the office of the Honorable James Bellett, of Claiborne, Alabama. In this study he is said "to have grasped the practical as well as the theoretical side of the subject." Like many another young man, he was forced to support himself while preparing himself for his profession. This he did by teaching school both at Monroeville and at Claiborne. While engaged in this work, he fell in love with one of his pupils, Rosanna Cato, a girl from one of the leading families of the district, and they were married October 26, 1828.[4] Soon afterward, Travis was admitted to the bar and, on August 8, 1829, his son, Charles Edward Travis, was born.[5]

Travis set up his own law practice and was doing well in his profession when a sudden blight fell upon his life. Whether or not the tale was true, he was made

1 Milledge L. Bonham, *James Butler Bonham, a Consistent Rebel* (MS.).
2 Correspondence with D. W. Stallworth of Waco, Texas.
3 "The Reminiscences of Mrs. Dilue Harris," *Texas Historical Quarterly*, IV, 104.
4 Travis's family Bible. State Library Archives.
5 Ibid. These two entries are made in Travis's handwriting.

to believe that his young wife was unfaithful to him, so in anger and despair, he left her and his infant son and came to Texas. It is generally stated that Travis left Alabama in financial straits, but this is probably not true, since he is known to have left a bank account of a considerable amount for the support of his wife and child. It is true, however, that he left all that he had for the support of his family, and carried with him only enough to make a start on his way to Texas.[6] He joined an emigrant train which went by way of New Orleans and Nacogdoches. After reaching Texas he immediately applied for headrights. In one of these 1831 applications, he describes himself as a bachelor, and in the other as a widower.[7]

He soon settled at Anahuac, where he set up a law office. There he came into contact with John Bradburn, the Mexican Military Commandant. Travis took a leading part in resisting Bradburn's tyranny, and in 1832, along with others, he was seized and imprisoned in the barracks of the garrison. After considerable disturbance, he and his fellow prisoners were released without trial. From that time on Travis was one of the foremost leaders of what was known as the "war party," a faction of the Texans who were always ready to assert and to maintain their rights, by force if necessary. Like his close friend, Henry Smith, Travis utterly distrusted and despised all Mexicans.

In 1832, he removed to San Felipe, the capital of Austin's colony, and formed a law partnership with one Willis Nibbs.[8] There, he had to compete with the best lawyers in Texas, such as R. M. Williamson, T. J. Chambers, Ira R. Lewis, William H. and Patrick C. Jack, Luke Lassassier and others of less note. There, in 1834, he became secretary of the ayuntamiento, and probably had a hand in drawing up the able petition, praying for the release of Stephen F. Austin after his incarceration in Mexico City.[9]

In January, 1835, Santa Anna sent a small detachment of troops under Captain Tenorio, to garrison the post at Anahuac and to reopen the custom house. This act caused great excitement among the people who felt that the conditions of 1832 were to be reestablished. A meeting was held at San Felipe on the night of June 21, presided over by James B. Miller, the political chief. Just what happened at that meeting is not completely understood in detail, but it is thought that a resolution was adopted for defense of the country against military occupation, and that it was resolved that the troops of Anahuac should be disarmed and ordered to leave Texas. Smarting under the wrongs that he had received at the hands of Bradburn, and honestly believing that Tenorio and his soldiers were a tyrannical expression of Mexican injustice, Travis raised a company of 25 volunteers

6 Travis family traditions told to me February 1930 by D. W. Stallworth of Waco, Texas.

7 Spanish Archives, *Register for Milam's Colony*, Book A, p. 97, General Land Office.

8 *Texas Republican*, February 14, 1835.

9 Thrall, *History of Texas*, 699, attributes this document to Travis, but more recent and credible
   authorities believe that it was chiefly the work of R. M. Williamson.

and captured and disarmed Tenorio and his men on June 29. In the meantime, however, the people had begun to feel that affairs were moving too rapidly on the road to revolution. They resented Travis's apparent effort to precipitate war, and upon his return to San Felipe, he found himself severely criticized for his attack on Tenorio. There was nothing that he could do but tell the truth, and say that all that he had done had been performed with the most patriotic motives, and to ask the people to suspend judgment until he could make a public explanation. But a large meeting at Columbia on June 28, followed by meetings in other communities, disavowed his act and declared their loyalty to Mexico and their desire for peace.[10] The progress of events, however, soon drove them from their position. In September, General Cos issued a requisition for the arrest of Travis, Williamson and seven other "obnoxious Texans" who had been leaders in the recent agitations. He ordered Ugartechea at San Antonio to enforce the decision, and declared that he would not receive a peace commission until the men were delivered. At the same time he himself pressed on to San Antonio with large reinforcements.

Not daunted by this order for his arrest, Travis hastened to join the Texan army as soon as it was called into service under Austin's leadership, and he was given an important position on the scouting corps. In November, 1835, while out on a scouting expedition, he captured two hundred Mexican horses about forty miles from San Antonio.[11]

After the Provisional Government had elected Houston commander-in-chief of the army, Travis was stationed at San Felipe as chief of the recruiting service there; but he did not remain in that position very long, for in December he was raised to the rank of major of artillery. Feeling, however, that the artillery was not the branch of the army in which he could render the best service, he resigned the commission and asked for a position with the cavalry.[12] Consequently, on December 24, 1835, Governor Smith gave him a commission as Lieutenant-Colonel of Cavalry.[13] In January, 1836, as we have seen, Governor Smith ordered Travis to reinforce Neill at Bexar. He went reluctantly; he pleaded with his friend and superior officer, Smith, to relieve him of the necessity of carrying out the order. He could see no need of his going to Bexar; moreover, he was eager for cavalry activity on the border. It is very probable that he hoped to be made the chief leader of the Matamoros expedition.[14] It is certain that he had little confidence in the success of a volunteer army under the stress and strain of a long siege; and

10 Barker, *Mexico and Texas, 1821-1835*, 137-139; Ibid., *The Life of Stephen F. Austin*, 474-477; *Lamar Papers*, I, 202-206.

11 William B. Travis to General Austin, November 16, 1835, Book No. 3, p. 75-76, Archives of the State Department. This document is Travis's own account of the incident.

12 Travis to J. W. Robinson, December 17, 1835, *Lamar Papers*, I, 264..

13 *Governor and Council Papers*, State Library.

14 Travis to J. W. Robinson, December 17, 1835, *Lamar Papers*, I, 264.

the troops at Bexar, by a large majority, were volunteers.[15] Smith, however, did not rescind the order, so there was nothing that a good soldier could do but obey. Travis was pre-eminently the good soldier, for while it is probable that no man in Texas did more than he did to initiate the revolution, certainly none fought more bravely, served more faithfully, or died more heroically.

At the time of his death Travis was in his twenty-seventh year. In person, he was about six feet tall and weighed around 175 pounds, being inclined to be sinewy and raw-boned. His complexion was fair and ruddy; hair auburn and crisp—almost curly; eyes blue-grey; beard reddish; chin, broad and dimpled; forehead, high and wide. With intimates the young man was genial, often jolly, but he was given to reverie, and toward mere acquaintances he often appeared stern. His temper was quick and only fairly well controlled, and when aroused, his eyes flashed defiance, his form seemed to grow taller and more commanding, but his courteous, courtly manner was never laid aside, and this fact, even in moments of anger, saved the man from abruptness.[16] Travis was a man of charming personality. He had the power of making friends with various classes and degrees of men. Toward women and children his attitude was that of true courtesy. Indeed, the contemporary writers were prolific in their choice of adjective for this man. They always wrote "the gallant Travis," and *gallant* in its best meaning aptly describes him.

As a lawyer and politician he was well trained for his day; he was practical, astute, and youthfully ambitious. His future lay before him, and it is evident that he dreamed dreams and saw visions of success in his profession, of "splendid fortune," and honorable position in the political and social life of Texas. But even so, Travis was not a happy man.[17] The wreck of his family life must have weighed heavily on his spirits, especially during 1834 and 1835. Only a few months after he left his home, a second child, a daughter, was born to him,[18] and in 1835, his wife came to Texas, bringing both children with her. No records can be found that give satisfactory information concerning the meeting between the estranged husband and wife. It is general knowledge, however, that she demanded that he either make a home for his family and live with them, or give her a written statement that he would not do so. He gave her the written statement. She returned

15 Travis to the Governor and Council, December 3, 1835, *Army Papers* (1835), State Library.

16 Thrall, *History of Texas*, 627-628; Frank Templeton, *The Fall of the Alamo*, 230; Materials collected by Judge D. W. Stallworth, and hints found in various letters. These sources have been carefully compared for the compilation of this description.

17 Many items hint at Travis's unhappiness. The following quotation is illustrative of them. "I almost think something that was you with me, that even you could enjoy some pleasure." Robert Wilson to W. B. Travis, June 9, 1835. *Judge Benjamin C. Franklin Papers*, University of Texas Archives.

18 Travis Bible, "Born 4th of August 1831, Susan Isabelle Travis, daughter of William B. Travis and Rosanna C. Travis."

to her father's house with their little daughter, leaving the young son in Texas with his father.[19] Immediately upon her return to Alabama, Mrs. Travis sued for a divorce, and in November, 1835, it was granted her by the state legislature of Alabama. On February 15, 1836—just twenty days before Travis fell at the Alamo—she was married to Dr. Samuel G. Cloud, a wealthy planter, of Mississippi. They removed to New Orleans where both died of yellow fever in 1848. There is some indication that W. B. Travis was engaged to a Miss Cummins of San Felipe.[20] How much his interest in Miss Cummins influenced his decision to divorce his wife might never be known.

A side of Travis that is decidedly clear, however, was that his heart was filled with solicitude for the welfare of his children. In may of 1835, he made a will in which he divided all of his property "share and share alike," between his son and his daughter, excepting such portion as might come to him from his father's estate. That, he specifically stated, was to go to his daughter, Susan Isabelle, in addition to her half of his estate. The will also gave explicit instructions concerning the education and guardianship of both children.[21] From the Alamo on March 3, 1836, along with the letters and official reports sent from the Alamo, Travis wrote a brief note to a friend, charging him with the care of his little boy in the event of his own death.

No satisfactory picture of William Barret Travis can be found. It is very doubtful whether an authentic likeness of the man ever existed, for he lived before the day of even daguerreotype photography, and his financial condition as well as other circumstances of his life preclude the probability of a painted portrait. Since, however, there are three or four pictures in existence that sometimes pass for authentic likenesses of the man, it seems well to mention them here. As a frontispiece for his book, *Margaret Ballentine, or the Fall of the Alamo*, Frank Templeton presents a rough pen sketch of Travis, made by Wiley Martin. Martin certainly was not a trained artist; whatever talent he may have had was wholly that of an amateur; but he and Travis were intimately associated, and it is possible that he was able to draw a sketch that somewhat resembled his friend.

The Travises of Alabama have two pictures that they believe to be likenesses of their famous kinsman. But skilled photographers have declared that the more probable of these pictures is a reconstruction or a picture, made by reworking some other photograph. Indeed, this picture bears such a close resemblance to the authentic portrait of Benjamin Milam, painted by Benjamin West, that one is forced to conclude that some clever photographer has deceived the Travises with a reconstruction based upon Milam's portrait. The other picture owned by the Travises and believed by them to be a likeness of William B. Travis is one of

19 Mark Travis to Samuel E. Asbury, University of Texas Archives.
20 Mary Austin Holley, *Manuscript Notes*, University of Texas Archives.
21 Travis's Will, "Domestic Correspondence, 1822-1835," State Library.

which Mark Travis of McKenzie, Alabama, gave Mrs. Adele Looscan a copy. Here, again one must doubt the authenticity of the picture, for the style of the thing betrays it—the dress, the photography, and other earmarks, plainly show that the picture was made in the 1860's or 70's, not in the 1830's when Travis lived.

The image that probably looks more like Travis than any other in existence is frankly an idealized portrait, painted by the artist H. A. McArdle. The original painting is said to be in existence, but it cannot be located at the present time; many copies, however, have been made of it. While this picture represents an artist's conception of what Travis might have, or should have looked like, it is not merely an artist's whim. McArdle studied the Alamo episode long and diligently in all its minutest details in order to paint his "Dawn at the Alamo" which now hangs in the senate chamber of the Texas State Capitol. During his long study, McArdle learned that Travis and Martin D. McHenry were often called "doubles" by their friends, because they looked so much alike. This fact gave him the idea of idealizing a photograph of Martin D. McHenry into a portrait of Travis. The artist himself called his finished product "The Personification of Bravery and Self-Sacrifice," but this picture has been frequently presented in books and magazine articles over the name of William Barret Travis, and many non-critical, non-inquisitive persons accept it as a true likeness of the hero of the Alamo.

JAMES BOWIE

James Bowie, the third son of Rezin Bowie and Elve Jones Bowie, was born in Elliott Springs, Tennessee, in 1795.[1] His parents were typical citizens of the frontier, ever on the move westward. They were both natives of and were married in Georgia. They moved to Tennessee, Missouri, Kentucky, and finally to Louisiana. The father is described as a man of strong mind and good judgment,[2] the mother, as a woman of keen intellect, fair education and sincere piety.[3] They had a family of six children, four boys and two girls, all of whom lived to be grown.

Living mostly in wild regions, these children had little opportunity for getting an education from books. John J., the eldest son, said that their mother gave to all her children the rudiments of an education, but except for this statement not a word can be found concerning the formal schooling of James Bowie. There are, however, a considerable number of letters and other documents from his pen, which are to be found in the archives of the Texas State Library, and among various other collections of papers in the state; these show that either by formal or informal methods, he had acquired a fair education, for these letters do not suffer from a critical comparison with the writings of other prominent men of the times who are known to have had college training. His brother, Rezin P. Bowie, at one time said that he and James were equally at home in the use of the English, French, and Spanish languages.[4] This statement is probably not literally true, for a few specimens of James Bowie's written Spanish remain, and while they are usually grammatically correct, they show little ease in the use of Spanish idioms; in fact, Bowie did not write Spanish as well as he wrote English. He may have been more "at home" with the spoken Spanish. No examples of his use of French could he found, but it is easy to believe that he wrote and spoke Louisiana French, because for seven or eight years of his life he is known to have spent his winters in New Orleans; moreover, as a boy at Opelousas, he probably learned Creole French.

In 1814, at the age of eighteen, Bowie left his father's home to face the world for himself. He settled at Bayou Boeuf in Rapides Parish, Louisiana, and alone cleared a small tract of land which he tilled. His chief money income, however, came from the sale of lumber which he sawed with a common whip ripsaw and boated down the river to New Orleans. The boy was poor, proud, and ambitious, without rich family connections or influence, but at this early date he determined to be something in the world. His brother says of him that he was

---

1 John S. Moore to W. W. Fontaine, April 14, 1890, *Fontaine Papers*, University of Texas Archives; W. W. Bowie, *The Bowies and Their Kindred*, 267.
2 *Galveston Daily News*, September 8, 1875, account by J. S. Moore, grandson of Rezin P. Bowie.
3 *Ibid.*
4 Bowie, *The Bowies and Their Kindred*, 267.

always careful to form his friendships and associations with only the best class of this backwoods community, but that he was always friendly with everybody.[5] He loved all manner of sports, but took particular delight in fishing, hunting and the catching of wild horses. He was an expert with the lasso, and he furnished great amusement for his neighbors by roping and riding wild horses. In fact, it is said that he often roped and rode the alligators in the bayou.[6]

When his farm increased in value as the country settled up around it, Bowie sold it, and for a few months in the early part of 1819, he was connected with the Long Expedition. In the fall of 1819 he and his brother, Rezin P. Bowie, entered into partnership for the development of sugar plantations. During the seven or eight years of this partnership these brothers owned and developed several valuable estates in the La Fourche, the Rapides, and the Opelousas districts. On one of their plantations, Arcadia, they introduced the first steam mill for grinding sugar cane ever used in Louisiana.

They finally sold Arcadia for $90,000. To their plantation interests, the Bowie brothers, John J. (who lived in Arkansas), Rezin P., and James, added a sideline. They fitted out small boats at the mouths of the Calcasieu and the Sabine Rivers, and from 1818 to 1821, they engaged in the slave trade. Jean Lafitte and his privateers were, at this time, harrying all commerce on the Gulf. They would capture slave ships—mostly under the Spanish flag—and would carry their prizes to Galveston Island where Lafitte had established a regular pirate colony. From this station many slaves were sold into the United States, sometimes directly to planters, but more often through agents such as the Bowies. John J. Bowie[7] said that they paid Lafitte a dollar a pound for negroes, or an average of $140 per head, and then transported their purchase, by means of their small boats, to the mouth of either the Calcasieu, or of the Sabine. Thence on foot, through the swamps of East Texas and Louisiana, they'd make their way to a custom house official.

The law of the day concerning the slave trade was rather irregular. Slave trading was illegal, but smuggling was common, and the question of what to do with the negroes after they had been smuggled into the United States was puzzling. Most of the southern states had laws that permitted such slaves to be sold by a United States marshal to the highest bidder; half of such sale price was given to the person or persons who informed the government of the fact of such smuggling. Thus, the Bowie brothers would carry their slaves, bought from Lafitte, to

---

5 *DeBow's Review*, XIII, 378.

6 Caiaphos K. Ham in Ford's *Journal* (MS.), University of Texas Archives. Ham had lived near neighbors to the Bowies in Louisiana. He had come to Texas with Bowie on his return from New Orleans in 1830 and had fought by his side in the Indian expeditions, and had for two years been an occupant of Bowie's home. He probably knew Bowie as intimately as men knew each other at the time.

7 *DeBow's Review*, XIII, 378.

a custom house officer and become informers. The marshal would then sell the
negroes at auction, the Bowies becoming a second time the purchasers, but receiving back, as informers, half the price they paid. After this double dealing had
been consummated, their title to the negroes was legalized and they were then
free to sell them at a profit, anywhere in the South.[8] But there was considerable
risk in this business. Often they had to keep the negroes for some time before
they found sale for them. Transportation risks were heavy. On one occasion,
James Bowie was convoying thirty slaves through the wilds of East Texas. They escaped from him while he slept and were captured by the Comanche Indians. He
trailed them to the Colorado River, but ultimately had to abandon his property.
But notwithstanding these disadvantages and losses, the brothers had within two
or three years made $65,000 at the business.[9]

     With money thus earned, James Bowie began to speculate in Louisiana lands.
He bought up large tracts of wild land and sold or traded it as opportunity offered. This new enterprise kept him constantly in the woods, but he loved the
woods and all wildlife, so his natural inclinations gave to his employment a peculiar fascination. He was in constant danger, however, from both wild beasts and
from Indians, and it was at this time that Rezin P. Bowie designed a hunting knife
for his brother, and had his plantation blacksmith, Jesse Cliffe, make one from an
old file. This knife was eight and one quarter inches long and one and a quarter
inches wide. It was sharp on only one edge and had a curved point. The knife was
designed to be used solely for hunting purposes, and except for a notorious brawl
on the sandbar of the Mississippi River, it was not used by Bowie in dueling.[10]

     Mr. John S. Moore, grandson of Rezin P. Bowie, was a merchant of New Or-
leans. He possess his grandfather's papers and manuscripts, and consequently had
a broad, and probably an accurate, knowledge concerning the Louisiana Bowies.
He gives the "brief and unvarnished facts" concerning the sandbar incident, an
event that has been variously garbled by many writers. He says that while engaged in the land business in Louisiana, James Bowie became involved in political
party squabbles of the day. At this time, he had his headquarters at Alexandria, on
the Red River. In September of 1827, six or seven men of prominence became
involved in an altercation over an election and the argument terminated in a
riot. In this brawl, Bowie, in sheer self-defence, killed a man named Wright.
Bowie had been shot through the breast, had a broken leg and was lying prostrate
on the sand, unarmed except for his hunting knife. Wright charged upon him
with a sword, whereupon, Bowie raised himself on his broken leg and thrust
the hunting knife through his antagonist's body. Mr. Moore gives the story in

8 E. C. Barker, "The African Slave Trade in Texas," *Texas Historical Quarterly*, VI, 149.

9 Bowie, *The Bowies and Their Kindred*, 270; John S. Moore to W. W. Fontaine, April 25, 1890, *Fontaine Papers*, University of Texas Archives; *DeBow's Review*, XIII, 379.

10 John S. Moore to W. W. Fontaine, April 25, 1890, *Fontaine Papers*, University of Texas Archives.

detail concerning the affair, but all that is of interest for this sketch is the fact that Bowie did not provoke the quarrel. He was not the aggressor, only a loyal supporter to one of the principals and, although he did kill another man, it was in self-defense. At a later day, he and his other antagonists in this affair became good friends. It is said, however, that Bowie vowed never to be without that hunting knife again, and so had a scabbard made for it, and wore it during the remainder of his days.[11] The knife was lost in 1885 but members of the Bowie family still have the scabbard.[12]

From land trafficking in Louisiana, James Bowie cleared from $15,000 to $20,000. In the operation of this business he established an office in New Orleans and spent several winters in that city. By 1828 he had disposed of most of his negroes and land, and then decided to go to Texas and play the land game in that newly opened country. He arrived in Texas in the early days of 1828, and spent several months in a fruitless search for the famous silver mines chronicled in old Spanish records. It is said that he never gave up the dream of some day reopening those mines.[13] He set up his headquarters at Bexar, and on June 26, 1828, was baptized into the Roman Catholic Church, Juan Martin and Joseph Navarro de Veramendi standing sponsors in his baptism.[14] He returned to Louisiana, but at just what time, records do not make clear. However, in February, 1830, he came back to Texas, bearing to Stephen F. Austin a letter of introduction from Thomas F. McKinney of Nacogdoches, which said:

> Permit me to introduce to you Mr. James Bowie, a gentleman who stands highly esteemed by his acquaintances, and merits the attention particularly of the citizens of Texas as he is disposed to become a citizen of that country and will evidently be able to promote its general interests. I hope that you and Mr. Bowie may concur in sentiments and that you may facilitate his views.[15]

Later in the same year, S. Rhoads Fisher, writing to Austin from Pennsylvania, says:

> I hope our friend Bowie may be successful—and no man is better calculated...Colonel, I give you a gratuitous opinion—The most valuable emigrant you have ever had is James Bowie. I consider him of the best order of men.[16]

11 This last sentence is based on lore. While it is frequently found in accounts of Bowie's prowess, the author could find no responsible authority for it.

12 John S. Moore to W. W. Fontaine, April 25, 1890, *Fontaine Papers*, University of Texas Archives.

13 *Ibid.*

14 Baptismal Records of the San Fernando Parish Church of San Antonio de Bexar.

15 Thomas F. McKinney to S. F. Austin, February 13, 1830, *Austin Papers*, II, 331.

16 S. Rhoads Fisher to S. F. Austin, August 14, 1830, *Austin Papers*, II. 465.

During the early months of 1830, Bowie invested from $1,000 to $1,500 in Texas lands, and set up his residence at Bexar. There, he quickly made friends with the most influential families of the town, and became popular both in social and in business circles. On April 22, 1831, he was married to Ursula María de Veramendi. Refugio de la Garza, the same priest who had baptized him in 1828, read the marriage ceremony, José Ángel Navarro and Juan Francisco Bueno, stood as sponsors for the marriage.[17] By the terms of the pre-nuptial contract we learn that at this time Bowie's estate was valued at some $250,000, and that he endowed his bride with his worldly goods to the amount of $15,000, including the deeds to machinery for cotton mills, already purchased but still located in Boston.[18]

This marriage was a real romance. On the wedding tour, Bowie carried his bride to New Orleans to introduce her to his kindred and friends. The whole trip was a series of ovations. At New Orleans the beauty critics pronounced Ursula Bowie to be one of the most beautiful women of the South, and when the couple went abroad, upon the streets they were "the observed of all observers."[19] James Bowie adopted his wife's people as his own, and even at the time of his death, he still considered himself as one of the Veramendi sons. By blood and relationship Bowie's marriage touched almost every prominent Mexican family at San Antonio, and toward them all Bowie was "consistently courteous, sympathetic, kind and affectionate; and they returned his affections in full measure."[20]

Bowie's domestic happiness would be short-lived. At the time of his marriage, Bowie had formed a partnership with Veramendi for the establishment of cotton mills at Saltillo. Since a foreigner could not engage in manufacturing within Mexican territory, letters of citizenship were granted to him by the Congress of Coahuila-Texas on September 30, 1830.[21] After the mills were set up, however, Bowie left the business of their operation to his father-in-law, who consequently established a residence at Saltillo as well as at Bexar, and spent much time there. This was convenient, because as vice-governor of Coahuila-Texas he had to be in Saltillo frequently on political business.

The Veramendi family also had a summer home at Monclova. In the year of 1833, Bowie had to be away from home a great deal, frequently on expeditions against the Indians and in the operation of his various interests. In June of that year, finding it necessary to make a protracted trip to New Orleans, he urged his wife to accompany her father's family to Monclova, promising to join her there in September or October. While on this visit to her father, Mrs. Bowie, her two

17 Marriage Records of the San Fernando Parish Church of San Antonio de Bexar.
18 Records of the Bexar County Court House, San Antonio, Texas.
19 Bowie, *The Bowies and Their Kindred*, 270.
20 Rodrigues, *Memoirs*, 17, 20-21.
21 Gammel, *Laws of Texas*, I, 277, Decree No. 159.

young children, her father, her mother, and several other members of the family died of cholera, all within three days' time.[22]

Self-controlled and calm as Bowie habitually was, the death of his family seemed had overturned the foundations of his life. Upon hearing of the tragic news, he rushed off to Monclova. While there he lost all interest in his manufacturing enterprise and sold the machinery at Saltillo at a great sacrifice. By the middle of October he was again in Louisiana. After making his will on October 31, 1833, at Natchez, Mississippi,[23] he immersed himself in the heart of his Bowie clan to mourn his loss. But Bowie's nature could not tolerate inactivity, and before Christmas he was back in Texas.

Records do not give a clear account of what he was doing in 1834, but glimpses show that he was in Saltillo, Monclova, New Orleans, Bexar, and we know that it was in 1834 that he became implicated as John T. Mason's agent in the infamous 400-league land deals. During the early months of 1835 he was still in Monclova, but by July he had returned to Texas and Louisiana, for John Forbes in writing to a friend on July 24, 1835, says: "Colonel Bowie is ever alive to the interests of Texas," and continues with an account of how Bowie on certain occasions had boldly intercepted dispatches from the Mexican government to its consul at New Orleans.[24]

Contrary to the expressed hope of their mutual friends, it seems that Bowie and Stephen F. Austin never became warm friends. The cause for this restraint between them is not definitely clear. Possibly it resulted from a conflict of financial interests, or from repellent personalities; but more probably it was because Austin believed that speculators of Bowie's type were a menace to the progress of Texas.[25] It will be remembered that Bowie came to Texas to traffic in land. The law authorized the government to sell land in large tracts only to Mexicans, and even to them there was a limitation of eleven leagues to an individual.[26] Bowie schemed to get much more than this amount. In 1830, and again in 1831, he went to Saltillo and induced Mexicans to apply for these eleven-league grants that were permitted to them. After the titles were secured to the individual Mexicans, Bowie bought the land from them. By this method he secured sixteen of those eleven-league grants—nearly a million acres of land.[27] In addition to those holdings, he bought headrights in all the empresario grants. Moreover, he was implicated in transactions concerning the infamous 400-league sale, made by

22 J. A. Navarro to S. M. Williams, September 26, 1833, *Williams Papers*, Rosenberg Library Archives.

23 Harried Smither (ed.), "Adolphus Sterne's Diary," *Southwestern Historical Quarterly*, XXX, 306.

24 *Ibid.*; *Telegraph and Texas Register*, January 21, 1841, and February 3, 1841.

25 Austin to Williams, March 21, 1832, *Austin Papers*, II, 759; *Ibid.*, May 31, 1833.

26 Gammel, *Laws of Texas*, I, 129.

27 Johnson & Barker, *Texas and Texans*, I, 186.

the legislature at Monclova before it was dispersed in May of 1835,[28] a sale that caused intense indignation in Texas. No doubt, Austin was right in his attitude concerning speculation. History has repeatedly proved it to be a curse to any country. But on the other hand, it must be granted that there were many men in Texas in 1835 who were speculators, yet who loved Texas and were ceaselessly active in her welfare. One such was James Bowie, and he had given and continued to give his adopted country much good service.

In 1830 he was elected a colonel in the Texas Rangers and, during the five years from that time until 1835, he engaged in many skirmishes with depredating Indians. In the winter of 1831 and in the spring of 1832, an extensive expedition was made against the Tehuacanas and other tribes. This terminated in the Battle of San Saba, of which Bowie's own official report remains to us.[29] During the years that Bowie was active in Ranger service, he won the confidence and loyalty of all his men, because of his prudent though sometimes reckless daring, and because of his kindness and fellowship among his men, and his unvarying fairness to friend and foe. His men nicknamed him "the young lion," but the Indians called him "the fighting devil."[30] In August, 1832, he led the engagement against the Indians and Mexicans at Nacogdoches which resulted in Jose de las Piedras and his garrison being taken prisoners. After the battle it became Bowie's duty to march 300 prisoners from Nacogdoches to San Felipe, where they were brought before Stephen F. Austin. Concerning the success of this task we have Bowie's own report.[31]

His great sorrow over the loss of his wife and children was upon him in the latter part of 1833 and in 1834. Concerning this period there are few available records, but in the early months of 1835, as has already been mentioned, he was actively engaged in land speculations. In July and September of that year he was again working in the interest of Texas at Nacogdoches and New Orleans. We are told, too, that during this period he was exerting all the influence that he possessed to hold the Mexicans to whom he was related by marriage, as well as others who held power at San Antonio, steady in their allegiance to the Texan cause.[32]

The Texas Revolution broke out on October 2, 1835. Though there are many documents concerning Bowie's activities between October of 1835 and January, 1836, they are difficult to interpret with accuracy. It appears, however, that he

---

28 *Telegraph and Texas Register*, January 2, 1841; *Ibid.*, February 3, 1841; Smither (ed.), "Diary of Adolphus Sterne," *Southwestern Historical Quarterly*, XXX, 307.

29 Bowie to the Political Chief at Bexar, April 23, 1832, *Domestic Letters*, State Library.

30 C. K. Ham's account, Ford's *Journal* (MS.), University of Texas Archives; Bowie, *The Bowies and Their Kindred*, 272.

31 Bowie to Austin, August 8, 1832, *Austin Papers*, II, 832-833.

32 Rodrigues, *Memoirs*, 71.

never held any rank in the army except the nominal one of "Volunteer Aid,"[33] although for a time the First Division of the First Battalion was marginally under his and Captain Fannin's joint command.[34]

Hard feelings arose between he and Austin, the details of which are not known, but it was rumored through the camp that Bowie felt aggrieved because no definite command had been given him,[35] and because, even in the division that he was supposed to command with Captain Fannin, he was actually a mere figurehead, a sort of guide and adviser, but not in actual authority. A shade of truth is given to this rumor by the fact that Bowie sent to Austin two resignations within the span of only a week.[36] The first was on October 26, but almost immediately afterward Austin called on Bowie for service. Bowie obeyed so promptly and efficiently as to merit and to receive Austin's unabashed praise for his skillful and successful conduct of the Battle of Concepción on October 28.[37] But Bowie's grievance was not healed. An incident that doubtless wounded his pride and his feelings still deeper was a bit of failed diplomacy that he attempted with General Cos. The plan was for Bowie to write a letter to Cos, offering negotiations for the Mexican general's peaceful capitulation. If the letter was not favorably received, the Texans were to make a sudden attack on San Antonio. The letter was drawn up and sent.[38] Cos refused to negotiate but, contrary to the plan, Austin delayed the attack until it would have been futile to attempt it.[39] So, on November 2, Bowie submitted his second resignation which was worded thusly: "I take the liberty to tender to you my resignation of the nominal command I hold in the army."[40]

In retrospect, it is clearly understood that the failure of this diplomatic scheme was due to the lack of organization and subordination within the Texan army, and not to willful neglect on Austin's part to thwart Bowie's plan. There is no doubt, however, that Austin was ungenerous to Bowie in the matter of army appointment. On the other hand, Bowie, very probably, was one of the "aspiring men" who gave Austin so much trouble during the few weeks that he served as commander-in-chief of the Texan forces.[41] How high these aspirations mounted can only be conjectured from the fact that Houston, upon hearing a report that

33 "Gen. Austin's Order Book for the Campaign of 1835," *Texas State Historical Quarterly*, XI, 32.
34 *Ibid.*, 22.
35 Charles M. Barnes, "Maverick Memoirs," *San Antonio Express*, January 22, 1905.
36 Bowie to Austin, October 26, 1835, *Army Papers*, State Library; *Ibid.*, November 2, 1835;
     "General Austin's Order Book for the Campaign of 1835," *Texas Historical Quarterly*, XI, 34.
37 *Ibid.*, 26, 33-34.
38 Bowie to Cos, October 31, 1835, *Army Papers; John Adriance Papers*, University of Texas Archives.
39 *Galveston News*, June 10, 1893; Barnes, "Maverick Memoirs," *San Antonio Express*, January 22, 1905.
40 Bowie to Austin, November 2, 1835, *Army Papers*, State Library.
41 Barker, *The Life of Stephen F. Austin*, 487.

Bowie had been put at the head of the army, wrote congratulating both Bowie and the army.[42]

On November 18, Austin received the announcement of his selection by the Consultation to go to the United States, and he set about preparing the army for his departure. On the 24th the army elected Edward Burleson to the chief command in Austin's stead, and on the next day Austin left for San Felipe. Burleson and Bowie were warm friends, and from that time until he was stricken down with typhoid-pneumonia on February 24, 1836, Bowie was continuously active.[43] He led his men in the Grass Fight on November 26, and was conspicuous at the storming of Bexar, December 5-9, 1835.

As the Honorable Seth Shepard said, James Bowie was by no means the rude, uncultivated man, or the desperado that legends make of him. He was a frontiersman, a self-made man, with the good and the bad characteristics of that type. On the other hand, he was a man of fair education and polite and courteous manners, a man who enjoyed and who was welcomed into polite society at Bexar, Nacogdoches, New Orleans and elsewhere. He had engaged in deadly duels which were common in his time, but he was never known to be unfair or cruel to an adversary. The universal testimony of those who knew him best was that he was a man of high sense of honor, sincere and candid in all his dealings, kind, generous, gentle in his dealings with men, and reverential in his regard for women.[44]

His brother, John J. Bowie, said that his disposition was mild, calm and affectionate, but when his temper was aroused by insult or injury that the display of his anger was terrible.[45] Yoakum says, "he was not quarrelsome, but mild and quiet even at moments of action, and he had a wonderful art of winning people to him."[46] William H. Wharton declared, "Bowie is a name synonymous with all that is manly and indomitable in the character of men,"[47] while Houston wrote, "There is no man on whose forecast, prudence and valor I place a higher estimate;"[48] and John Linn calls him "high-toned, chivalrous Jim Bowie."[49]

All stress the fact that for his times he was unusually temperate, and that while he would take "a glass in merry mood," he was seldom drunk. According to W. B. Travis and John J. Baugh, Bowie departed from his habitual temperance while at the Alamo. This may have been because of his knowledge of his illness, or

42 Barker, *The Life of Stephen F. Austin*, 487; Gen. Houston to Col. Fannin, November 13, 1835, *Army Papers*.
43 *Comptroller's Military Service Records*, No. 1513, State Library.
44 Seth Shepard, *The Fall of the Alamo*, 17.
45 *DeBow's Review*, XIII, 378.
46 Yoakum, *History of Texas*, I, 270.
47 W. H. Wharton, "Address to Texas," *Lamar Papers*, I, 363.
48 Houston to Smith, January 30, 1836, *Army Papers*.
49 Linn, *Reminiscences of Fifty Years in Texas*, 303.

as a result of the illness itself. Concerning his bravery it is said that he did not understand the meaning of the word "fear." Juan N. Seguin said that Bowie was known among the Mexicans from Saltillo to Bexar, and that whether they loved or hated him depended upon whether they were for or against Texas, but that whether they liked him or not, they all knew that he was absolutely brave, and that they could always depend upon his being fair to foe and loyal to friend.[50] It is said that after the fall of the Alamo when Santa Anna was looking at the bodies of the massacred Texans, at first he gave orders for Bowie to be buried, saying that he was too brave a man to be burned like a dog; but the generous mood passed.[51]

While he was in New Orleans in 1834, Bowie had his portrait painted by the celebrated artist, Benjamin West. The original portrait is in the possession of his kinsmen in New Orleans, but an oil copy hangs on the walls of the old Alamo chapel in San Antonio. This portrait is said to be an excellent likeness of the man. John J. Bowie describes his brother as being six feet, one inch tall, weighing 180 pounds, with an especially well-made body and limbs. His hair was chestnut brown—not quite red; his eyes dark grey-blue and deep set in his head, calm, quiet, but penetrating in their glance. His complexion was fair, and where unexposed to the sun was white as milk. His hands were long, slender, white, and very capable, with a grip like steel. Altogether, he was a manly, fine-looking person.

50 Juan N. Seguin to W. W. Fontaine, April 10, 1874, *Fontaine Papers*, University of Texas Archives.
51 Bowie, *The Bowies and Their Kindred*, 272; Thrall, *History of Texas*, 506; Lenore Bennett, *Historical Sketches and Guide to the Alamo*, 94-95.

DAVID CROCKETT

David Crockett was born August 17, 1786, in eastern Tennessee. His father, John Crockett, was born in Ireland and was of an old and noble family. John Crockett came to America as a child and grew up in Pennsylvania. He was a soldier of the American Revolution and participated in the Battle of King's Mountain. After the Revolution was over, Crockett moved to Lincoln County, North Carolina, where he married Sara Rebecca Hawkins, a sister of John Sevier's first wife. The ancestors of these Hawkins sisters had played high roles in the history of both France and Scotland. In fact, so far as blood counts, David Crockett was decidedly well-born. But John Crockett was a true pioneer and was ever on the move, a characteristic that was inherited by the son. From North Carolina the Crocketts went into East Tennessee. There they had much trouble with Indians who killed Mrs. Crockett's father and mother. But a home was established, and six of their nine children were born there, with David arriving fifth in the birth order.

John Crockett was a farmer and was perpetually poor. His children had scant educational advantages. David himself said that by the age of twelve, he had never been to school a day, had never heard a sermon preached and had never read a book, but in spite of all that, he was not so ignorant as one might suppose. At a very early age, he said, he had been admitted to the school of experience, and had even entered the university of hard knocks where he had become learned in self-reliance and independence. But in his twelfth year, David's father sent him to a school that had been organized in the community. He and the teacher could not agree, and so this course lasted just four days, because the elder Crockett took the teacher's side in the difficulty, and was about to give the boy a sound thrashing, whereupon young David ran away from home and was gone for three years.

During those three years the boy led a checkered life. He was often on the road with wagoners as a lackey boy, sometimes hired out by the month. Though he always had work, he was always penniless. Finally, at the age of fifteen, he came to realize that he was almost a man yet did not know a "letter in the book," nor could he write his name. The opportunity was given him to return home, and he decided to take it. Upon his arrival, he found his father in his normal condition, "heels over head in debt." John Crockett struck a bargain with the returned prodigal, and told his son that if he could work off a debt of $36 for him that never again need he submit to paternal authority. David agreed and worked for six months to pay the debt. Then, without his father's knowledge, he agreed to work another six months in order to cancel another note of his father's, drawn for forty dollars. This last creditor was an old Quaker—stern, but just, and very kind to the boy.

It was in this old Quaker's home that David experienced his first love affair. The girl was the Quaker's young niece, and she did not reciprocate the boy's affection. After he was somewhat over the hurt of this affair, he decided that the cause of his misfortune was his utter ignorance of books, so he determined to get an education. He made arrangements with his employer whereby he could go to school four days in the week and work two to pay for it. This agreement continued for six months, and this was all the formal schooling that David Crockett ever got. During this time he learned to read a little and to write his name, and upon this foundation he later worked out for himself a fair degree of understanding of the printed page, as well as a gift for clear and picturesque expression of his own opinions in writing. As a mature man he wrote in a clear, legible hand,[1] but was known to say that he never let grammar and spelling get in his way when he wanted to say something.

His schooling might have continued longer but for the fact that he was in love again. By this time he was eighteen and known as the "crack shot" of the neighborhood; he was also getting a reputation as a great hunter. But his second love affair was even less fortunate than the first, for the "heartless jade" plainly jilted him. The wound did not strike deep, however, for in a short time he had found a new love, a fair-haired, blue-eyed, Irish girl—pretty little Polly Finley. This time David was determined to win, although from the start he had a rival. Consequently he began what he called "a close courtship," a plan he defined as sitting up so close that the other fellow had no chance to get at the girl. The plan was successful, for, after some difficulty with her mother, he and Polly were married, and had a "rousing big" reception at his father's house, the only present that John Crockett was able to give his son. In the meantime, Polly's mother had relented and gave the young couple two cows and calves. David had a horse of his own, so he rented a piece of ground and settled down. Polly had a good spinning wheel and was an expert spinner and weaver, so the young couple prospered and were happy. It may be well to state here that if David Crockett was well-born, he was doubly well-married, for Polly Finley was in direct line of descent from royal blood, being the daughter of the William Finley who accompanied Daniel Boone to the west. This William Finley was a descendent in direct line, from MacBeth, son of the Earl of Moray, King of Scotland.

But pioneer blood ran in David Crockett's veins and the impulse to move on-ward—westward, ever westward—never left him contented for long at any one place. We find him next in Lincoln County, in middle Tennessee, a wild country on the Elk River. Here he remained until after the War of 1812. He participated in this war, fought in the Creek War and went with Jackson on the Florida campaign, where he was the hero of many adventures, some perilous, some amusing.

1 *Comptroller Military Service Records*, No. 13, State Library.

Not long after this campaign, faithful little Polly Finley died, but David soon consoled himself by marrying "a soldier's widow who owned a snug little farm and lived quite comfortably." This widow, Elizabeth Patton, had lost her husband in the Creek War.

Scarcely had David and his new wife settled down together before the urge to move struck him again. He left Lincoln County and went into the Creek country. In this wild new country, the settlers got together and organized a civil government, of which David Crockett was elected a magistrate. He was utterly ignorant of government and all its forms and rules, and he found great embarrassment in his new task of issuing warrants and keeping a docket. In fact, few of the nice forms of common law were observed; rather a sort of natural law held sway, whereby crude justice was administered, the payment of debt was enforced, and thieves were tied up to stakes and soundly flogged. This experience gave David a taste of politics. He was next elected colonel of the Tennessee state militia, and soon afterward, with some urging on the part of his friends, he became a candidate for the legislature. His methods of campaigning were frank and unique, highly amusing, yet based upon good common sense, and he was elected by a majority of two to one.

He tells in his autobiography how soon after his election, he met at Pulaski, James K. Polk who remarked, "Well, Colonel, I suppose we will have a radical change of the judiciary at the next session of legislature." Crockett says that he replied, "Very likely, sir, very likely"; and discreetly withdrew. "Well," he further comments, "if I know'd what he meant by 'judiciary,' I wish I may be shot. I had never heard there was such a thing in all nature." But from this time the man's self-education began, and he proved an apt scholar. In the legislature he acquired a good store of sound information which he was shrewd enough to improve upon and put to good account.

It was just about this time that the disasters of a flood rendered him penniless, and again we find him on the move, this time to West Tennessee to a wilderness filled with Indians. But, by 1823, he had again entered politics and was elected to the legislature from a district composed of eleven counties of West Tennessee. By this time he was well known and popular, the result of his hard common sense, absolute honesty, and a deep, broad vein of humor in his nature that gave him an intuitive understanding of the men about him. From 1823 to 1835 David Crockett was much in the public eye. In 1827, he was elected Congressman from Tennessee, and was a strong Jackson man, but in 1829 he voted against Jackson's Indian Bill. This act let loose the enemy's venom, and he was defeated for a third term by a petty political trick of his opponents. At the next congressional election, however, he was triumphantly elected as an anti-Jackson man, in the face of all of Jackson's influence.

Crockett now took part in debates in Congress in which the State of Tennessee was especially interested, always basing his speeches, not on political theory, but on the "plain common sense view." He had a knack for speech making and, while he could "talk bar" to backwoodsmen with the best of them, it is a mistake that the world has made to believe that he used, in cultivated circles, the grammar and pronunciation usually attributed to him. The truth is that he had sufficient mastery of the English language to use it without attracting unusual attention to his abuse of it.[2] David Crockett was shrewd and clever. He loved the limelight, and was a rather accomplished actor. When his backwoods lingo would gain for him center stage, he used it freely—even in the cultured environs of Boston.

He remained a strong anti-Jackson man, and some of his writings and speeches were prominent among the anti-Jackson literature of the times. There were persons who perhaps served in a speech-writing capacity for Crockett, but he thought out the problems for himself, and fearlessly voted according to his convictions of what would be best for the country, irrespective of his party's policy. Thus, we find him voting against the instructions of the legislature of his own state regarding the public lands of Tennessee. He favored internal improvement by the government, and in a speech in Congress in 1830 he said, "I would vote to go through any gentleman's estate with a road or a canal if it was for the good of the whole Union, and I do not believe I will ever give up this doctrine." This speech gained for him popularity in the Northern and commercial states. He was invited to Philadelphia, New York, Boston, and Cincinnati; his whole journey brought ovation after ovation. He also introduced a set of resolutions, favoring the abolition of the West Point Military Academy on the grounds that if the government had bounties to bestow, they should be to the poor and destitute and not to the rich and influential.

Despite the popularity he had found in certain sectors of the country, in 1835 David Crockett was defeated for Congress. This defeat weighed heavily on his spirits. He was loath to give up popular favor and high position—the sweets which he had tasted. The iron of defeat sank deep into his soul, but after grieving over his downfall for a time, his old motto reasserted itself—"Be sure you are right, then go ahead"—and gave him courage to begin life anew. It is said that in a speech to his constituents, he told them to go to hell…that he would just head to Texas. A short time later, he shouldered his favorite rifle, Betsy, and started westward again. If his *Autobiography* can be trusted, it traces his footsteps through Arkansas en route to his fate in Texas.

After reaching Texas, he can be tracked from Nacogdoches to Washington-on-the-Brazos thence to San Antonio through official documents. At Nacogdoches, he was elected colonel of a company of Tennesseeans who were on their way to

2 Emerson Hough, *The Way to the West*, 147-148, 165.

San Antonio.[3] There were some sixteen in this band when it left Nacogdoches. Possibly only twelve of them entered the Alamo with Crockett,[4] although one or two others of the company, no doubt, went into the fort a few days later.

After reaching San Antonio, he was cordially received by Travis, the commander of the post, and was offered a command. He refused the command, but at the urgent demand of the soldiers, he mounted a goods box and gave them a speech.[5] Mrs. Dickenson, one of the survivors of the massacre, told that Colonel Crockett was very popular with all the soldiers at the Alamo and after the siege began, constantly cheered and encouraged the men.[6] She also said that Crockett often "played tunes on his fiddle" when the fighting was not brisk; and that sometimes he played in competition with John McGregor's bagpipes.

Others, who knew Crockett after he came to Texas, praise his oratory skills and his sterling honesty, but describe him as quaint and rather uncouth. The man was certainly eccentric, perhaps he purposely appeared queer. At any rate, upon leaving Tennessee, he cast aside all garments except those made from the skins of animals that he had slain. His cap was of coonskin, his breeches of buckskin; fur peltries covered his shoulders when it was cold, while in warm weather he wore a buckskin jacket ornamented with horn buttons. His feet were usually shod in moccasins like those worn by Indians.[7]

The last letter that Crockett probably ever wrote gives us an insight into the magnitude of the man's courage, shrewdness and egoism. His spirits and his belief in himself had not been so crushed by political defeat that he could not again turn his thoughts and his hopes westward and plan bigger things in both a financial and a political way for his future than he had experienced in the past. The letter reads:

> San Augustine, Texas
> January 9, 1836
>
> My Dear Son and Daughter:
>
> This is the first time I have had the opportunity to write to you with convenience. I am now blessed with excellent health, and am in high spirits, although I have had many difficulties to encounter. I have got through safe and have been received by everybody with open arms of friendship,

3 John Forbes to J. W. Robinson, January 12, 1836, *Lamar Papers*, I, No. 294; *Comptroller Military Service Records*, Nos. 10, 13, 208, 226, 1361, State Library; Letter from a "Volunteer of 1836" to Mr. Teulon, *Austin City Gazette*, April 4, 1841.

4 DeShields (ed.), "John Sutherland's Account..." *Dallas News*, February 5, 1911.

5 *Ibid*; Barnes, *San Antonio Express*, February 12, 1905.

6 Morphis, *History of Texas*, 173-178; Gray, *From Virginia to Texas*, 136.

7 Barnes, *San Antonio Express*, February 12, 1905.

I am hailed with a hearty welcome to this country, a dinner and a party of Ladys have honored me with an invitation to participate with them, both in Nacogdoches and this place; the cannon was fired here on my arrival and I must say as to what I have seen of Texas: it is the garden spot of the world, the best land & best prospects for health I ever saw is here, and I do believe it is a fortune to any man to come here; there is a world of country to settle, it is not required to pay down for your league of land; every man is entitled to his headright of 4,438 acres and they may make the money to pay for it off the land.

I expect in all probability to settle on the Bodark or Chocktaw Bayou of Red River, that I have no doubt is the richest country in the world, good land, plenty of timber, and the best springs, and good mill streams, good range, clear water & every appearance of health—game a plenty. It is in the pass where the buffalo passes from the north to south and back twice a year and bees and honey a plenty.

I have a great hope of getting the agency to settle that country and I would be glad to see every friend I have settle there, it would be a fortune to them all. I have taken the oath of the government and have enrolled my name as a volunteer for six months, and will set out for the Rio Grande in a few days with the volunteers of the U. S., but all volunteers are entitled to a vote for a member of the convention and these members are to be voted for; and I have but little doubt of being elected a member to form the Constitution for the Provence. I am rejoiced at my fate. I had rather be in my present situation than to be elected to a seat in Congress for life. I am in great hopes of making a fortune for myself and family...I have not wrote to William but have requested John to direct him what to do. I hope you show him this letter and also your brother John as it is not convenient at this time for me to write them. I hope you will do the best you can and I will do the same. Do not be uneasy about me, I am with my friends. I must close with great respects.

Your affectionate father, Farewell

David Crockett[8]

(Children alluded to are from his first marriage. None of them came to Texas.)

There are several authentic pictures of David Crockett in existence. Crockett enjoyed having his portrait painted and his eccentric personality, as well as his popularity, induced friends and politicians to have his portrait painted a number of times, always without cost to the clever David. Two of these portraits were

8 Crockett to his daughter, Margaret and her husband Wiley Flowers, January 9, 1836. Published in *Dallas News*, January 1, 1913.

painted by the celebrated Benjamin West, while there are others by less famous artists.[9]

---

9 The main part of this sketch is based on the following sources: David Crockett, *Autobiography*, edited by W. H. Graham; *Ibid.*, edited by G. G. Evans; *Ibid.*, edited by J. Limbird; *Ibid.*, edited by Everett McNeill; James J. Roche, *David Crockett;* John S. C. Abbott, *Ibid.*; W. F. Cody, *Ibid.*; E. S. Ellis, *Ibid*; William C. Sprague, *Ibid.*; Marcus J. Wright, *Ibid.*; *Arkansas Advocate*, April 4, 1836, March 13, 1835; *Augusta Sentinel*, May 24, 1836; Hough, *The Way to the West*.

ANTONIO LÓPEZ DE SANTA ANNA

Antonio López de Santa Anna was born at Jalapa, Vera Cruz, February 21, 1792. Has father was a Spaniard, respectable though poor; his mother was a Mexican woman of mixed blood. He received an education of the barest rudiments, for his father planned for him to be a merchant and deemed it unnecessary to waste time and money on books. But the boy's inclination toward the military was so prevalent that, at the age of fourteen or fifteen, he was taken into the military family of General Davila, the Intendent of Vera Cruz, and for the next five or six years he served with the king's troops in Texas and Tamaulipas. During the war of Mexican independence, he served near Vera Cruz, principally engaged in suppressing guerilla chieftains like Victoria and Guerrero. When the Plan de Iguala was proclaimed, Santa Anna left Vera Cruz and turned against his old master and benefactor. He placed himself at the head of some irregular troops which he'd managed to raise and, with this crude cavalry, he seized the city and drove Davila into the castle of San Juan d'Ulloa. For a time he seemed to have complete control but the tables soon turned and he was repulsed. Subsequently, he entered the city again, got complete possession, expelled the Spanish troops, and reduced royal Spanish power in Mexico to the castle. It is told that following this event Davila had an interview with his erstwhile favorite, in which the old patron told his former protege that he was destined to play an important role in the history of his country. "And now," said the old soldier, "I will give you some good advice—always go with the strongest party." Of this advice Santa Anna was ever mindful.

But while Santa Anna had been one of the first to join Iturbide and to acclaim him emperor, his loyalty hardly outlasted the year, for feeling himself slighted by the emperor, he decided to overthrow him, and was actually one of the first to proclaim a republic. Thus, the story runs throughout his long career—all men of position came to distrust his loyalty and to fear his power. To be rid of him, President Victoria gave him a command in Yucatán. In spite of this practical exile from the center of the political game, he managed to make himself governor of that state, and by 1828 was in control of Vera Cruz again. It is not the purpose of this sketch, however, to give a full account of Santa Anna's career, for that would necessitate the tracing of the history of Mexico for fifty years; so it is sufficient to say here that he was promoted (often self-promoted) step by step until he made himself president of Mexico in February, 1833. His heart's desire was to be emperor, but that goal he never reached.

Indeed, Santa Anna's life is so full of anomalies, so full of contradictions, that it is difficult to make isolated plausible statements about his character. It may be said with equal truth that he was an extremely affable man, full of anecdote and humor and sympathy, fascinating and agreeable as a companion; but on the other hand, a bigoted, cowardly, merciless tyrant whose path was marked by death, fire, famine, and desolation. Mexico came to regard this man as ancient Greece did her Alcibiades—she loved him, she hated him, she exiled him, but always called him back, for she seemed not to be able to get on without him.

But Mexico's love for Santa Anna was unrequited, it seems. He did not care deeply for his country, its growth and prosperity, although he was ever full of bombastic talk about patriotism. He was always curiously unwilling to take up the ordinary duties of public life, and whenever a crisis came, he was shrewd enough to retire to private life and let someone else bear the brunt of unpopular reform. He would figure only in spectacular affairs, and left hum-drum details to others. He was overweening in his ambition, but only for wealth, riches and self-aggrandizement. The following story pretty thoroughly represents the man: On the day that he was raised to the rank of major, in 1820, instead of seeming joyful and proud, he was sad and weary looking. A friend congratulated him on his promotion, but chided him for his unhappy countenance, whereupon Santa Anna shrugged his shoulders and said: "If they could make me God I would still want something higher."

His conscience seems to have been rather capricious; actions that revolted most men never disturbed Santa Anna. Still, such ferocious, inhuman cruelty as he exhibited in Texas was not in keeping with his previous career, which had not, except in his treatment of Zacatecas, been marked by inhumanity. It may truthfully be said that he was not habitually cruel.

Although rated by many as both a statesman and a great general, he was truly neither. Though in the field he was at times unbelievably successful, he lacked personal bravery, sagacity and loyalty. Nor did he stand high intellectually. Though for successive periods of from two or more years at a time, he exercised almost absolute control over Mexico, no intelligent person believed in his honesty or his patriotism, rather, he was thought to be ever, according to historian Justin H. Smith, "a wonderful combination of imperious will, mental quickness…unmatched ambition, audacity and unscrupulousness." His knowledge of Mexicans and their natures was almost uncanny, and he could play upon their ignorance and superstitions as he willed. Nature had also endowed him with a genius for action which he most effectively brought into play whenever it would serve his own purpose. Another factor that both made and marred his career was the fact that men much shrewder and morally worse than himself, but lacking in leadership abilities, were ever ready to support him in order to use his powers to their own purposes. Nor did he have any firm set of political principles; the only principle he knew was greed for wealth with which he could gratify his own pleasures and his lust for self-aggrandizement.

Texans are apt to think of Santa Anna's career as ending with his defeat at San Jacinto, but this is not so. He figured in Mexican history, first in almost absolute power, then in exile, then in power again until 1855, when he was sent on his last exile. His magnificent estates were seized and confiscated, restored, then seized again. In the end, he was stripped of his great wealth and left with but a small competence in his old age. In 1867 he made a last effort to regain power. It was a complete failure, and he would have been executed had the Mexican courts not decreed that he was in his dotage. In 1870, he began writing his memoirs, which are as full of falsehood and bombast as was the life of the man. In 1874, now an old crippled man, he was allowed to return to Mexico under an amnesty law; but nobody recognized in the poor old decrepit creature the arrogant "El Presidente" of former days, and even when his identity was made known, it caused no comment. Mexico was no longer proud of him; she no longer needed him. Upon his return to the country, he went to Mexico City, where he rode unnoticed in an old dilapidated public hack through the very streets where he had once commanded in grandeur. A stranger owned his kingly estate, Manga de Clavo. In a poor, obscure boarding house he lived out his last two years, wholly ignored, and he died in squalor on June 21, 1876. The only notice of his death was this simple statement in a leading Mexico City newspaper, *Two Republics*:

> General Antonio López de Santa Anna died in this city on the 21st inst. However he may have been condemned by parties, his career formed a brilliant and an important part of the history of Mexico, and future historians will differ in their judgment of his merits. Santa Anna outlived his usefulness and his ambitions. He died at the ripe age of eighty-four. Peace to his ashes.

As may be supposed, there are many authentic portraits and photographs of Santa Anna, and they portray the many different conditions of his life. When McArdle was painting his "Dawn at the Alamo," he wrote to the War Department of the Mexican government and asked for a photograph of Santa Anna that was authentic and a good likeness of the man. The picture sent is of the period of his dictatorship. He wears a full-dress uniform of the rank of a general. His face is clean-shaved, his mouth is grim, and his eyes are moody. This picture is that of an older looking man than the Santa Anna who invaded Texas in 1836. At that time he was regarded as a very handsome man. He was 5 feet, 10 inches in height and rather spare. His complexion was dark, black hair, short black whiskers, without mustache, moderately high forehead and large, black, expressive eyes. He was graceful, genteel and dignified in deportment, a man of agreeable even fascinating manners. His conduct in Texas, however, placed a stigma of heartless cruelty and treachery upon his reputation that even a century has not obliterated.[1]

---

1 The facts of the above sketch are compiled from the following sources: Caro, *Verdadera Idea*, transl. by C. E. Castañeda; Filisola, *Guerra de Tejas*, transl. by C. E. Castañeda; Santa Anna, *Memoirs*, translated by Willye Ward Watkins; Rives, *The United States and Mexico*, I, 207-210; Bancroft, *The History of Mexico*, V, 138-139; Justin Smith, "Santa Anna," *American Historical Association Reports*, 1917, 357-358; C. H. Wharton, "El Presidente," *Boston Evening Transcript*, June 17, 1836.

CHAPTER VII
ROLL OF THE ALAMO OCCUPANTS

THE TOTAL NUMBER OF INMATES AT THE ALAMO

There are many historical problems growing out of the siege and fall of the Alamo, some of which may never be definitely settled. It is the purpose of this chapter, however, to discuss those problems and to present such answers at which I have tentatively arrived.

How many souls were in the Alamo when the siege began, and how many died there? Authorities vary in their attempt to answer this question, some putting the number of persons at the Alamo as low as 150; others report more than 200. This discrepancy is due largely, I think, to differences in interpreting Travis's reports. Those who give the low numbers always cite Travis's letters as proof of their statements, but in his reports from the Alamo after February 23, Travis counted only able-bodied men upon whom he could depend for effective service.

At no time after the siege of San Antonio in December of 1835, were there fewer than twenty or thirty sick and wounded men in the hospital of the Alamo.[1] Dr. Amos Pollard sent to the Council, on December 28, 1835 the names of twenty-two men who had been wounded at the taking of Bexar.[2] Five of that twenty-two—all reported by Pollard as having been severely wounded—are on the roll of 187 victims that I have verified by reliable documents. Those men were probably never fit for service during the siege of March of 1836. Moreover, in all the letters from Pollard to Smith,[3] he writes of the numerous sick soldiers and of how busy he is attending them. One suspects that a good deal of this distress was bluster on Pollard's part to magnify his service, but the fact remains that there were in all probability more than twenty sick men at the Alamo. Travis never mentioned even Bowie after he had fallen ill of pneumonia, and after a little thought one is convinced that it was a wise policy for him not to enumerate any of his disabled men in his reports while asking for reinforcements, but in estimating the number of persons at the fort, they must be considered.

There were also twenty or thirty non-combatants, citizens of Bexar—men, women, and children—who had taken refuge in the Alamo upon the arrival of the Mexican army. Some of those frightened Mexicans left before the final assault, but the majority were there to the end. In fact, my study of this question

1 "Jesse B. Badgett's Account of the Alamo Massacre," Little Rock *Advocate*, April 15, 1836; DeShields (ed.), "John Sutherland's Account of the Fall of the Alamo," *Dallas News*, February 3, 1911; Seguin, *Memoirs*, 7, University of Texas Archives; Memorial No. 131, File 82, Archives of the State Department.
2 Amos Pollard to Gov. Smith and the Council, December 28, 1835, *Army Papers*, State Library.
3 There are a number of Pollard letters among the *Army Papers*, State Library.

leads to the opinion that there were some 215 or 220 persons in the fortress on the morning of March 6, 1836. Between 185 and 200 of this number were soldiers, the others were the non-combatants. If we remember, however, that Travis counted only efficient fighting men, it will be clearly seen that this estimate does not conflict with his reports. Before the arrival of the thirty-two from Gonzales on March 1, there were probably never more than 145 or 150 men at the Alamo who were fit for service.

Travis never made a complete return to the Texan government of his forces at the Alamo and whatever muster rolls he may have used in his command of the fort were apparently destroyed by the Mexicans after they took possession of it. The roster of the Alamo dead, therefore, must necessarily be a reconstruction. Many attempts have been made to compile it, but no complete or accurate roll has ever been made, and probably no absolutely accurate roster of those brave men will ever be made. The list of 187 names which follows, compiled from an exhaustive study of all available sources, is, in the author's opinion, as nearly complete and accurate as it is possible to make it. In addition to this verified list, an additional lists is presented. These are the names of men who probably died at the Alamo. There is some evidence that these twelve men died at the Alamo, but it is not sufficiently clear to justify my putting them on the verified roll.

VICTIMS OF THE ALAMO MASSACRE
VERIFIED BY RELIABLE DOCUMENTS

Abamillo, Juan	Brown, George
Allen, R.	Brown, James
Andross, Miles DeForest	Buchanan, James
Autry, Micajah	Burns, Samuel E.
Badillo, Juan Antonio	Butler, George D.
Bailey, Peter James	Campbell, Robert
Baker, Isaac G.	Cane (Cain), John
Baker, William Charles M.	Carey, William R.
Ballentine, John J.	Clark, Charles
Ballentine, Robert W.	Cloud, Daniel William
Baugh, John J.	Cochran(e), Robert
Bayliss, Joseph	Cottle, George Washington
Blair, John	Courtman, Henry
Blair, Samuel	Crawford, Lemuel
Blazeby, William	Crockett, David
Bonham, James Butler	Crossman, Robert
Bourne, Daniel	Cummings, David P.
Bowie, James	Cunningham, Robert
Bowman, Jesse B.	Damon (Raymon), Squire

Darst (Durst, Dust), Jacob C.
Davis, John
Day, Freeman H. K.
Day, Jerry C.
Dearduff, William
Dennison, Stephen
Despallier, Charles
Dickenson, Almaron
Dillard, John H.
Dimkins, James R.
Dover, Sherod J.
Duel (Dewell), Lewis
Duvalt (Devault), Andrew
Espalier, Carlos
Esparza, Gregorio
Evans, Robert
Evans, Samuel B.
Ewing, James L.
Fishbaugh (Fishback), William
Flanders, John
Floyd, Dalphin Ward
Forsyth, John Hubbard
Fuentes, Antonio
Fuqua, Galba
Furtleroy, William H.
Garnett, William
Garrand, James W.
Garrett, James Girard
Garvin, John E.
Gaston, John E.
George, James
Goodrich, John Calvin
Grimes, Albert Calvin
Guerrero, Jose Maria
Gwin (Gwynne), James C.
Hannum, James
Harriss, John
Harrison, Andrew Jackson
Harrison, William B.
Haskell (Heiskill), Charles M.
Hawkins, Joseph
Hays, John M.

Hendricks, Thomas
Herndon, Patrick Henry
Hersee (Hersey), William
Holland, Tapley
Holloway, Samuel
Howell, William D.
Jackson, William Daniel
Jackson, Thomas
Jameson, Green B.
Jennings, Gordon C.
Johnson, Lewis
Johnson, William
Jones, John
Kellogg, Johnny
Kenney, James
Kent, Andrew
Kerr, Joseph
Kimball, George C.
King, John G.
King, William P.
Lewis, William Irvine
Lightfoot, William J.
Lindley, Jonathan L.
Linn, William
Losoya, Toribio Domingo
Main, George Washington
Malone, William T.
Marshall, William
Martin, Albert
McCafferty, Edward
McCoy, Jesse
McDowell, William
McGee, James
McGregor, John
McKinney, Robert
Melton, Eliel
Miller, Thomas R.
Mills, William
Millsaps, Isaac
Mitchasson, Edward F.
Mitchell, Edwin T.
Mitchell, Napoleon B.

Moore, Robert B.

Moore, Willis A.

Musselman, Robert

Nava, Andres

Neggan, George

Nelson, Andrew M.

Nelson, Edward

Nelson, George

Northcross, James

Nowlan, James

Pagan, George

Parker, Christopher

Parks, William

Perry, Richardson

Pollard, Amos

Reynolds, John Purdy

Roberts, Thomas H.

Robertson, James

Robinson, Isaac

Rose, James M.

Rusk, Jackson J.

Rutherford, Joseph

Ryan, Isaac

Scurlock, Mial

Sewell, Marcus L.

Shied, Manson

Simmons, Cleveland Kenlock

Smith, Andrew H.

Smith, Charles S.

Smith, Joshua G.

Smith, William H.

Starr, Richard

Stewart, James E.

Stockton, Richard L.

Summerlin, A. Spain

Summers, William E.

Sutherland, William D.

Taylor, Edward

Taylor, George

Taylor, James

Taylor, William

Thomas, B. A. M.

Thomas, Henry

Thompson, Jesse G.

Thomson, John W.

Thurston, John M.

Trammel, Burke

Travis, William Barret

Tumlinson, George W.

Walker, Asa

Walker, Jacob

Ward, William B.

Warnell (Wornel), Henry

Washington, Joseph G.

Waters, Thomas

Wells, William

White, Isaac

White, Robert W.

Williamson, Hiram J.

Wilson, David L.

Wilson, John

Wolfe, Antony

Wright, Clairborne

Zanco, Charles

_____, John

Possibly, twelve other names should be on the foregoing list but I could not locate conclusive evidence to justify putting them there, so I present these possible victims in a separate roll.

Anderson, George Washington (?)	Kedison, _____
Ayers (Ayres), _____	Olamio, George
Burnell, John (?)	Pixon, John
George, William	Robbins. George S.
Ingram, _____	Spratt, John
Jackson, John	Warner, Thomas S.

ROLL OF THE GONZALES MEN

Perhaps the bravest and the most self-sacrificing incident in the defense of the Alamo was the entrance on March 1, of thirty-two men from Gonzales. In answer to Travis's call for help, these men, commanded by Captain George C. Kimball and Albert Martin and guided by John W. Smith, rode to San Antonio and entered the Alamo. They well knew that there was little hope that the Alamo would be strongly reinforced, but they went with the determination to sacrifice their lives, if need be, in order to encourage and strengthen their friends and compatriots. The following list is a roll of those brave souls:

Baker, Issac	King, William P.
Cane, John	Lindley, Jonathan
Cottle, George W.	Martin, Albert (Captain)
Cummings, David F.	McCoy, Jesse
Damon, Squire	Miller, Thomas R.
Darst, Jacob C.	Millsaps, Isaac
Davis, John	Floyd, Dalphin Ward
Dearduff, William	Fuqua, Galba
Despallier, Charles	Garvin, John E.
Fishbaugh, William	Gaston, John E.
Flanders, John	George, James
Jackson, Thomas	Neggan, George
Kellogg, Johnny	Summers, William E.
Kent, Andrew	Tumlinson, George
Kimball, George C. (Captain)	White, Robert
King, John G.	Wright, Clairborne

THE QUESTION OF THE COURIERS

Little official or definite information can be found concerning the couriers whom Travis dispatched from the Alamo, but from various statements, found here and there, it seems certain that he must have sent out between fifteen and twenty men during the eleven days of the actual investment of the fort. He himself in his letter of March 3, to the Convention, says that he had "repeatedly sent messengers to Fannin." Herman Ehrenberg[1] says: "At the risk of their lives one or two [messengers] came daily through the enemy lines and brought us the pleadings of the garrison, especially the private letters of Travis, the Commander, and of Bowie and Crockett." John Sowers Brooks[2] mentions the arrival at Goliad of four different messengers from the Alamo between February 25 and March 9, but does not give their names. W. F. Gray, in his book *From Virginia to Texas*, mentions four messengers from Travis who arrived at San Felipe, and it is certain that as many were sent to Gonzales. But who those messengers were, and on exactly what days they were sent out, cannot be fully determined. My investigation of this problem, however, seems to show rather conclusively that those who went from the Alamo at some time between February 23, and March 6, were as follows:

James L. Allen	Byrd Lockhart
John W. Baylor	Albert Martin
James Butler Bonham	William S. Oury
Robert Brown	Juan N. Seguin
Antonio Cruz y Arocha	John W. Smith
Alexandro de la Garza	Lancelot Smithers
Benjamin F. Highsmith	Andrew Sowell
_____ Johnson	John Sutherland

Besides those on the above list, the following men were probably also messengers from the Alamo, but the evidence found concerning them was not conclusive in establishing the fact:

Samuel G. Bastian
Gerald Navan
Captain William Patton
Francis de Sauque
W. K. Simpson
Henry Warnell

In addition to these suggestions, John Sutherland tells us that Nat Lewis, a merchant of Bexar, who was in the Alamo on February 23, for a few hours, at

---

1 Herman Ehrenberg, *Fahrten Und Schicksale Eines Deutschen in Texas*, 159, University of Texas Archives.

2 *Texas Historical Quarterly*, IX, 178-192.

least, together with Captain Philip Dimmitt and Lieutenant B. F. Nobles, left Bexar on the afternoon of February 23. They were not sent out by Travis, and the circumstances of their going exclude them from being classed as official messengers. Still they did a good deal to spread the news of the siege of the Alamo, and of the dire needs of that fortress. It is possible that Samuel G. Bastian accompanied these men in their flight.

THE TENNESSEE MOUNTED VOLUNTEERS

There is yet another problem or moot question concerning the fall of the Alamo that involves the reconstruction of a roll of men: Did David Crockett go to the Alamo as colonel of a company of men, or did he enter practically alone?

As has previously been stated, there is conclusive evidence that Crockett went to San Antonio with a band of men over whom he held at least a nominal command. Dr. John Sutherland says that he "brought twelve men with him direct from Tennessee."[3] Another writer who signs himself simply "A Volunteer of 1836" says that he was one of a few volunteers who arrived at Nacogdoches in January, 1836, on their way to join the Texan army. They took the oath of allegiance on January 14, and sixteen or seventeen of them having secured horses, formed a company of "mounted volunteers" under Colonel David Crockett, and proceeded on their way to San Antonio by way of Washington-on-the-Brazos.[4]

Among the Comptroller Military Service Records, there are seven documents, all requisitions on the Provisional Government of Texas, signed by David Crockett and others of his band for board for a company of "Tennessee Mounted Volunteers" while they were resting at Washington and while they were on the way from that town to Bexar. These documents show that there were eighteen or more men in the company, including Colonel Crockett and Captain William B. Harrison, and that they went by way of Gonzales to San Antonio. Among the men signing these documents "in behalf of the squad" were David Crockett, William B. Harrison, M. Autry, P. J. Bailey, D. W. Cloud and B. A. M. Thomas.[5]

At the General Land Office, the *Muster Roll Book*, pp. 115-117, gives three separate lists which contain, altogether, the names of more than a hundred volunteers who took the oath of allegiance before John Forbes at Nacogdoches on January 14, 1836. On these lists are names of fifteen men who certainly belong on the roll of the Alamo dead; probably there are three or four others that belong there also.

---

3 DeShields (ed.), "John Sutherland's Account of the Fall of the Alamo," *Dallas News*, February 5, 1911.

4 "A Volunteer of 1836" to Mr. Teulon, March 22, 1841, *Austin City Gazette*. CMSR, No. 644, points to A. L. Harrison of William B. Harrison's company at the anonymous "Volunteer of 1836." He fell sick on the way to San Antonio and could not go on with his company, thereby escaping the massacre of March 6, 1836.

5 CMSR, Nos. 10, 13, 14, 208, 226, 664 & 1361, State Library.

But Dr. Sutherland says that only *twelve* men arrived with Crockett at the Alamo. Very probably that statement is correct, for there is evidence that for some reason B. A. M. Thomas was lagging behind "the squad" while on the way,[6] and there were others, no doubt, who did likewise, for these young men were eager to "spy out the land" and find good locations for the headrights that they expected to apply for. We know that John Harris was a first cousin of David Crockett and that he came to Texas with Crockett and was a member of the Tennessee Mounted Volunteers, yet Harris's headright certificate designates him as a resident of Gonzales. The reason for this is that, on his way to San Antonio, he stopped at Gonzales and selected a location for his headright land.

In fact, various documents show that most of Crockett's men were professional men—doctors, lawyers, civil engineers—who had been enticed to Texas by the cheap lands and the opportunity to make a fortune. They were willing to help Texas fight for independence, but fighting was not their sole objective in coming. There is abundant proof that many of the young men who came to Texas in 1836 did a good deal of land prospecting even on their way to the battle grounds. So it is probable that all of the Mounted Volunteers from Tennessee did not arrive in San Antonio with Crockett on February 8, 1836, but it is certain that most of them joined him there before the coming of the Mexicans on February 23.

Reliable documents show that the following list of men were members of the Tennessee Mounted Volunteers, and that they either went to the Alamo with Crockett, or followed him there a few days later:

Name	Age	From
David Crockett	50	Tennessee
Joseph G. Washington	28	Tennessee
Micajah Autry	43	Tennessee
B. A. M. Thomas	18	Tennessee
John Purdy Reynolds	27	Tennessee
John W. Thomson	27	Tennessee
William McDowell	40	Tennessee
Joseph Bayliss	28	Tennessee
William B. Harrison	26	Tennessee
William H. Smith	24	Tennessee
Robert Campbell	25	Tennessee
John Harris	23	Kentucky or Tennessee
Peter J. Bailey	24	Kentucky
Daniel William Cloud	21	Kentucky
William H. Furtleroy	22	Kentucky
Richard L. Stockton	18	Virginia
William Irvine Lewis	28	Pennsylvania

6 CMSR, No. 13, is a requisition on the Texan Government for board for the Tennessee Mounted Volunteers, signed by David Crockett and others. It is dated January 23, 1836. Record No. 10, also a requisition for board, and presented by the same tavern keeper as Record No. 13, is dated January 24 and is signed "B. A. M. Thomas, one of D. Crockett's Company."

At the Alamo most of these men were ranked as privates, although Crockett and Washington bore courtesy titles of "colonel" and William B. Harrison is listed among the captains of the fortress. It is said that upon the arrival of this company of Tennesseeans, Travis welcomed them cordially and offered Crockett a command while the soldiers all demanded a speech. Crockett refused the command, but made the speech, saying that he had come to identify himself with the Texans in their cause, and desired no higher honor than that of defending as a private the liberty of the country. We are told that upon the arrival of the Mexicans on February 23, Crockett once more offered his services, saying: "Here, am I, Colonel, assign us to some place and I and my Tennessee boys will defend it all right."[7]

Travis assigned to him and his band the duty of protecting the low wall and stockade on the south side of the fort, and there they died, fighting desperately. It thus appears that there was some sort of understanding that Crockett and his men should fight together, and although it is said that Crockett had no official command, he evidently was an active leader and commander during the twelve or thirteen days of the siege of the fort. It is also said that after Travis and John J. Baugh had been killed on March 6, the command of the entire post fell upon Crockett. This authority, however, if the statement is true, was brief—lasting less than an hour—and ended in the complete annihilation of all the combatants of the fortress.[8]

THE SURVIVORS OF THE MASSACRE

Who were the survivors of the Alamo tragedy? Concerning the answer to this question the sources are confused and conflicted. All agree, however, that no white male occupant of the Alamo remained alive, and the majority of the records indicate that there were fifteen or more persons spared. These were:

Mrs. Almaron Dickenson & Angelina, her 15 month-old daughter
Mrs. Horace Alsbury & her 18 month-old son, Alijo
Gertrudis Navarro (she later married John M. Cantu);
Mrs. Gregorio Esparza & her four sons
Mrs. Toribio Losoya—later Mrs. Milton—& her three young children
Madam Candalaria

Besides these, Mexican accounts claim that there were eight or ten other Mexican women and a number of small children in the Alamo who went through the massacre unharmed. This statement is possibly true. Enrique Esparza, son of Mrs. Gregorio Esparza, in his account adds to the list given above the name of Trinidad Saucedo, a very beautiful young Mexican girl, and Doña Petra, a very

7 DeShields (ed.), "John Sutherland's Account of the Fall of the Alamo," *Dallas News*, Jan. 5, 1911.
8 Little Rock *Advocate*, April 4, 1836.

old woman, but he emphatically denies that Madam Candalaria was there. There
is evidence to indicate that Esparza's claim may well be true. Mrs. Candalaria, in
giving her account of those who perished at the Alamo, gave the names of four
Mexican fighters who died in the service of Travis. Documents at the General
Land Office, however, show that those four Mexicans fought at the storming
of Bexar in December of 1835, were honorably discharged on dates between
December 20, 1835 and February 16, 1836, and were re-enlisted in the army in
time to participate in the Battle of San Jacinto. Had Mrs. Candalaria herself been
in the Alamo, she would most probably have known of the discharge of these men
prior to the arrival of the Mexican forces. However, since a preponderance of
sources declare that Mrs. Candalaria was Bowie's nurse, or at least attempted to
be, her name is listed among the survivors. The evidence is inconclusive.

Joe, Travis's negro slave boy, said that one woman was killed during the fight.
He thought that her death was accidental. It seems that she had attempted to
cross the large area of the Alamo, for her body was found lying between two
guns.[9] Besides the women and children, two negro slave boys were left alive,[10]
Joe, the servant of Travis, and Sam, Bowie's man. And then, there was Anselmo
Borgarra, who claimed to have been a servant to Travis and in the Alamo during
the final assault, though not a combatant. It was he who first reached Gonzales
with the news of the disaster.

After the fighting had ceased, the Mexican women and children were given
immediately into the care of their friends and relatives at Bexar. Enrique Esparza,
an eight year old child who survived the massacre, said in his account of the
events:

> After the fall of all the men of the fort, the women and children were
> all huddled in the southwest corner of the church in a small room
> to the right of the entrance doors. A guard was placed over them,
> but orders soon came for them to be carried to the home of Ramon
> Musquiz. There, Santa Anna held a sort of court, hearing [each of
> their stories] and turning them over to friends. Before dismissing her,
> he gave to each woman a blanket and two silver dollars.[11]

The negro boys were taken to a fortification in the town and detained for several days. Santa Anna questioned Joe concerning conditions in Texas and the state
of the Texan army, especially whether many soldiers were in the army from the
United States, and if many more were expected. He told Joe that he had enough
men in *his* army "to march straight to Washington."[12] Mrs. Dickenson and her child

9 Gray, *From Virginia to Texas*, 137.
10 *Ibid.*
11 *San Antonio Express*, May 12, 1907.
12 Gray, *From Virginia to Texas*, 137.

were taken to Santa Anna's camp, where they were treated with consideration, even kindness. Soon, Santa Anna put them on a horse and sent them to General Houston, then at Gonzales. He sent his own negro servant, Ben, along with them.

Some fifteen miles from San Antonio, this little party came upon Joe, Travis's servant, who had escaped the guard at Santa Anna's camp. They all journeyed on together. About twenty-five miles from Gonzales, they met Deaf Smith, Robert B. Handy and Captain Henry Karnes, who had been sent out by Houston to investigate conditions at Bexar, for on Tuesday night, March 8, Anselmo Borgarra and Andrés Barcena had arrived at Gonzales with the awful news concerning the Alamo. Houston had arrived in the little town only a few hours earlier with about five hundred soldiers, on his way to carry relief to Travis and his men.

Borgarra, not knowing anything about Houston, who he was, or that he was in the town, did not carry his news to army headquarters, but circulated it pretty thoroughly among the citizens of the place. The grief and the excitement created by this report amounted almost to madness. In order to allay the excitement and calm the fears of the people, Houston ordered that Borgarra and Barcena be arrested and imprisoned as spies, although he himself was convinced that their story was true. By Thursday night, John W. Smith arrived with the twenty-five troops whom he had undertaken to lead to San Antonio.[13] They confirmed Borgarra's story. By Friday night Mrs. Dickenson had arrived. There was no hope left—all had to believe the truth of the awful message she bore. That was a black day for Gonzales. There was hardly a home that had not lost a beloved member. In this little town, the fall of the Alamo had left thirty-three widows and almost a hundred fatherless children.

THE ASHES OF THE TEXAN DEAD

As has been previously stated here, the bodies of the slain Texans were stripped, mutilated, and burned.[14] Two to four pyres (accounts differ here) were built of alternate layers of wood and dead bodies. Then grease and oil were poured over the pyres and the torch applied. C. M. Barnes, in his discussion of an excavation on the site and the pyres, says that it took two days to for the fires to consume the bodies. To the modern mind this seems a far more humane way to dispose of great numbers of dead bodies than was the fate meted out to some of Santa Anna's dead soldiers. But in 1836 cremation on a funeral pyre at the order of the victor was regarded as the greatest cruelty and dishonor that could be shown a fallen foe.

Events moved swiftly in Texas during the next few months. Momentous happenings crowded one upon the other so rapidly that it was almost a year after the massacre before the fragments and ashes of the Alamo defenders had a proper

13 DeShields (ed.), "John Sutherland's Account of the Fall of the Alamo," *Dallas News*, February 12, 1911; Houston to Fannin, March 11, 1836, *Army Papers*, State Library.
14 Francisco Ruiz, *Texas Almanac*, 80, 1860; Caro, *Verdadera Idea*, 11; Filisola, *Guerra de Tejas*, 13-14.

Christian burial. But after the victory at San Jacinto, with Santa Anna captured, with the invading Mexicans all driven out of Texas, with the government of the new republic established under its own constitution, with the fears of the people calmed, with peace and prosperity fairly established—only then it was that General Houston had the time to concern himself with the more refined sentiments of civilized man. Accordingly, he ordered Colonel Juan N. Seguin, then in command of the post at Bexar, to collect the bones and ashes of the Alamo dead and give them the honors of a military burial. On February 25, 1837, Seguin obeyed this order and performed his duty with a considerable ceremony, an account of which appeared in the *Telegraph and Texas Register* of March 28, 1837.

But even concerning this final event, like most everything related to the Alamo, accounts differ. Dr. John Sutherland says that the *Telegraph's* account of the burial of the ashes of the Alamo dead was all a hoax. He claimed that:

> Sometime after the Battle of San Jacinto, a company of rangers, under Captain Byrd Lockhart, passed through Bexar, and halting at the dismantled fortress of the Alamo, searched out and found the ashes of the brave men who died there. These remains they gathered into a substantial coffin and interred them with military honors at a spot, then a peach orchard, not far from the scene of the last charge and struggle.[15]

Still another writer[16] says: "After the battle of the Alamo, it is said that by the authority of the alcalde, Don Francisco Ruiz, the remains of the Alamo heroes were tenderly gathered together and placed beneath the sod." But to further complicate the records of this event, Colonel Seguin, in reply to an inquiry from General Hamilton P. Bee, concerning the burial of the Alamo men, wrote on March 28, 1889: "I collected the fragments, placed them in an urn and buried it in the Cathedral of San Fernando, immediately in front of the altar—that is in front of the railing and near the steps." The clergy of San Fernando vehemently deny the truth of this statement; nevertheless, it is believed by many Texans.[17] It is possible that all of these accounts were written of the same occasions. It is possible that Byrd Lockhart and his men were a part of the funeral procession as pall bearers. Rodrigues may have erred in thinking that the ceremony was at the command of Alcalde Ruiz or, perhaps, Ruiz did issue orders that the town should take part in the ceremony.

15 DeShields (ed.), "John Sutherland's Account of the Fall of the Alamo," *Dallas News*, February 12, 1911.

16 Rodrigues, *Memoirs*, 7.

17 E. C. Barker, "The Funeral of the Heroes of the Alamo," *Texas Historical Assn. Quarterly*, V, 69.

MEXICAN LOSSES

There is probably more disagreement among the sources concerning the number of Mexicans killed in the siege and last assault of the fort than upon any other one point of the entire Alamo subject. Santa Anna's official report of seventy killed and three hundred wounded[18] is too absurd to be considered (in the same report, he listed the Texan dead at 600) but, on the other hand, some of the unofficial Mexican reports seem to exaggerate the number of Mexicans who were slain. Francisco Becerra, a sergeant in General Sesma's division, says that during the siege and final assault of the Alamo, the Mexicans lost 2,000 killed and 300 wounded.[19] Francisco Ruiz, the alcalde of Bexar, the man whom Santa Anna ordered to bury his dead, says the Mexican dead numbered 1,600.

Upon their arrival at Gonzales, Mrs. Dickenson and Joe, Travis's servant, both reported this same number of Mexican dead as Ruiz; but the *Telegraph and Texas Register*, March 24, 1836, says, the enemy loss, killed and wounded was 1,500. The messenger from the Navarro family to Seguin at Gonzales gave the same number, while the messenger from the Mexican citizens of Bexar to their representatives at the Convention, reported 521 dead and as many wounded. On April 15, 1836, Jesse B. Badgett, a member of the Convention, was on a visit to his old home in Little Rock and gave to the press of that city an account of the Alamo disaster. He said that according to the best information to be obtained in Texas when he left, the Mexicans had lost 881 killed and over 700 wounded, and that of this loss 521 were killed during the final assault, and an equally great number wounded. Colonel Edward Stiff relates that Ben, Santa Anna's negro cook, told him that he heard the Mexican officers talk among themselves about their loss, and they said they had 1,200 killed.

In writing his *History of Texas,* Yoakum was very conservative in his estimate of the Mexican loss at the Alamo. He said that it was about three times that of the Texan loss. Wooten puts the number of dead at 521, with as many wounded. Captain R. M. Potter, afraid that he would exaggerate the estimate, reasoned out by military calculations that the Mexicans lost only 500 killed and wounded. We know that his estimate is far too conservative. Sutherland also worked on this problem. He says:

> The most conclusive witness that I have concerning the number of Mexicans lost at the Alamo was secured after the Battle of San Jacinto. It came from Ramón Caro, the private secretary of Santa Anna. During my interview with this man, I requested Captain Patton, the interpreter, to ask him how many men they had in the siege of the Alamo, and what was their loss there. Patton did so, and the answer was: "We brought to San Antonio more than 5,000

18 Santa Anna to the Minister of War, March 6, 1836, *University of Texas Transcripts*, Guerra, Frac. 1, Leg. 3, Op. Mil. 1836, Campana de Tejas.

19 John S. Ford, *Journal* (MS.), University of Texas Archives.

men, and we lost during the siege 1,544 of the best of them. The Texans fought more like devils than like men." Santa Anna and Almonte were both present at this conversation and they did not contradict the statement.

In his account Sutherland goes on to figure out that Caro meant 1,544 men were killed or mortally wounded, and he cites Ruiz's estimate of 1,600 to back up his reasoning.[20]

Sutherland's reasoning may be correct. A study and comparison of all these statements with one another and with correlated accounts convinces me that Caro gave a truthful answer to Patton's question, and the majority of the sources indicate, as Sutherland thought, that he meant 1,544 killed. But we must remember, as the Mexican reports clearly show, that the Texans themselves were not wholly responsible for that figure, for during the first part of the final assault, the Mexicans were distributed and arranged in such a way for the attack that they practically battled against themselves.

Moreover, their hospital service was very deficient. Many of the wounded died for lack of medical attention, beds, shelter and surgical instruments. Dr. John Bernard recorded in his journal that on April 16, 1836, Ugartechea sent a courier from San Antonio to the command at Goliad asking that surgeon who could amputate limbs be sent to him. Drs. Bernard and Shackelford volunteered to go and arrived in April 20. On the 21st, Dr. Bernard writes in his journal:

> Yesterday and today we have been around with the surgeons of the place to visit the wounded, and a pretty piece of work "Travis and his faithful few" have made of them. There are now about 100 of the wounded here. The surgeons tell us that 400 of them were brought into the hospital the morning they stormed the Alamo, but I think from the appearance there must have been many more than that number. I see many around the town who were crippled then, apparently two or three hundred, and the citizens tell me that three or four hundred have died of their wounds... Their surgical department is shockingly conducted—not an amputation performed before we arrived, although there are several cases even now that should have been operated upon at the first, and how many have died of the want of operation is impossible to tell, though it is a fair inference that there have not been few. There has scarcely been a ball cut out as yet, every patient carrying the lead he received that morning...
>
> We have been treated well by the officers here. It is evident that they have a high opinion of our skill, and if the surgeons that I have seen

20 Texas Almanac, 1860, 80; Linn, Reminiscences of Fifty Years in Texas, 144; Morphis, History of Texas, 186; A. J. Sowell, Rangers and Pioneers of Texas, 140; Telegraph and Texas Register, March 24, 1836; John S. Ford, Journal (MS.), 73, University of Texas Archives; Arkansas Gazette, April 15, 1836; Edward Stiff, Texas Emigrant, 8; Yoakum, History of Texas, II, 82; Wooten, History of Texas, I, 242; Potter, "The Fall of the Alamo," Magazine of American History, January 1878; DeShields (ed.), "John Sutherland's Account of the Fall of the Alamo," Dallas News, February 12, 1911.

among them are a fair sample of their medical talent, I can safely say without the least spark of vanity that they have reason to think well of us. The head surgeon of the garrison came for me the other day to visit his wife who was in the greatest distress and he did not know what to do for her. On going to his house to see her, I found that she merely had a toothache. This man amputated the leg of one of the wounded men on the day we arrived. The man died the next day. We have amputated but one limb, and the patient is doing well. A dozen more need this service, but they will die anyway, so there is no need to do it.[21]

The disposal of the Mexican dead was a serious problem for Santa Anna, but even a greater one for the citizens of Bexar. Santa Anna ordered Francisco Ruiz, the alcalde of Bexar, to have them buried, but Ruiz himself reports that there was not room enough for them in the cemetery. Moreover, the work of digging even trench graves for so large a number was too great a task for the facilities he had for the work, so he had many of the bodies thrown into the San Antonio River. Some of those bodies floated off below, but many lodged against the banks and other obstructions and choked the river. Great flocks of vultures hovered over the city for weeks afterward. All the citizens who had remained at Bexar now fled, if they could find a way to go. Many who remained fell sick of fever and other diseases, caused by the stench and unsanitary conditions. Santa Anna himself was one of the victims of illness.

---

21 John Ford, *Journal* (MS.), "Dr. John H. Bernard's Journal from December 1835–March 27, 1836, and Scraps from then on till May 30," University of Texas Manuscripts.

CHAPTER VIII
ANNOTATED ROLL OF THE DEAD

The foregoing is an annotated roll of the 187 names of men who died at the Alamo that have been verified by reliable documentation. Since my verified roll is itself a reconstruction, it is necessary to explain the methods used in its compilation and to describe the sources from which I have worked. First, I made a collection of all lists that had been previously made of men who were supposed to have fallen at the Alamo. Such lists are numerous. Some are more or less contemporaneous with the fall of the Alamo, while others were made later. From all these lists, I compiled a working list which contained every name mentioned on any previously made roll or from any other source obtainable. Such a compilation yielded over 300 names, although contemporary authority is practically in agreement that the number of Alamo victims was less than 200, most writers hovering around 182 or 183.

The work of verification and elimination began at the General Land Office because, according to the various ordinances and decrees of the Provisional Government, decrees that were later converted into law by the Republic of Texas, the heirs of each Texan soldier who died in the service had the right, according to the lowest calculations, to about 4,000 acres of land. The first task was to check the working list against the <u>Bounty and Dona-tion Register</u>. This register is a large ledger which is supposed to contain the name of every individual to whom Texas has ever issued land as a bounty or a donation for service of any kind. It lists the name of the person who rendered the service, the number of the certificate issued, the amount of land granted, the land district issuing the certificate, the location of the land and the file number of the certificate. (Bounty documents are called "warrants" and donation documents "certificates," but for the sake of convenience, they are all referred to as certificates in this explanation.)

There must be a separate certificate for each location. That is, if a man is granted 640 acres located in three different tracts, there must be three certificates totalling 640 acres, but each showing that the specific location is only a part of the 640 acres granted. For this reason, one name on the <u>Bounty Register</u> may carry more than a dozen certificates because rarely was a man's entire bounty or donation located in a single tract, or even granted by a single land district.

Each original certificate is supposed to show the time of the service and whether the man was killed, dismissed or honorably discharged, and on what date. In the case of the loss of an original certificate, the Land Office could, upon good evidence of loss, issue a duplicate certificate. Many duplicates were carelessly prepared, and very few indicate the service for which the original grant was made.

Besides the <u>Bounty Register</u> there are three other indices or registers of land grants. They are called <u>Headright Registers</u>. There are three classes of headrights...The first class certificates (Class I) were issued to those who came to Texas prior to March 2, 1836; the second class of certificates (Class II) were granted to those who came after independence was declared but before 1838; and the third class of certificates (Class III) were issued by land agents, usually to those who came after 1838. These <u>Headright Registers</u> give about the same information to be found in the <u>Bounty Register</u>, however, the headright certificates rarely show the service for which the headright is granted. Related papers in the same file, though, frequently give such information.

The use of these registers would have rendered the task of verification relatively easy but for a few difficulties. The first difficulty was that none of the sources from which my work was compiled gave the full Christian name, or even the initials, of the men listed. Moreover, where Christian names or initials were given, they varied widely in the different sources, and the spelling of surnames also differed so greatly that considerable imagination had to be exercised to determine whether the same man was intended. After I had spent about ten days of checking by the trial and error method, the Land Commissioner and the file clerk both advised me that the simplest and surest way to get a true check would be to draw out each file box and inspect each certificate in it. Bear in mind that there are more than 16,000 of these bounty and donation documents, issued by twenty-eight land districts. But the work was done. Even that did not clear up all of the difficulties, for many of the original certificates were lost or missing, and the service for which the grants were made was seldom cited by the duplicate certificates or by the surveys and field notes.

The next step was to check the working list against the headright registers and files. These, as a rule, do not state the service for which land was granted, but I obtained such information from them for twenty-five of the names on my final list.

The second difficulty was the fact that in a considerable number of cases, two or more men of exactly the same name served in the Texan Army in 1836. For example, there were five John Joneses, only three of whom had a distinguishing second initial, and those three did not always use the middle initial in signing documents. There were three John Blairs, two William Henry Smiths, two William Gilmores, three William Lightfoots, six John Wilsons and an even greater number of John Jacksons. This fact caused great confusion in verification. It was the Court of Claims files that helped to straighten out this tangle.

The Court of Claims files are a valuable source of information. There are some forty boxes of these records, each box containing from 300 to 500 documents, filed alphabetically. Most of the documents are numbered but they are not arranged in consecutive order. They consist of proofs of heirship, depositions, affidavits, letters and statements, all originally submitted to the various land boards in support of claims.

Then, of course, there are three <u>Muster Roll Books</u> in the General Land Office. Two of these volumes are compiled from incomplete originals supplemented from the memories of men contemporary with the revolution. The third volume is a typewritten copy of the other two volumes. Most of the original rolls were burned in a disastrous fire that occurred in the Adjutant General's Office in 1855, but it is doubtful whether a true return of the Alamo men was ever made after February 12, 1836, and Travis's roster, no doubt, was destroyed by the Mexicans at the Alamo when they left San Antonio. These reconstructed muster rolls are as nearly accurate as diligent effort and the mere memory of men could make them, but they show considerable error when checked against other documents. These muster rolls also frequently fail to give Christian names or distinguishing initials, while the spelling of the surnames varies from list to list.

In the State Library, there is a voluminous collection of papers, known as the Comptroller Military Service Records. There are some eighty boxes of this material, covering the period from 1835-1877. It is arranged chronologically but is otherwise unorganized. Each box contains from 200-500 documents which related to nearly everything of a military nature that could pass through the Comptroller's office. There are requisitions on the Provisional Government for board for soldiers and horses, as well as for other supplies of various kinds; there are reports that relate to equipment and expenditures for equipment; and then there are claims and affidavits of administrators concerning the pay of dead soldiers. This material has been of great value in the reconstruction of my roll of the Alamo soldiers. There are also at the State Library the collections of papers classified as Domestic Correspondence, the Governor and Council Papers, and the Army Papers, all of which have been utilized for this work.

Three other sources have been found valuable in constructing and checking the verified list presented in this section. The first is a set of thirty-four volumes of the Southwestern Historical Quarterly; the second is the six volumes of Lamar Papers; and the third is the Austin Papers in three volumes.

Newspaper files have also been canvassed but not, perhaps, with the comprehensiveness that might be desired. My use of newspapers has been restricted almost entirely to Texas publications. Papers of other states might yield scattered items.

Several abbreviations have been used in the citations to sources of this section. They are as follows:

(1) Bounty or Donation certificates are indicated by the name of the land district granting the certificate, followed by the file number of the document. For example, "Bexar 138" indicates that the file number of the document is 138, and that it is to be found among the Bounty and Donation files of the Bexar land district.

(2) The headright certificates are indicated by the class number preceding the name of the granting district and file number, such as "1 Bexar 100.

(3) The initial letters CMSR are used to indicate the Comptroller's Military Service Records.

ANNOTATED LIST OF VICTIMS

ABAMILLO, JUAN: Private; native and resident of San Antonio. Sources: R. M. Potter to General William Steele, July 10, 1870 in *Texas Telegraph* July 17, 1874; E. M. Pease to General William Steele, July 14, 1876, in *Austin City Gazette* July 17, 1874; see also H. A. McArdle, *Book of the Alamo* in the State Library Archives. These sources all say that in 1873 and again in 1874, Juan N Seguin gave to R. M. Potter a list of nine soldiers who were under his command and who, including himself, constituted ten of the twenty-five men who went to the Alamo with Travis on February 3, 1836. These soldiers were enlisted for six months. They were a part of a company of 24 Mexicans who had served under Seguin as captain at the storming of Bexar in December of 1835. In February of 1836, several of the twenty-four were on furlough, while the others were with Houston's troops at Gonzales. Seven of the ten who went to the Alamo died there. Seguin and two of his men, Antonio Cruz y Arocha, and Alexandro de la Garza, were sent out as messengers. The bounty and donation files fully verify four of the seven whom Seguin listed as Alamo victims. E. M. Pease, Frank Templeton and J. J. Linn include these seven Mexican names on the lists of the Alamo dead which they compiled. Seguin's nine soldiers were: Juan Abamillo, Antonio Cruz y Arocha, Juan Antonio Badillo, Gregorio Esparza, Antonio Fuentes, Alexandro de la Garza, Jose Maria Guerrero, Toribio Losoya and Andres Nava.

ALLEN, R.: Private. Sources: The *Muster Roll Book*, 2-3; *Telegraph and Texas Register*, March 24, 1836; W. F. Gray, *From Virginia to Texas*, 138; The Alamo Monument; and every list that has ever been made of Alamo victims. The name cannot be verified by bounty, donation or headright certificates, but the *Comptroller's Military Service Records*, No. 74, in the State Library Archives makes it clear that the name should be on the verified list. This conclusive document, CMSR No. 74 is a requisition on the Provisional Government, made by Captain John H. Forsyth for board for himself and six men. R. Allen is one of the six. It is on record that three of these six men deserted.[1] The other two can be verified as Alamo victims by bounty certificates. So, unless R. Allen was sent out as a messenger, and no suggestion of that fact is found, he evidently died at the Alamo.

ANDROSS, MILES DE FOREST: Age 27, Private. Sources: I San Patricio 647; Memorial No. 110, File No. 3, Archives of the Department of State; Court of Claims Application No. 1427, File A-B; Muster Rolls, p. 20. Most of the lists that include this name write it "Mills D. Andross," but the Court of Claims records show clearly that it should be written as it is here.

---

1 Travis to Smith, January 29, 1836, *Army Papers*, State Library. Contains the names of deserters.

AUTRY, MICAJAH: Age 43, Private; a native of North Carolina, but immigrated to Texas from Tennessee. Sources: Robertson 211, 326; I Robertson 274; I Fort Bend 37; CMSR No. 9163; Adele B. Looscan, "Micajah Autry," in the *Texas Historical Quarterly*, XIV, 315; *Lamar Papers*, I, 295; Muster Rolls, p. 117.

BADILLO, JUAN ANTONIO: Sergeant; a resident of San Antonio. Sources: See note under entry for "Juan Abamillo." *Lamar Papers*, VI, 297. (There this name is given "Antonio Padillo.")

BAILEY, PETER JAMES: Age 24; Private; native of Springfield, Logan County, Kentucky; came to Texas in January, 1836. Sources: Fannin 368, 544; I Milam 1420; Muster Rolls, p. 117; CMSR Nos. 1361, 1408. This last cited document shows that Peter J. Bailey was a lawyer by profession; *San Antonio Express*, November 24, 1901, prints a letter from defender Daniel William Cloud to his mother, in which he writes of "Mr. Bailey" in highly complimentary terms; Adele Looscan, "Micajah Autry," *Texas Historical Quarterly*, XIV, 321; W. P. Orndorff to Adjutant General William Steele, February 21, 1875, and G. W. Bailey to William Steele, March 6, 1875, *Adjutant General's Miscellaneous Papers*, Archives of the Texas State Library. These letters tell that Peter J. Bailey, Archer Thomas (aka B. A. M. Thomas), Daniel W. Cloud, William Furtleroy and Jo Washington were all from Logan County, Kentucky, and that they came to Texas together.

BAKER, ISAAC G.: Age 32; Private; immigrated to Texas from Arkansas, and became a resident of DeWitt's Colony and lived at Gonzales. Sources: Gonzales 29, 30; I Gonzales 208; Muster Rolls, p. 256; Ethel Z. Rather, "DeWitt's Colony," *Texas Historical Quarterly*, VIII, 163; Miles S. Bennett, "The Battle of Gonzales," *Texas Historical Quarterly*, II, 314; *The Spanish Archive Register*, General Land Office, shows that Isaac Baker arrived in DeWitt's Colony, June 14, 1832. He was one of the thirty-two men from Gonzales who entered the Alamo on March 1, 1836.

BAKER, WILLIAM CHARLES M.: Captain; native of Missouri but came to Texas from Mississippi. Sources: Bexar 411; Travis 293; I Galveston 17; Muster Rolls, pp. 2, 256; *Lost Book of Harris*,[2] p. 86, General Land Office; James E. Winston, "Mississippi and the Independence of Texas," *Southwestern Historical Quarterly*, XXL, 41.

BALLENTINE, JOHN J.: Private; resident of Bastrop, Texas. Sources: I Bexar 1809; see J. H. Walker to Amelia Williams, April 5, 1930, Archives of the University of Texas. Mr. J. H. Walker, the present Land Commissioner, states that for

---

2 *The Lost Book of Harris* is a ledger that contains the land grants issued by the Land Board of Harris County. This book was lost for several years, hence the name.

thirty-three years he has been familiar with the details of the various files at the General Land Office. Twenty years ago he had occasion to work on the problem of the identity of J. J. Ballentine and R. W. Ballentine. He has satisfactorily proved that these were different men, and that both died at the Alamo on March 6, 1836. The evidence of this fact is filed at the Land Office.

John J. Ballentine, as is shown by I Bexar 1809, was a single man who lived at Bastrop for several years prior to 1836. On Muster Rolls, p. 2, he is listed as "Voluntine," while on page 256, he appears as "J. Ballentine." See also Muster Rolls, p. 20; "Notes and Fragments," *Texas Historical Quarterly*, V, 355, shows that in 1895, Benjamin F. Highsmith made an affidavit in which he stated that in 1836 he was well acquainted with all the soldiers in the Republic of Texas, and that he was well acquainted with R. W. Ballentine who was also known as J. J. Ballentine. In 1836, Mr. Highsmith was a young man under nineteen years of age. He, no doubt, was a brave and daring young man, for Travis sent him from the Alamo with a dispatch, but even so it is unlikely he could have known all the soldiers in the Texan army in 1836, nor have remembered them for sixty years.

BALLENTINE, ROBERT W.: Age 22; Private; a native of Scotland, but immigrated to Texas from Alabama. Sources: Milam 1498, 1541, 1630; Muster Rolls, p. 2. On the Muster Rolls the name is written "R. W. Valentine (Ballentine)"; Frank Templeton, *Margaret Ballentine, or The Fall of the Alamo*; *Texas Historical Quarterly*, V, 355; also see note under entry for "John J. Ballentine."

BAUGH, JOHN J.: Age 33; Captain; immigrated to Texas from Virginia. Sources: CMSR, No. 174; Muster Rolls, pp. 2, 20, 25, 26; E. C. Barker, "The Texas Revolutionary Army," *Texas Historical Quarterly*, IX, 237; James E. Winston, "Virginia and the Independence of Texas," *Southwestern Historical Quarterly*, XVI, 279; Herman Ehrenberg, *Fahrten Und Schicksale Eines Deutschen in Texas*, 110; John J. Baugh to Henry Smith, February 13, 1836, *Army Papers*, Texas State Library; *Arkansas Advocate*, April 15, 1836. Here Jesse B. Badgett tells that after the death of Travis, John J. Baugh became the commander of the Alamo but that he was soon killed, whereupon the command fell briefly to David Crockett.

BAYLISS, JOSEPH: Age 28; Private; came to Texas from Tennessee in January, 1836. Sources: Robertson 761, 924; Milam 1508; I Milam 1773; Muster Rolls, p. 117; Court of Claims, Special Acts Vouchers, No. 1323. This last document shows that Joseph Bayliss was a single man; that his father, John B. Bayliss, and his mother, Patience Bayliss, were his heirs; that they lived at Clarksville, Tennessee; and that Bayliss belonged to "Colonel Crockett's band."

BLAIR, JOHN: Age 33; Private; came to Texas from Tennessee in February, 1835. Sources: Houston 9, 173; Milam 1114; I Harrison 101; I Milam 1154; Muster Rolls, pp. 2, 256; CMSR, Nos. 1922, 7855. The various records show that there were three John Blairs in the Texan army in 1836. Two of them were still living in 1838, but the *Register of the Spanish Archives*, General Land Office, shows that the John Blair who registered in Zavala's colony in February of 1835, was a married man who died at the Alamo, March 6, 1836.

BLAIR, SAMUEL: Age 29; Captain; native of Tennessee, resident of McGloin's Colony. Sources: Bexar 609, 876; I Bexar 996, 1122; Muster Rolls, pp. 2, 20, 25, 256. CMSR, No. 9663, shows that James McGloin was his administrator; Memorial, No. 154, shows Samuel Blair as a single man of McGloin's Colony; *Register of the Spanish Archives*, General Land Office, shows that he registered for a headright of land, September 10, 1834.

BLAZEBY, WILLIAM: Age 41; Captain; native of England, came to Texas from New York. Sources: *Lost Book of Harris*, 116, General Land Office; CMSR, No. 6673; I Fannin 908; Muster Rolls, pp. 2, 25, 256.

BONHAM, JAMES BUTLER: Age 29; Lieutenant; native of South Carolina, came to Texas, December, 1835. Sources: Milam 507; Robertson 968, 976; I Milam 688; Muster Rolls, pp. 2, 3, 256; CMSR, 7474; *Lost Book of Harris*, 86; Judge M. L. Bonham to Amelia Williams, March 3, 1930; M. L. Bonham, Jr., *James Butler Bonham* (MS.); *Southwestern Historical Quarterly*, XXXV, 124-136.

James Butler Bonham was born February 20, 1807, at Red Banks, South Carolina. His elementary education was received in the country schools of his neighborhood, but in 1824 he entered South Carolina College. He did not graduate, however, because of his participation, along with other members of his class, in a protest against regulations that required prompt attendance at classes in stormy weather, and against poor food that was served by the college commons. The entire senior class was expelled because of this insubordination. Bonham then studied law, and in 1830 set up an office at Pendleton, South Carolina. He was successful in his practice of law, but an unhappy love affair caused him to leave Pendleton and go to Montgomery, Alabama. There he began the practice of his profession in 1834.

During the Nullification excitement in 1832, Bonham served as an aide on the staff of Governor James Hamilton, with the rank of colonel. He also commanded a company of artillery in Charleston, which company he drilled in anticipation of conflict with the national government.

As young boys William Barret Travis and James Butler Bonham attended the same country school, and there they became fast friends. When the Travises

moved to Alabama in 1818—some writers say 1820—these boys began a correspondence which was kept up by an occasional exchange of letters, until 1835.
In the early fall of 1835, Travis wrote Bonham a letter recounting the glories of
Texas, her struggles, her hopes of independence, and ended with the statement
that "stirring times are afoot here; come out to Texas and take a hand in affairs."

Bonham decided to go. Lacking money sufficient for the venture, he closed his
law office in Montgomery, and rode horseback from Alabama to South Carolina
in order to borrow money for his Texas trip. He arrived in Texas in December,
1835, soon after General Cos left San Antonio. He went immediately to San
Felipe and joined Travis, who was at that time superintendent of the recruiting
office at that town. It was not long before Bonham was given a commission as
lieutenant of cavalry, a position that he held at the time of his death (James B.
Bonham to General Sam Houston, December 31, 1835, *Army Papers*; also *Comptroller Military Service Records*, No. 7474), but for a short while he was associated
with Travis in the recruiting office. On January 18, 1836, Houston sent him with
Bowie to the Alamo, and there he remained for the rest of his life, except for the
two trips that he made out as a messenger.

The Bonham family of South Carolina say that they have never had a portrait
of James Butler Bonham, but that he is described as an unusually handsome man.
He was more than six feet tall and "straight as an Indian." He had a rich olive
complexion to match black, wavy hair and dark brown eyes. While he was brave
to rashness, his manner was thoughtful and gentle. He loved sports and was an
expert swordsman and a graceful daring horseman. His high sense of honor and
loyalty are eminently manifested by his last return to the Alamo to die with his
friend and comrade.

BOURNE, DANIEL: Age 26; Private; native of England, resident of Gonzales.
Sources: Robertson 567, 575; I Robertson 609; Muster Rolls, pp. 3, 20, 256.

BOWIE, JAMES: Age 40; Colonel of volunteers; native of Louisiana, resident of
San Antonio. Sources: Bexar 962; Fannin 1496; Muster Rolls, pp. 2, 256; CMSR,
No. 1513; Memorial No. 451, Archives of the State Department.

BOWMAN, JESSE B.: Private. Sources: I Lamar 109; I Bowie 119; I Red River
670; Court of Claims Vouchers, No. 17, File (A-B).

BROWN, GEORGE: Age 35; Private; native of England, resident of Gonzales.
Sources: I Liberty 317; Muster Rolls, pp. 2, 256. The Muster Rolls are not
definite for this name. They give merely "Brown." The records show four George
Browns in the Texan army in 1836, but the headright files and CMSR, No. 728,
show that but one of them died at the Alamo.

BROWN, JAMES: Age 36; Private; came to Texas from Pennsylvania in 1835. Sources: Bexar 962; I Nacogdoches 399, 681; I Washington 193; Muster Rolls, pp. 2, 20, 256 (the Muster Rolls give only the last name); James E. Winston, "Pennsylvania and the Independence of Texas," *Southwestern Historical Quarterly*, XVIII, 266; *Telegraph and Texas Register*, March 24, 1836; the *Register of Spanish Archives*, General Land Office, shows that this man registered in DeLeon's Colony, April 17, 1835.

BUCHANAN, JAMES: Age 23; Private; came to Texas from Alabama in 1834. Sources: Montgomery 64, 77-1/2, 78; *Register of Spanish Archives*, General Land Office, shows that this man and his wife, Mary, registered in Austin's Colony in 1834.

BURNS, SAMUEL E.: Age 26; Private; native of Ireland, resident of Natchitoches. Sources: I Nacogdoches 467; I Fannin, 1748; Muster Rolls, p. 3; Court of Claims Vouchers, Nos. 71, 93, File (A-B); CMSR, 793; *Telegraph and Texas Register*, March 24, 1836, and every list that has been made of Alamo victims. The name on all these former Alamo lists, however, is simply "Burns."

BUTLER, GEORGE D.: Age 23; Private; native of Missouri, but came to Texas from New Orleans. Sources: I Bexar 254, 1296; I Milam 1721; I Fannin 1617; Court of Claims Vouchers, No. 58, File (A-B); Muster Rolls, p. 3; *Telegraph and Texas Register*, March 24, 1836; W. F. Gray, *From Virginia to Texas*, 140.

CAMPBELL, ROBERT: Lieutenant; came to Texas from Tennessee in January, 1836. Sources: CMSR, No. 644.

CANE (CAIN), JOHN: Age 34; Private; native of Pennsylvania, resident of Gonzales. Sources: I Gonzales 361; Muster Rolls, pp. 5, 520; Miles S. Bennett, "Battle of Gonzales," *Texas Historical Quarterly*, II, 314; Ethel Z. Rather, "DeWitt's Colony," *Texas Historical Quarterly*, VIII, 159. John Cane was one of the immortal thirty-two who went to the Alamo on March 1, 1836.

CAREY, WILLIAM R.: Age 30; Captain; native of Virginia, came to Texas from New Orleans. Sources: Milam 179, 184; I Milam 629; Muster Rolls, pp. 2, 5, 20; CMSR, No. 9302. This last document states that William Carey was a single man. His father, Moses Carey, was his heir and came to Texas to administer his estate.

CLARK, CHARLES: Private; native of Missouri, came to Texas about November, 1835, probably with the New Orleans Grays. He was a single man, and his heir, a nephew, John Charles Clark, applied for lands due him in December, 1837. Sources: Milam 1425; Travis 648; I Robertson 1435; Court of Claims Vouchers,

891. Charles A. Clark, a cousin to this man, came to Texas with the New Orleans Grays, fought at San Jacinto and later was one of the Mier prisoners.

CLOUD, DANIEL WILLIAM: Age 22; Private; native of Kentucky, came to Texas, January, 1836. Sources.: Bastrop 253, 260; Milam 1601, 1337; I Travis 322; Muster Rolls, p. 117; CMSR, Nos. 1361, 4108; Adele B. Looscan, "Micajah Autry," *Texas Historical Quarterly*, XIV, 321; James E. Winston, "Kentucky and the Independence of Texas," *Southwestern Historical Quarterly*, XVI, 34; Letter from Daniel William Cloud to his mother, *San Antonio Express*, November 24, 1901.

COCHRAN(E), ROBERT: Age 26; Private; immigrated to Texas from New Jersey. Sources: Bexar 118, 119; I Bexar 1164; Muster Rolls, pp. 2, 205; see also the "Journal of Ammon Underwood, 1834-1838," *Southwestern Historical Quarterly*, XXXII, 130-133.

COTTLE, GEORGE WASHINGTON: Age 38; Private; a native of Tennessee, resident of Gonzales. Sources: Bexar 938, 1639; Fannin 857; Shelby 486; Muster Rolls, pp. 4, 5; CMSR, Nos. 4, 302; Ethel Z. Rather, "DeWitt's Colony," *Texas Historical Quarterly*, VIII, 159; Miles S. Bennett, "Battle of Gonzales," *Ibid.*, II, 315; *Register of the Spanish Archives*, General Land Office, shows that he arrived in DeWitt's Colony, September 12, 1832. He entered the Alamo on March 1, 1836.

COURTMAN, HENRY: Age 28; Private; emigrated from Germany to Texas. Sources: Muster Rolls, pp. 5, 25; Court of Claims Applications, No. 1965, File (C-D). This man belonged to Breece's company. His brother, George F. Courtman, died at Goliad.

CRAWFORD, LEMUEL: Age 22; Private; immigrated to Texas from South Carolina. Sources: San Patricio 105; Bexar 1175; I Bastrop 446; CMSR, Nos. 53, 69, 109, 141, 413; *Reminiscences of John H. Jenkins* (MS.), p. 123, University of Texas archives.

CROCKETT, DAVID: Age 50; Private; immigrated to Texas from Tennessee, January, 1836. Sources: Bexar 1040, 1240, 1286; Robertson 609; I Bexar 1248; CMSR, Nos. 13 (shows his signature), 3196; Muster Rolls, pp. 2, 5; *Telegraph and Texas Register*, March 24, 1836; *Arkansas Advocate*, April 15, 1836, states that Crockett had command of the Alamo after the death of Travis and John J. Baugh.

CROSSMAN, ROBERT: Age 26; Private; native of Pennsylvania, immigrated to Texas from New Orleans. Sources: Milam 774; Fannin 1298; I Fannin 1615; Muster Rolls, pp. 2, 5, 20, 25 (the Muster Rolls give this name as "Crosson" and

"Crasson," but other documents write it "Crossman"); James E. Winston, "Pennsylvania and the Texas Independence," *Southwestern Historical Quarterly*, XVII, 268.

CUMMINGS, DAVID P.: Age 27; Private; native of Georgia, resident of Gonzales. Sources: Bexar 907, 1034; I Bexar 1180; *Lost Book of Harris* 110, 263; Court of Claims Vouchers, No. 4271, File (A-C). This document shows two letters from D. P. Cummings to his father. One was written February 14, 1836, after his arrival at the Alamo.

CUNNINGHAM, ROBERT: Age 27; Private; native of Tennessee, immigrated to Texas from Arkansas. Sources: Milam 1052-1/2, 1186; Robertson 862; I Milam 952; Muster Rolls, pp. 3, 5, 20; CMSR, No. 440; *Register of the Spanish Archives*, General Land Office, shows that he registered in Austin's Colony, March 4, 1833.

DAMON (DAYMON), SQUIRE: Age 28; Private; native of Tennessee, resident of Gonzales. I Bastrop 513; Muster Rolls, pp. 5, 20; CMSR, 4202. One of the famous thirty-two men from Gonzales.

DARST (also seen as DURST or DUST), JACOB C.: Age 48; Private; native of Tennessee, resident of Gonzales, and one of the thirty-two who went to the Alamo on March 1, 1836. Sources: Gonzales 102, 71; Bexar 801; Muster Rolls, pp. 3, 5; CMSR, No. 9548; Miles S. Bennett, "Battle of Gonzales," *Texas Historical Quarterly*, II, 314-315; Ethel Z. Rather, "DeWitt's Colony," *Texas Historical Quarterly*, VIII, 159.

DAVIS, JOHN: Age 25; Private; native of Kentucky resident of Gonzales, and one of the thirty-two who went to Travis's aid on March 1, 1836. Sources: Gonzales 77, 131, 165 Milam 779; I Goliad 19; Muster Rolls, pp. 3, 5; CMSR Nos. 374, 378, 9456; Miles S. Bennett, *Texas Historical Quarterly*, II, 315; Ethel Z. Rather, *Ibid.*, VIII, 159.

DAY, FREEMAN H. K. (this name is generally found as F. H. K. Day): Age 30; Private. Sources: I Nacogdoches 521; I Fannin 973 (these files give definite information that he died at the Alamo); Muster Rolls, pp. 5, 20 (Muster Rolls are not definite.) On page 5 of the Muster Rolls, the name is Day; on page 20, it is H. K. Day. It is easy to confuse this name with that of H. B. Day who died at Goliad, and with that of H. R. Day who participated in the battle of San Jacinto, but a close study of the records makes it clear that these were three different men.

DAY, JERRY C.: Age 20; Private; immigrated to Texas from Missouri, lived near Gonzales. He was the son of Jeremiah Day who served the Texan forces from

1836 through 1838 as a wagoner. Sources: Bexar 1597; San Patricio 4; I Montgomery 97; Muster Rolls, p. 3. On the Muster Rolls this name merely appears as "Day."

DEARDUFF, WILLIAM: Private; native of Tennessee, resident of Gonzales, and was one of the brave thirty-two who went to the Alamo on March 1. Sources: Gonzales 113; Bexar 940; I Gonzales 405, 456; CMSR, 8746; Miles S. Bennett, *Texas Historical Quarterly*, II, 315; Ethel Z. Rather, *Ibid.*, VIII, 159.

DENNISON, STEPHEN: Age 24; Private; native of England, immigrated to Texas from Kentucky. Sources: Bexar 1840; Fannin 1257, 1057; I Fannin 1568; I Bexar 2001; Memorial, No. 102, State Department; Court of Claims Vouchers, No. 1114, File (D-G), shows claims for headright presented by H. F. Smith of Louisville, Kentucky.

DESPALLIER, CHARLES: Age 24; Private (Aid to Travis); native of Louisiana. He entered the Alamo on March 1 with the famous thirty-two from Gonzales. Conclusive documents state this fact; on the other hand, in a letter of February 25, Travis cites him for special bravery. It is evident from these two facts that he had been sent out as a messenger and returned with the men from Gonzales. We know that John W. Smith and Albert Martin of this same band had been sent out as messengers. Sources: Nacogdoches 347; Fannin 721; I Nacogdoches 825. These documents show that the heirs of Charles Despallier applied for land due him, or his heirs, in 1837. In 1852, bounty, donation and headright lands were patented to his heirs. These documents are definite in their information. They describe this man as the younger brother of Blaz Phillipe Despallier, who participated in the storming of Bexar in December, 1835. B. P. Despallier was a captain, or is spoken of as such, although the Muster Rolls list him as a private in York's company. Immediately after the fall of Bexar to the Texans, B. P. Despallier was associated with Travis in scout service, but on December 29, he was honorably discharged and went home sick. Upon reaching his home, Rapides Parish, Louisiana, his younger brother, Charles, was sent out to join the Texas army, reaching San Antonio about the middle of February. All this is shown by the Bounty and Donation files.

In 1837, Charles Despallier's mother, Madam Caudida Despallier, applied for lands due her son, but before they were granted, she and her two other sons, B. P. Despallier and Victor M. Despallier, had died of cholera in 1839. Then, the heir to Charles Despallier's lands was the young son of Blaz P. Despallier who was also named Blaz Phillipe. This child's guardians took up his claim to his uncle's Texas lands, and in 1852, headright, bounty, and donation lands were patented to him as the heir of Charles Despallier.

But in the archives of the Texas Department of State, Memorial No. 20, File 25, there are a number of affidavits, made in October 1855 by reputable Mexicans of San Antonio, in an attempt to assist Espalier's heir with her claim, affirming that Charles Despallier and Carlos Espalier were one and the same person. They say, at least, that they had never heard of a Charles Despallier and that they believe these names to be variants of the same name. They testify that Carlos Espalier was a young Mexican boy of San Antonio, seventeen years old and a protege of James Bowie. The evidence produced by these Mexicans seems sufficient and conclusive proof that young Espalier did die at the Alamo, but it is not sufficient to prove that Espalier and Despallier were the same man. In fact, similarity of name is the only strong point they had for such a conclusion. The heir of Carlos Espalier was Guardia de Luz, a very old Mexican woman of San Antonio.

Upon the evidence presented by these Mexicans, the Legislature of Texas granted to the old woman, Doña Guardia de Luz, the lands due to her nephew for his service. These facts have led to a good deal of confusion concerning these two men. Concerning this problem there are these facts: (1) two separate and distinct grants of headrights, donation, and bounty lands (see file numbers under the respective names); (2) two separate and distinct heirs; (3) two distinctly different descriptions of the men concerned, for Despallier was a twenty-four year old Frenchman from Rapides Parish, Louisiana, while Espalier was a seventeen year old Mexican boy of San Antonio. This comparison of data seems sufficient proof that these names represent two men who died at the Alamo, one Charles Despallier, the other Carlos Espalier. See also Travis's letter of February 25, 1836 in of this study.

DICKENSON (DICKINSON), ALMARON: Age 26; Captain; immigrated to Texas from Tennessee, resident of Gonzales. Sources: Fannin 297, 305; I Gonzales 99; CMSR, Nos. 13, 7688. This last document is a soldier's discharge and is signed by "Almaron Dickenson," captain, and William T. Austin, "Aid to Col. Burleson." It is dated December 13, 1835. Almaron Dickenson is generally rated as a lieutenant, but he had his commission as a captain of artillery and was in command of the artillery forces at the Alamo. There has been a great deal of confusion concerning the spelling of this man's name. Most of the better Texan historians—Yoakum, Wooten, Brown, Foote, and others—spell the name "Dickinson"; others write it "Dickenson," but CMSR, No. 7688, and an affidavit, made by Mrs. Dickenson's last husband, J. W. Hannag (*Miscellaneous Papers of the Adjutant General's Office*, State Library Archives), show conclusively that the name should be written "Almaron Dickenson."

DILLARD, JOHN H.: Age 31; Private; came to Texas from Tennessee, resident of Nashville-on-the-Brazos. Sources: Robertson 659, 673; I Milam 778; CMSR,

No. 6281.

DIMKINS (DIMPKINS), JAMES B.: Private; native of England. Sources: Robertson 569; Muster Rolls, pp. 2, 5; *Telegraph and Texas Register*, March 24, 1836; F. W. Gray, *From Virginia to Texas*, 140.

DOVER, SHEROD J.: Age 30; Private; native of England. Sources: I Shelby 514; I Bexar 2059; CMSR, 165; Court of Claim Applications, No. 1331, File (C-D).

DUEL (DEWELL), LEWIS: Age 24; Private; came to Texas from New York. Sources: Montgomery 283, 289; I Bexar 1264; Court of Claims Vouchers, No. 549, File (D-G); James E. Winston, "New York and the Independence of Texas," *Southwestern Historical Quarterly*, XVIII, 377. This man was a plasterer by trade. In Texas, he made his living as a brick mason.

DUVALT (DEVAULT), ANDREW: Age 32; Private; native of Ireland, resident of Gonzales. Sources: Bowie 38, 71, 87, 91; Muster Rolls, pp. 5, 20, 23; Miles Bennett, "Battle of Gonzales," *Texas Historical Quarterly*, II, 315; Ethel Z. Rather, "DeWitt's Colony," *Ibid.*, VIII, 159.

ESPALIER, CARLOS: Age 17; Private; resident of San Antonio. Sources: Bexar 1271, 1337, 1383; I Bexar 1348; See notes under entry for Charles Despallier.

ESPARZA, GREGORIO: Age 33; Private; native and resident of San Antonio. Sources: Bexar 1183; Travis 762; I Bexar 682; Court of Claims Applications, No. 572, File (D-G). This last cited document shows plainly that it was more difficult for the Mexicans who participated in the battles of the Texas Revolution, to secure warrants for the lands due for their services than it was for others. Esparza was one of Juan N. Seguin's soldiers. His family, wife and four children, were in the Alamo when it fell. His brother, in Santa Anna's army, with other friends, asked Santa Anna for the dead body of Esparza. Santa Anna granted the request, and his body was not burned with the rest of the victims, but was carried away by his friends and buried.

EVANS, ROBERT: Age 36; Master of Ordnance; native of Ireland, immigrated to New Orleans from New York, thence to Texas. Sources: Robertson 568, 580; Fannin 1131; I Robertson 610; Muster Rolls, p. 2; *Telegraph and Texas Register*, March 24, 1836; James E. Winston, "New York and the Independence of Texas," *Southwestern Historical Quarterly*, XVIII, 377.

EVANS, SAMUEL B.: Age 27; Private; came to Texas from Kentucky. Sources: Refugio 64, 74; Fannin 1311-1/2; Bexar 1620; I Fayette 37; CMSR, No. 9309;

Muster Rolls, p. 2 (Muster Rolls give only last name "Evans"). R. Potter to Adjutant General William Steele, July 10, 1874, *Adjutant General's Miscellaneous Papers,* Texas State Library. Here, Potter says that Samuel Evans was the son of Musgrave Evans, and the grandson of General Jacob Brown, of the U.S. Navy. CMSR, No. 9309 shows that Musgrave Evans was administrator of this Alamo soldier's estate.

EWING, JAMES L.: Age 24; Private; came to Texas from Tennessee. Sources: Bexar 628, 629, 230; I Bexar 742; Muster Rolls, pp. 3, 20; *Telegraph and Texas Register,* March 24, 1836.

FISHBAUGH (FISHBACK), WILLIAM: Private; resident of Gonzales, and was one of the thirty-two who went to the Alamo on March 1 to aid Travis. Sources: Bexar 932, 1893; I Gonzales 340; I Fannin 462; CMSR, No. 3; Miles S. Bennett, *Texas Historical Quarterly,* II, 315; Muster Rolls, p. 4 (here the name is spelled "Fishback.")

FLANDERS, JOHN: Age 36; Private; immigrated to Texas from Massachusetts by way of New Orleans, and was a resident of Gonzales, being one of the thirty-two from that place who went to the Alamo on March 1. Sources: Bexar 882, 890; I Harris 144; H. G. Flanders, Chicago, to Harriet Smither, July 26, 1932, Texas State Library. This letter is a pretty complete genealogy of John Flanders's family. For the purpose of this list, the most interesting items of it are: John Flanders, son of Levi and Mary (Sargent) Flanders, was born in Salisbury, Massachusetts, in 1800. As far as is known he never married. He was in business with his father. They had disagreement over a mortgage held by the son on a piece of property owned by a widow. John Flanders wished to foreclose, but his father opposed it. The disagreement developed into bad feelings and John Flanders left home and never communicated with his family. They heard of him, however, in New Orleans and later in Texas.

FLOYD, DALPHIN WARD: Age 29; Private; resident of Gonzales. Sources: Bexar 1141; Gonzales 32; I Gonzales 39; CMSR, No. 9224; Miles S. Bennett, *Texas Historical Quarterly,* II, 315; Ethel Z. Rather, *Ibid.,* VIII, 159. On the *Texas Almanac* list, this name is given as "Dolphin Ward."

FORSYTH, JOHN HUBBARD: Age 39; Captain; immigrated to Texas from New York. Sources: Jefferson 23, 30; Milam 879; Muster Rolls, p. 2; CMSR, Nos. 73, 9583; George Forsyth to E. M. Phelps, July 12, 1909, *Biographical and Historical Notes,* Texas State Library. The latter is a letter from George Forsyth, a nephew of John Hubbard Forsyth. His letter gives a biography of his uncle, the most interesting items of which are as follows:

Captain John Hubbard Forsyth, who fell in the battle of the Alamo on March 6, 1836, was the eldest child of Alexander and Mercy (Treat) Forsyth. He was born at Avon, Livingston County, New York, August 10, 1797. He grew to manhood on his father's farm near Avon, but he was better educated than the average farmer boy of those days. He studied medicine, but never practiced the profession. On April 3, 1822, at the age of 25 he married Deborah Smith, who died on December 25, 1828, leaving one child, a son, Edmund Augustus Forsyth, who grew to manhood at Rochester, New York. This boy married in 1853 and had several children. Shortly after the death of his wife, John Hubbard Forsyth left his infant son with his father's family and went west...At the Alamo he was the senior captain of the command, outranked only by Travis and Bowie. When I was still a very young boy, I remember that my father tried to secure title for the son, Edmund, to Texas lands due to his father. I do not know the outcome of the effort.

FUENTES, ANTONIO: Age 23; Private; native and resident of San Antonio. Sources: Bexar 1285; Memorial No. 71, File 29, Archives of the State Department; see, also, the notes under the entry for "Juan Abamillo."

FUQUA, GALBA: Age 16; Private; native and resident of Gonzales. Sources: Bexar 1253, 1360; Milam 1358; I Bexar 1287; CMSR, Nos. 294, 295, 306; Miles S. Bennett, *Texas Historical Quarterly*, II, 315; Ethel Z. Rather, *Ibid.*, VIII, 159; Muster Rolls, p. 4. He was one of Gonzales's famous thirty-two who entered the Alamo on March 1.

FURTLEROY (FONTLEROY), WILLIAM H.: Age 22; Private; came to Texas from Kentucky in January, 1836. Sources: Muster Rolls, p. 117; James E. Winston, *Southwestern Historical Quarterly*, XVI, 34; *Ibid*, XIV, 315; W. P. Orndorff to William Steele, February 21, 1875; also George W. Bailey to William Steele, March 6, 1875; both letters are among *Adjutant General's Miscellaneous Papers*, Texas State Library. Orndorff and Bailey both say that William H. Fontleroy (Orndoff spells the name "Fauntleroy") came to Texas with Peter James Bailey, Daniel William Cloud, Joseph Washington and Archer (B. A. M.) Thomas, all from Logan County, Kentucky, all of who went into the Alamo with Crockett. They all took the oath of allegiance before John Forbes, January 14, 1836. Forbes's records spell the name "Furtleroy" and that is the spelling which has been used in this study. No evidence has been found that the heirs of this man ever applied for the land due them.

GARNETT, WILLIAM: Age 24; Private; immigrated to Texas from Tennessee, resident of the Falls of the Brazos. Sources: Fort Bend 32, 33; I Milam 292; I Fort Bend 36; Court of Claims Vouchers Nos. 1824, File (E-G). This last document shows that Garnett was a Baptist preacher, and his friends testify that "he was a man of unblemished character," who lived in Robertson's Colony at the Falls of the Brazos. He was a great admirer of Travis.

GARRAND, JAMES W.: Age 23; Private; came to Texas from Louisiana. Sources: I Fannin 1343; Muster Rolls, p. 20; Memorial No. 25, File 31, Archives of Department of State.

GARRETT, JAMES GIRARD: Age 30; Private; native of Tennessee, came to Texas by way of New Orleans. Sources: Nacogdoches 655, 670; Robertson 1167; I Robertson 1332, 1279; Muster Rolls, pp. 2, 13; *Telegraph and Texas Register*, March 24, 1836.

GARVIN, JOHN E.: Age 27; Private; resident of Gonzales. Sources: Milam 1263, 1264; I Fannin 1439; I Bexar 1545; CMSR, No. 2; Miles S. Bennett, *Texas Historical Quarterly*, II, 315; Ethel Z. Rather, *Ibid.*, VIII, 159; *Telegraph and Texas Register*, March 24, 1836. One of the Gonzales thirty-two.

GASTON, JOHN E.: Age 17; Private; resident of Gonzales and was another of the brave men who went into the Alamo on March 1. Sources: Bexar 1240, 1359; Milam 1352, 1355; I Bexar 1284; CMSR, No. 9599; Bennett, *Texas Historical Quarterly*, II, 315; Rather, *Ibid.*. VIII, 159.

GEORGE, JAMES: Age 34; Private; resident of Gonzales. Sources: Gonzales 106, 150; Travis 354; Milam 750; I Goliad 48; I Gonzales 437; CMSR, Nos. 369, 8747, 197; Muster Rolls, p. 12; Bennett, *Texas Historical Quarterly*, II, 315; Rather, *Ibid.*, VIII, 159; *Telegraph and Texas Register*, March 24, 1836.

GOODRICH, JOHN CALVIN: Age 27; Private; came to Texas from Tennessee. Sources: Montgomery 59, 77-1/2, 78; I Montgomery 1; CMSR, No. 5137; Benjamin Briggs Goodrich to Edmund Goodrich, March 15, 1836, UT Archives.

GRIMES, ALBERT CALVIN: Age 23; Private; native of Georgia, resident of Texas, near present Navasota. Sources: Fannin 205; Milam 982, 715; I Milam 1188; CMSR, No. 5180; Rufus Grimes to E. M. Pease, July 20, 1875, *Adjutant General's Miscellaneous Papers*, Archives of the Texas State Library.

GUERRERO, JOSE MARIA: Age 43; Private; resident of Laredo. Sources: I San Patricio 320; I Bexar 143, 237; see notes under entry for "Juan Abamillo." This man was usually spoken of as "old one-eyed Guerrero."

GWYNNE (GWIN), JAMES C: Age 31; Private; native of England, came to Texas from Mississippi. Sources: Bexar 787; Victoria 124; I Milam 1144; CMSR, No. 55; Muster Rolls, p. 2. This man's name is spelled "Groyn" on the Alamo Monument.

HANNUM (HANNAN, HANUAM), JAMES: Age 21; Private; Milam 1212, 1288; Refugio 154; I Milam 53, 202.

HARRIS, JOHN: Age 23; Private; came from Kentucky, resident of Gonzales. Sources: Bexar 664; Rusk 80; Nacogdoches 648, 649; I Sabine 19; I Houston 386; Muster Rolls, pp. 3, 15; CMSR, No. 1077; Court of Claims Vouchers, No. 2627, File (H-L); Bennett, *The Texas Historical Quarterly*, II, 315; Rather, *Ibid.*, VIII, 159.

HARRISON, ANDREW JACKSON: Age 27; Private. Sources: Milam 1109, 1111; Robertson 1064; I Milam 374; Court of Claims Vouchers, No. 579, File (H-L).

HARRISON, WILLIAM B.: Age 25; Captain; native of Ohio, came to Texas, January, 1836, from Tennessee. Sources: Bexar 410; Houston 161, 256; Austin 49; I Houston 186; CMSR, Nos. 14, 226, 208, show his signature, while No. 7421 is his administrator's claim on the government; Muster Rolls, p. 2 (only last name given); *Telegraph and Texas Register*, March 24, 1836. Harrison was the captain of the Tennessee Volunteers, the so-called Crockett men.

HASKELL (HEISKILL), CHARLES M.: Age 23; Private; native of Tennessee, came to Texas from Louisiana. Sources: Milam 727, 729; Muster Rolls, pp. 2, 13; Houston to White, January 30, 1860, *Houston Letters*, State Library. From this letter it is apparent that Charles M. Haskell left the Alamo with Grant or Johnson, but returned to it with Bowie.

HAWKINS, JOSEPH M.: Age 37; Private; native of Ireland, came to Texas from Louisiana. Sources: Victoria 71; CMSR, No. 76; Muster Rolls, pp. 2, 13, gives the name "____ Hawkins, Ireland, La."; W. F. Gray, *From Virginia to Texas*, 139, writes the name, "Col. Hawkins, Louisiana." *Lamar Papers*, I, 307, in a letter to Governor Smith, the man himself signed his name "M. Hawkins." The bounty certificate Victoria 71, gives Joseph Hawkins, Louisiana. From the man's own signature it seems that he was known by his middle name, and there is some evidence that it was Mark. His letter shows that he was a man of intelligence and influence.

HAYS, JOHN M.: Age 22; Private; immigrated to Texas from Nashville, Tennessee. Sources: Milam 1012, 1195; I Bexar 942; *Lost Book of Harris*, p. 86; Muster Rolls, p. 2; *Telegraph and Texas Register*, March 24, 1836.

HENDRICKS, THOMAS: Age 21; Private. Sources: Fannin 366; Muster Rolls, p. 20; Court of Claims Vouchers, No. 474, File (H-L).

HERNDON, PATRICK HENRY: Age 31; Private; native of Virginia, resident of Navidad, Texas. Sources: Bexar 1104, 1107; I Montgomery 267; I Bexar 1121; CMSR, Nos. 122, 157.

HERSEE (HERSEY), WILLIAM D.: Age 32; Sergeant; native of England, came to Texas from Louisiana. Sources: Fannin 1081, 1082; I Fannin 1324; Muster Rolls, pp. 13, 20. The Muster Rolls show that William Hersee was wounded at the storming of Bexar in December of 1835. So, while he was at the Alamo during the siege and final attack, it is possible that he was not an efficient soldier during that time, depending upon the severity of his previous wounds.

HOLLAND, TAPLEY: Age 24; Private; resident of Grimes County, Texas. Sources: Robertson 500-1/2, 728; Fannin 610; Bastrop 96; I Robertson 524; Muster Rolls, p. 20; Court of Claims Vouchers, No. 16, File (H-L). All authorities who recount the "Rose Story," tell that when Travis drew the line with his sword and invited all who were willing to die with him to cross it to his side, Tapley Holland was the first man to leap across it to stand beside his chief.

HOLLOWAY, SAMUEL: Age 28; Private; native of Philadelphia, Pennsylvania; came to Texas from Louisiana. Sources: Robertson 1031, 1032, 1034; I Robertson 913, 1324-1/2; Muster Rolls, pp. 2, 20; *Telegraph and Texas Register*, March 24, 1836.

HOWELL, WILLIAM D.: Age 45; Surgeon; native of Massachusetts, came to Texas from New Orleans. Sources: Bexar 1550, 1603, 1618; Muster Rolls, pp. 2, 13, 20; *Telegraph and Texas Register*, March 24, 1836. The Alamo Monument incorrectly spells this name "Homrell."

JACKSON, THOMAS: Private; native of Ireland, resident of Gonzales, and was one of the thirty-two who went to the Alamo on March 1. Sources: Bexar 999; Milam 984; Gonzales 173; I Gonzales 484; CMSR, Nos. 1, 373; Miles S. Bennett, *Texas Historical Quarterly*, 11, 315; Rather, *Ibid.*, VIII, 159; *Telegraph and Texas Register*, March 24, 1836; *Register of the Spanish Archives* shows that this man registered in DeWitt's Colony, May 1, 1831, and that he died at the Alamo.

JACKSON, WILLIAM DANIEL: Age 29; Private; native of Ireland, came to Texas from Kentucky. Sources: I Fannin 354, 362; Muster Rolls, p. 3 gives "_____ Jackson, Ireland"; W. F. Gray, *From Virginia to Texas*, p. 140, lists this name as "Dan'l Jackson, sailor;" *Telegraph and Texas Register*, March 24, 1836.

JAMESON, GREEN B.: Age 29; Ensign; native of Kentucky, resident of Brazoria. Sources: Liberty 197; Milam 1487; I Robertson 1212, 1213; CMSR, No. 1806; Muster Rolls, pp. 2, 16. It is well to explain that all engineers of the Texas Revolutionary Army were called "ensigns." Jameson is listed on all rolls as an ensign. He was the chief engineer of the Alamo fortress. See also Bowie's despatch to Batres in this study. Here Bowie, refers to this man as "Benito Jameson."

JENNINGS, GORDON C: Age 27; Private; came to Texas from Missouri. Sources: Travis 3940; I Bastrop 414; I Milam 844; CMSR, No. 12.

JOHNSON, LEWIS: Private; native of Wales, resident of Nacogdoches. Sources: Milam 780, 786; Travis 316; I Travis 281; CMSR, No. 4199; Muster Rolls, pp. 2, 20; *Telegraph and Texas Register*, March 24, 1836.

JOHNSON, WILLIAM: Private; immigrated to Texas from Pennsylvania. Sources: Milam 787, 1585, 1611; Liberty 186; Court of Claims Letters, File (A-Z). Among these letters there is one from M. M. Grant of Galveston, written to the Court of Claims, March 30, 1861. Grant explains that William P. Johnson and William R. Johnson (who is shown on the Muster Rolls as having died with Fannin at Goliad) are one and the same man, and that the correct middle initial is "P." This William P. Johnson belonged to King's company. He furthermore explains that the Land Commissioner got William Johnson, from Philadelphia—the man listed above—and William P. Johnson confused in his records. Grant goes on to restate clearly that William Johnson from Philadelphia died at the Alamo, while William P. Johnson died at Goliad. He did not state how or why he knew these facts, but it is true that there is confusion in the bounty files concerning these names.

JONES, JOHN: Age 26; Lieutenant; immigrated to Texas from New York. Sources: *Lost Book of Harris*, p. 15; CMSR, Nos. 6551, 6692. This last document shows John Jones as a lieutenant in Blazeby's Company of New Orleans Grays, Muster Rolls, pp. 2, 16, 20. There are five John Joneses recorded in the Texan army in 1836. The records for them are very confusing, but the references, cited above, prove clearly that one John Jones died at the Alamo on March 6, 1836.

KELLOGG, JOHNNY: Age 19; Private; resident of Gonzales. Sources: I Bastrop 240; I Bexar 553; Miles S. Bennett, *Texas Historical Quarterly*, II, 315; Rather, *Ibid.*, VIII, 159. This man was the son of John Kellogg, Sr., of Gonzales, and he was one of the thirty-two who went to the Alamo on March 1.

KENNY, JAMES: Age 23; Private; came to Texas from Virginia. Sources: Bexar 1264, 1336, 1342; Travis 323; I Travis 323; CMSR, No. 4201; *Telegraph and Texas Register*, March 24, 1836.

KENT, ANDREW: Age 38; Private; resident of Gonzales, and went to the Alamo on March 1. Sources: Nacogdoches 320; Fannin 604; Milam 1548; I Houston 261; CMSR, No. 166; *Telegraph and Texas Register*, March 24, 1836; Miles Bennett, *Texas Historical Quarterly*, II, 315; Rather, *Ibid.*, VIII, 159.

KERR, JOSEPH: Age 22; Private; came to Texas from Lake Providence, Louisiana. Sources: Nacogdoches 417; Affidavits of S. L. Chambliss and of Mary E. Martin, on January 9, 1875, among the *Adjutant General's Miscellaneous Papers*, Texas State Library.

KIMBALL, GEORGE C.: Age 27; Lieutenant; resident of Gonzales, and he went to the Alamo with the famous thirty-two from that place. Sources: Gonzales 190, 191; I Bexar 341; CMSR, No. 8366; Muster Rolls, p. 4, 17; *Telegraph and Texas Register*, March 24, 1836; Miles S. Bennett, *Texas Historical Quarterly*, II, 315; Ethel Z. Rather, *Ibid.*, VIII, 159.

KING, JOHN G.: Age 26; Private; resident of Gonzales. Sources: Gonzales 97; I Gonzales 205; Muster Rolls, p. 17; CMSR, Nos. 7928, 8748. He went to the Alamo, March 1, 1836, with the band from Gonzales.

KING, WILLIAM P.: Age 24; Private; resident of Gonzales. Sources: Gonzales 65, 78, 89; I Gonzales 204; Muster Rolls, pp. 4, 6; *Telegraph and Texas Register*, March 24, 1836; Miles S. Bennett, *Texas Historical Quarterly*, II, 315; Rather, *Ibid.*, VIII, 159. William P. and John G. King were brothers and lived some ten or fifteen miles above Gonzales.

LEWIS, WILLIAM IRVINE: Age 23; Private; native of Wales, immigrated to Texas from Pennsylvania. Sources: Bexar 183, 184; I Victoria 70; CMSR, No. 7795; Muster Rolls, p. 3; *Telegraph and Texas Register*, October 21, 1840. In this newspaper there is a copy of a letter from the mother of William Irvine Lewis, begging for some memento of her son who died at the Alamo. A stone of the Alamo ruins, carved into a small monument was sent to her in Philadelphia.

LIGHTFOOT, WILLIAM J.: Age 25; Third Corporal; native of Virginia, resident of Gonzales. Sources: Bexar 1715; I Washington 43, 78; I Brazoria 62; Muster Rolls, pp. 18, 20; CMSR, No. 4319 (Name here "John W. Lightfoot"); Court of Claims Vouchers, No. 63, File (H-L). He is easily confused with Wilson T. Lightfoot and William W. Lightfoot, both of whom participated in the Battle of San Jacinto.

LINDLEY, JONATHAN L.: Age 31; Private; native of England, resident of Gonzales. He went to the Alamo on March 1. Sources: Nacogdoches 304, 369; Rusk

50, 81; I Montgomery 370; CMSR, No. 9189; Muster Rolls, p. 20; *Telegraph and Texas Register*, March 24, 1836.

LINN, WILLIAM: Private; immigrated to Texas from Massachusetts. Sources: Fannin 124-1/2, 1307, 1242; I Robertson 1298; I Victoria 41; Muster Rolls, pp. 3, 20, 25; *Telegraph and Texas Register*, March 24, 1836.

LOSOYO, TORIBIO DOMINGO: Private; native and resident of San Antonio. Sources: Bexar 1354, 1638; Fannin 1156; I Goliad, 230; I Fannin 505; see notes under entry for "Juan Abamillo."

MAIN, GEORGE WASHINGTON: Age 29; Private; immigrated to Texas from Virginia. Sources: San Patricio 168, 294; Robertson 1175; Refugio 142; I San Patricio 486; I Houston 8; Muster Rolls, pp. 19, 20.

MALONE, WILLIAM T.: Age 18; Private; came to Texas from Alabama. Sources: Robertson 1117; Milam 1495; I Robertson 101; Muster Rolls, p. 20; CMSR, No. 7733; *Lost Book of Harris*, 114, 268; G. A. McCall, *Texas Historical Quarterly*, XIV, 325-327.

MARSHALL, WILLIAM: Age 29; Private; native of Tennessee, came to Texas from Arkansas. Sources: Bastrop 466; I Harris 51; I Bastrop 466; Muster Rolls, pp. 19, 25 (Breece's Company); Court of Claims Vouchers, Nos. 2, 1454, File (M-R).

MARTIN, ALBERT: Age 30; Captain; native of Tennessee, resident of Gonzales. Sources: Bexar 643; Montgomery 130; I Fannin 699; Muster Rolls, p. 4; *Telegraph and Texas Register*, March 24, 1836; Miles S. Bennett, *Texas Historical Quarterly*, 11, 315; Rather, *Ibid.*, VIII, 159. Albert Martin was sent out during the early days of the siege to get reinforcements. He returned on March 1, as captain of the thirty-two from Gonzales and its environs.

McCAFFERTY, EDWARD: Lieutenant; resident of McGloin's Colony. Sources: Memorial, No. 154, File 78, Archives of the Texas Department of State.

McCOY, JESSE: Private; resident of Gonzales. Sources: Bexar 931; Milam 1246; I Bexar 1360; Muster Rolls, p. 4; CMSR, Nos. 5, 428; *Telegraph and Texas Register*, March 24, 1836. Jesse McCoy was one of the thirty-two from Gonzales who went to the Alamo on March 1.

McDOWELL, WILLIAM: Age 40; Private; came to Texas from Tennessee in January, 1836. Sources: Bexar 1710; I Fannin 1838; *Lamar Papers*, V, 159. This last document is a letter from George M. McDowell to Lamar or to Peter W. Grayson. He stated that his brother, William McDowell, went to Texas in January,

1836, to join the Texan army, that he left Tennessee with John Purdy Reynolds. Reynolds took the oath of allegiance under John Forbes at Nacogdoches, January 14, 1836 (per Muster Rolls, p. 117.) In this same Muster Roll appears the name of one William McDowelly. The addition of the "y" to the name is, no doubt, a clerical error. See, also, Adele B. Looscan, *Texas Historical Quarterly*, XIV, 315. There was another William McDowell who served in the Texan army in 1836. He fought at the storming of Bexar, December, 1835, and was living in 1838. He should not be confused with this man who died at the Alamo, March 6, 1836.

McGEE, JAMES: Private; native of Ireland, resident of Gonzales. Sources: Montgomery 39; Bexar 1599; I Bexar 869; CMSR, Nos. 551, 6674; Muster Rolls, p. 20. The Muster Rolls show that James McGee was wounded at the storming of Bexar. He probably was not an efficient soldier during the siege of the Alamo, but he died there March 6, 1836.

McGREGOR, JOHN: Age 34; Second Sergeant; native of Scotland, resident of Nacogdoches. Sources: Nacogdoches 428; Muster Rolls, p. 19; *Telegraph and Texas Register*, March 24, 1836; W. F. Gray, *From Virginia to Texas*, 140. In 1926, Mrs. Susan Sterling, a granddaughter of Alamo survivor Mrs. Dickenson, retold to me many of the stories that she as a child and young woman had heard from her grandmother concerning the fall of the Alamo. One story that always amused her was Mrs. Dickenson's account of John McGregor and his bagpipes. She said that when the fighting would lull, and the Texans had time for rest and relaxation, John McGregor and David Crockett would give a sort of musical concert, or rather a musical competition, to see which one could make the best music, or the most noise—David with his fiddle, and John with his bagpipes. She said McGregor always won so far as noise was concerned, for he made "strange, dreadful sounds" with his queer instrument.

McKINNEY, ROBERT: Age 27; Private; native of Tennessee, came to Texas from New Orleans. Sources: Fannin 1087; Travis 591; I Bexar 1611; see, also, *Reminiscences of John H. Jenkins* (MS.), p. 123, Archives of the University of Texas.

MELTON, ELIEL: Age 40; Lieutenant-Quartermaster; native of South Carolina, resident of Nashville-on-the-Brazos. Sources: Robertson 279, 365, 366; I Robertson 599; Muster Rolls, pp. 2, 19; CMSR, No. 9067; *Telegraph and Texas Register*, March 24, 1836; W. F. Gray, *From Virginia to Texas*, 140.

MILLER, THOMAS R.: Age 41; Private; native of Tennessee, resident of Gonzales, and one of the thirty-two who went to the Alamo on March 1. Sources: Bexar 555, 556; I Bexar 660; Muster Rolls, p. 4; CMSR, Nos. 183, 1087, 8770;

Telegraph and Texas Register, March 24, 1836; Miles S. Bennett, *Texas Historical Quarterly*, II, 315; Ethel Z. Rather, *Ibid.*, VIII, 159.

MILLS, WILLIAM: Age 21; Private; native of Tennessee, came to Texas from Arkansas. Sources: Memorial, No. 257, File. 64; Court of Claims Vouchers, Nos. 351, 426, File (M-R).

MILLSAPS, ISAAC: Age 41; Private; native of Mississippi, resident of Gonzales. Sources: Milam 379; Victoria 66; I Milam 909; I Robertson 627; Muster Rolls, p. 4; *Telegraph and Texas Register*, March 24, 1836; Miles S. Bennett, *Texas Historical Quarterly*, 11, 315; Rather, *Ibid,*, VII, 159. Isaac Millsaps was one of the band of thirty-two who went to the Alamo on March 1. He was survived by his blind wife and seven young children.

MITCHASSON (MITCHERSON), EDWARD F.: Age 29; Surgeon; native of Virginia, but came to Texas from Missouri. Sources: Nacogdoches 73; Bexar 1179, 1580; I Shelby 375; Muster Rolls, pp. 2, 19; *Telegraph and Texas Register*, March 24, 1836; CMSR, Nos. 8454, 8493.

MITCHELL, EDWIN T.: Age 30; Private; immigrated to Texas from Georgia. Sources: Fannin 736, 737; I Fannin 859; Muster Rolls, pp. 2, 19; *Telegraph and Texas Register*, March 24, 1836.

MITCHELL, NAPOLEON B.: Age 32; Private; Sources: Travis 219, 225; I Travis 159; I Goliad 38; Muster Rolls, pp. 19, 20 (the initials on the Muster Rolls are A. B. instead of N. B.). See also the *Reminiscences of John H. Jenkins* (MS.), 123, Archives of the University of Texas.

MOORE, ROBERT B.: Age 55; Private; native of Virginia, came to Texas from New Orleans. Sources: *Lost Book of Harris* 111; I San Patricio 498; I Bastrop 401; CMSR, No, 7852; Muster Rolls, pp. 3, 19, 20, 25; *Telegraph and Texas Register*, March 24, 1836.

MOORE, WILLIS A.: Age 28; Private; immigrated to Texas from Arkansas. Sources: Travis 657, 688, 775; Goliad 198; Fannin 979; I Goliad 281; Muster Rolls, pp. 2, 19. The Muster Rolls give merely the surname "Moore." Also, see *Telegraph and Texas Register*, March 24, 1836.

MUSSELMAN, ROBERT: Age 31; Sergeant; native of Ohio, came to Texas from Louisiana. Sources: Robertson 1151; Fannin 1478; I Fannin 1724; Muster Rolls, pp. 2, 19, 20, 25; *Telegraph and Texas Register*, March 24, 1836; James M. Musselman to E. M. Pease, *Domestic Correspondence*, Texas State Library.

NAVA, ANDRES: Age 26; Private; native and resident of San Antonio. Sources: Court of Claims Applications, No. 416, File (M-R). The claim was filed by John Burlage on March 25, 1861. Burlage later made a note, saying that the heirs were too poor to carry their claim any further. See also notes under entry for "Juan Abamillo."

NEGGAN, GEORGE: Age 28; Private; native of South Carolina, resident of Gonzales. Sources: Nacogdoches 653, 715; Lamar 133; I Nacogdoches 826; Muster Rolls, p. 21; Court of Claims Vouchers, No. 790, File (M-R); *Telegraph and Texas Register*, March 24, 1836.

NELSON, ANDREW M.: Age 27; Private; native of Tennessee. Sources: Milam 1421; Red River 118; I Robertson 1203; Muster Rolls, pp. 2, 4 (the roll on page 4 of the Muster Rolls gives three "Nelsons" by surname only); *Telegraph and Texas Register*, March 24, 1836, also gives three Nelsons, as does also Gray's list, published in 1837.

NELSON, EDWARD: Age 20; Private; came to Texas from South Carolina. Sources: Travis 5; I San Patricio 487; Lost Book of Harris, p. 34; CMSR, Nos. 8951, 9263; Muster Rolls, pp. 2, 4, 21; *Telegraph and Texas Register*, March 24, 1836; W. F. Gray, *From Virginia to Texas*, 140.

NELSON, GEORGE: Age 31; Private; came to Texas from South Carolina. Sources: Milam 1455; I Fannin 1659; CMSR, No. 7123; Muster Rolls, pp. 2, 4, 21; *Telegraph and Texas Register*, March 24, 1836. George and the above Edward Nelson were brothers.

NORTHCROSS, JAMES: Age 32; Private; native of Virginia, resident of Mina, Texas. Sources: Red River 120, 136; Bastrop 254; I Milam 647; Muster Rolls, pp. 20, 21; *Register of Spanish Archives*, General Land Office, shows that this man registered in Benjamin Milam's Colony, April 22, 1835, and that he died at the Alamo on March 6, 1836.

NOWLAN (NOWLIN), JAMES: Age 27; Private; native of England. Sources: Goliad 68, 84, 92-1/2; I San Patricio, 597; Court of Claims Vouchers, Nos. 402, 1416, File (M-R); Muster Rolls, pp. 21, 20 (this shows that James Nowlin was severely wounded at the Storming of Bexar, December, 1835.)

PAGAN, GEORGE: Age 26; Private; came to Texas from Natchez, Mississippi. Sources: I Bexar 170; Muster Rolls, pp. 20, 22.

PARKER, CHRISTOPHER: Age 22; Private; came to Texas from Natchez, Mississippi. Sources: Bexar 931, 848; Travis 609, 632-1/2; Milam 1392; Muster

Rolls, pp. 2, 22; Court of Claims Vouchers, No. 931, File (M-R); *Register of the Spanish Archives*, shows that Christopher Parker was a single man who registered in Vehlein's Colony, November 20, 1835, and that he died at the Alamo on March 6, 1836.

PARKS, WILLIAM: Age 31; Private. Sources: San Patricio 287, 289; I San Patricio 119; Muster Rolls, pp. 20, 22; Court of Claims Vouchers, No. 83, File (M-R). It is easy to confuse this man with William A. Parks who participated in the Battle of San Jacinto, but they were different men.

PERRY, RICHARDSON: Age 19; Private; native of Texas. Sources: Bexar 539; I Travis, 445; I Milam 1636; Muster Rolls, pp. 20, 22; CMSR, No. 9564.

POLLARD, AMOS: Age 33; Chief Surgeon of the Alamo; native of Massachusetts, educated and reared in New York, came to Texas from New Orleans, resident of Gonzales. Sources: Milam 1122, 1123; Brazoria 10; I Milam 1226; CMSR, Nos. 33, 348; *Telegraph and Texas Register*, March 24, 1836; among the *Army Papers*, Texas State Library, are several letters (originals) from Pollard to Governor Smith, written from the Alamo during January and February of 1836; see, also, the *Samuel E. Asbury Papers*, University of Texas.

REYNOLDS, JOHN PURDY: Age 29; Private (he was a well-trained surgeon, but held no official position as such at the Alamo); native of Philadelphia, came to Texas, January, 1836, from Tennessee. Sources: Harris 37; Montgomery 287; Bexar 2085; Muster Rolls, p. 117; Court of Claims, Special Acts Certificates, Files No. 14/56, July 5, 1881. This document contains the deposition of Stephen Cummings who swears that John Purdy Reynolds was the son of Judge David Reynolds of Mifflin County, Tennessee. He also states that J. P. Reynolds graduated (MD) from Jefferson College, Philadelphia, in 1827, that he practiced medicine for seven years at Mifflin, Tennessee, and then went to Texas in January of 1836, with David Crockett's company.

ROBERTS, THOMAS H.: Private. Sources: Travis 543; Court of Claims Vouchers, No. 1984, File (M-R).

ROBERTSON, JAMES: Age 32; Private; native of Tennessee, came to Texas from Louisiana. Sources: Goliad 227; Bexar 1917; Fannin 1304; *Lost Book of Harris* 96, 250. This last reference states that at the storming of Bexar, December, 1835, James Robertson was a member of Captain B. P. Despallier's company. The Muster Rolls do not show that B. P. Despallier was in command of a company at Bexar, but several other similar statements have been found in which Despallier is called Captain. See Muster Rolls, p. 24.

ROBINSON, ISAAC: Age 33; Private; native of Scotland, came to Texas from New Orleans. Sources: Goliad 65; I Goliad 180; Muster Rolls, pp. 3, 24 (on Muster Rolls the name is merely "Robinson;") Court of Claims Vouchers, No. 122, File (M-R); *Telegraph, and Texas Register*, March 24, 1836.

ROSE, JAMES M.: Age 31; Private; native of Ohio, but immigrated to Arkansas and from there to Texas. Sources: Nacogdoches 162; Colorado 144; I Colorado 132; CMSR, Nos. 2549, 9629; Muster Rolls, p. 2; *Telegraph and Texas Register*, March 24, 1836. If the Rose Story be true, there were two Roses at the Alamo—Moses Rose, the man who is said to have escaped, and James M. Rose. The sources that are cited are very definite in stating that James M. Rose died at the Alamo, so he should not be confused with the Moses Rose who, according to Abraham Zuber's retelling of Rose's account, escaped.

RUSK, JACKSON J.: Private; native of Ireland; resident of Nacogdoches. Sources: I Red River 46; Court of Claims Vouchers No. 67, File (M-R); *Register of Spanish Archives* shows that this man registered in Zavala's Colony, September 30, 1835, and that he died at the Alamo, March 6, 1836; see, also, Muster Rolls, pp. 3, 24; *Telegraph and Texas Register,* March 24, 1836; W. F. Gray, *From Virginia to Texas*, 140.

RUTHERFORD, JOSEPH: Age 35; Private; native of Kentucky, resident of Nacogdoches. Sources: Rusk 73; Fannin 1272; Memorial No. 36, File 75; Muster Rolls, pp. 20, 24; see Templeton, *Margaret Ballentine, or the Fall of the Alamo*, 231.

RYAN, ISAAC: Age 24; Private; resident of Opelousas, Louisiana. Sources: Milam 651, 653; I Milam 859; Muster Rolls, pp. 3, 20; Court of Claims Vouchers, No. 185, File (M-R).

SCURLOCK, MIAL: Age 27; Private; immigrated to Texas from Louisiana. Sources: Travis 216; Fannin 311; I Fannin 452; Court of Claims Vouchers, No. 134, File (S-Z).

SEWELL, MARCUS L.: Age 31; Private; native of England, resident of Gonzales. Sources: Bexar 1006; Goliad 162; I Nacogdoches 408; Muster Rolls, pp. 3, 20; *Telegraph and Texas Register*, March 24, 1836.

SHIED (SHEAD), MANSON: Age 25; Private; native of Georgia, resident of Brazoria, Texas. Sources: Fannin 443, 631, 1184; I Robertson 565, 816, 872; Muster Rolls, p. 20 (here the name is spelled "Shudd.") See, also, S. P. Hollingsworth to William Steele, July 22, 1876, *Adjutant General's Miscellaneous Papers*, Texas State Library.

SIMMONS, CLEVELAND (CLELLAND) KENLOCK: Age 26; Lieutenant of Cavalry; native of Charleston, South Carolina, came to Texas, January, 1836. Sources: Fannin 1128, 1129; I Fannin 1358; Travis to Houston, February 25, 1836; Charles B. Stewart to Moses A. Bryant, May 16, 1876, *Veteran Papers*, Archives of the University of Texas; Charles B. Stewart to E. M. Pease, July 26, 1876, *Adjutant General's Miscellaneous Papers*, Texas State Library; Pease to Wm Steele, August 13, 1876, *Ibid*. The bounty and the headright certificates record this man's name as "Clelland K. Simmons." Stewart writes it "Cleveland Kenlock Simmons."

SMITH, ANDREW H.: Age 22; Private; came to Texas from Tennessee. Sources: Gonzales 194; Muster Rolls, p. 2; Court of Claims Vouchers, No. 68, File (S-Z).

SMITH, CHARLES S.: Age 30; Private; native of Maryland, came to Texas from Louisiana. Sources: Bastrop 246, 247; I Bastrop 578; Muster Rolls, p. 2; CMSR, No. 4200; *Telegraph and Telegraph Register*, March 24, 1836.

SMITH, JOSHUA G.: Age 28; Private; native of North Carolina, resident of Bastrop, Texas. Sources: Fannin 855; Montgomery 293; I Shelby 458; Muster Rolls, pp. 2, 20, 25 (these rolls give only last name); CMSR, Nos. 810, 872; *Telegraph and Texas Register*, March 24, 1836.

SMITH, WILLIAM H.: Age 27; Private; resident of Nacogdoches. Sources: Fannin 376; I Milam 1337; Muster Rolls, pp. 3, 20 (only the surname "Smith" is given here); *Telegraph and Texas Register*, March 24, 1836; Court of Claims Vouchers, No. 4275, File (S-Z). This document gives a detailed explanation showing that in 1836 there were two men in the Texan army who signed their name "William H. Smith." The one identified by the Fannin 376 died at the Alamo and the other was still living in 1840.

STARR, RICHARD: Age 25; Private; native of England, resident of San Antonio. Sources: Robertson 570, 578; I Robertson 605; Muster Rolls, pp. 2, 20, 25; *Telegraph and Texas Register*, March 24, 1836.

STEWART (STUART), JAMES E.: Age 28; Private; native of England. Sources: Milam 1018; I Colorado 84; Court of Claims Vouchers, No. 68, Pile (S-Z); Muster Rolls, pp. 2, 25. Here and on the list printed in the *Telegraph and Texas Register*, March 24, 1836, the name is spelled "Stuart," but it is "Stewart" in the bounty and headright files.

STOCKTON, RICHARD L.: Age 18; Private; native of Virginia, came to Texas, January, 1836, with Crockett. Sources: Milam 525, 526; I Milam 1186; Muster Rolls, pp. 117, 25; James E. Winston, *Southwestern Historical Quarterly*, XVI, 279.

SUMMERLIN, A. SPAIN: Age 19; Private; native of Tennessee, came to Texas from Arkansas. Sources: Lamar 74; Bowie 92, 615; Nacogdoches 405; I Nacogdoches 1044; I Fannin 1315; Muster Rolls, pp. 20, 26.

SUMMERS, WILLIAM E.: Age 24; Private; native of Tennessee, resident of Gonzales. Sources: Bexar 405, 406; *Texas Almanac*, 1860, pp. 81-82. This list was made by Francisco Ruiz. He declared that he burned 182 bodies, but he listed only 112 names.

SUTHERLAND, WILLIAM D.: Age 18; Private; resident of Navidad, Texas. Sources: Goliad 48, 49; I Fannin 1766; Muster Rolls, p. 2; also see a letter from this boy's mother, Mrs. George Sutherland, to her sister in Alabama, June 5, 1836, University of Texas Archives. Mrs. Sutherland tells of her son's death, of the "Run Away Scrape," and of general conditions in Texas.

TAYLOR EDWARD: Age 18; Private; resident of Liberty, Texas. Sources: Robertson 196; Bexar 1093; Fannin 989; I Bexar 1782; I Montgomery 522; I Milam 1050.

TAYLOR, GEORGE: Age 22; Private; resident of Liberty, Texas. Sources: Harrison 47, 114; Milam 893; I Liberty 206; I Milam 1067; Court of Claims Vouchers, No. 1997, File (S-Z).

TAYLOR, JAMES: Age 20; Private; resident of Liberty, Texas. Sources: Bexar 967-1/2; Milam 894; Bexar, 1092; I Harrison 45; I Bowie 9. Edward, George, and James Taylor were brothers.

TAYLOR, WILLIAM: Age 37; Private; native of Tennessee, resident of Little, River community—now Milam County, Texas. Sources: Court of Claims Vouchers, No. 1479, File (S-Z). This document explains that there were three William Taylors in the Texan army in 1836, and that one of them died at the Alamo. The other two were living in 1840. See W. F. Gray's list in *From Virginia to Texas*, 140. It gives four Taylors as Alamo victims, as do several other lists. The confusing factor in the matter, however, is the fact that none of these early lists give Christian names.

THOMAS, B. ARCHER M. (generally found as B. A. M. Thomas): Age 19; Private; came to Texas from Kentucky, January, 1836. He was a member of the Tennessee Mounted Volunteers—commonly called Crockett's men. Sources: Bastrop 206, 215; Milam 702; I Milam 927; Muster Rolls, p. 117; Adele B. Looscan, *Texas Historical Quarterly*, XIV, 315; CMSR, No. 13. This document shows his signature. He also signed a requisition drawn on the Provisional Government for room and board, declaring himself "One of Crockett's men." See also the letters from G. W. Bailey and W. P. Orndorff to General William Steele, as quoted in sources under the entry for "Peter James Bailey."

THOMAS, HENRY: Age 25; Private; native of Germany. Sources: Court of Claims Applications, No. 1972, File (S-Z), says that this man was killed with Travis at the Alamo. There was some flaw in the proof of heirship on the part of those applying for the land due Henry Thomas, so the certificates were postponed until heirs could be properly identified. Several affidavits stated that Henry Thomas died at the Alamo. No certificates granting land in his name can be found. Muster Rolls, p. 20 (Neill's Return of Soldiers Left at the Alamo, February 12, 1836) shows this full name. Muster Rolls, p. 25 ("A Roll of Breece's Company and What Became of It"), shows "Henry Thomas killed at the Alamo."

THOMPSON, JESSE G.: Private; native of Arkansas, resident of Brazoria. Sources: Bexar 519; Fort Bend 51, 53; Colorado 97; CMSR, No. 7093; Court of Claims Vouchers, No. 954, File (S-Z); Muster Rolls, pp. 2, 28 (Here, only the surname "Thompson" is given.)

THOMSON, JOHN W.: Age 25; Private (surgeon); native of North Carolina, came to Texas from Tennessee, January, 1836. Sources: Bexar 2356-1/2, 2383, 2509, 2513; Telegraph and Texas Register, March 24, 1836; Court of Claims Vouchers, Special Acts Certificates, Nos. 14/63, 14/64, 14/65, 14/66, issued June 19, 1883. This file contains two depositions. One of these was made by Mrs. M. J. Rainey, the aunt of Thomson, who said that he belonged to Crockett's company. The other was made by Captain William Gilmer, who says that in January, 1836, he and Thomson went together to Washington, Texas, but there they separated, Thomson going on to San Antonio to join Crockett.

THURSTON, JOHN M.: Age 27; Second Lieutenant; native of Pennsylvania, came to Texas from Kentucky. Sources: Milam 159; Goliad 144; I Victoria 554; Muster Rolls, pp. 2, 28; CMSR, Nos. 5226, 5742, 7809; Telegraph and Texas Register, March 24, 1836. John Thurston lived at San Antonio and was a clerk in Francis De Sauque's store.

TRAMMEL, BURKE: Age 26; Private; native of Ireland, came to Texas from Tennessee. Sources: Bexar 463; Milam 1106; Fannin 460; I Bastrop 433; CMSR, No. 9566; Muster Rolls, pp. 20, 28 (the name is written "R. Tommel.")

TRAVIS, WILLIAM BARRET: Age 27; Lieutenant Colonel Commanding; native of South Carolina, came to Texas from Alabama. Sources: Travis 244; San Patricio 181; I Fannin 704; Muster Rolls, pp. 2, 28; CMSR, Nos. 652, 5926.

TUMLINSON, GEORGE W.: Age 27; Private; native of Missouri, resident of Gonzales and was one of the famous thirty-two who went to the Alamo on March 1, 1836. Sources: Milam 1335; I Gonzales 363; Muster Rolls, pp. 20, 28; CMSR, No. 5273; *Telegraph and Texas Register*, March 24, 1836.

WALKER, ASA: Age 23; Private; came from Tennessee, November, 1835, to Texas. Sources: Goliad 72; I Fayette 29; *Fontaine Papers*, University of Texas Archives, contains a letter from Asa Walker to W. W. Gant, November 28, 1835. With this letter are notes signed by Walker for $35 for a rifle, and $20 for an overcoat, and another for $35.88 for transportation from Columbia, Tennessee, to Washington, Texas, altogether an indebtedness of $96. As a passing comment on how the lands of dead soldiers were manipulated in those days, it may be stated that W. W. Gant became administrator of Walker's estate. The lands due Walker were more than 4,000 acres. After all the costs of administration, the debt of $96, and other costs were paid, the estate of this soldier remained $210 in debt to the administrator.

WALKER, JACOB: Age 31; Private; resident of Nacogdoches. Sources: Nacogdoches 38; I Robertson 89. Mr. J. W. Walker, the present land commissioner, says that Asa and Jacob Walker were first cousins, and that both were first cousins of his father. See J. M. Morphis, *History of Texas*, 176. There Mrs. Dickenson tells that the last man killed in the Alamo was Jacob Walker, a gunner from Nacogdoches. He was shot down at her side.

WARD, WILLIAM B.: Age 30; Sergeant; native of Ireland; came to Texas from New Orleans. Sources: Lamar 58; Bexar 1702; Court of Claims Vouchers, No. 378, File Box (S-Z). This is probably the man whom Potter speaks of as manning the south battery in his account of the fall of the Alamo.

WARNELL (WORNEL), HENRY: Age 24; Private; immigrated to Texas from Arkansas, a resident of Bastrop. Sources: Travis 160; Bowie 94, 99; Fannin 1080, 1099; Bexar 1647; I Bastrop 415; I Jefferson 108. These certificates all state that Henry Warnell died at the Alamo. See also, Muster Rolls, p. 20; and all lists of Alamo victims. These lists vary as to the spelling of the name, giving Warnell, Wornel, Warnal, Wurnall, but all give the initial H., or the name Henry. CMSR, No. 108, is an administrator's claim against the Texan government for $39.59 of salary due to the Alamo soldier, Henry Warnell. Edward Burleson was the administrator. Wherever the documents cited above give any personal description of the man at all, it is to state that he was a single man, but Court of Claims Voucher, No. 400, File (S-Z), states that Henry Warnell was married, that his wife died in Arkansas in November, 1834, whereupon he left his infant son, John, with friends and went to Texas. He arrived in January, 1835, and hired himself to Edward Burleson, at whose home he lived. CMSR, No. 108, proves that Burleson was the administrator of Warnell's estate. The Court of Claims document further describes this man as being twenty-four years old, small—weighing less than 118 pounds—blue-eyed, red-headed, freckled, and "an incessant tobacco chewer." It also states that he had been a jockey and a great hunter in Arkansas.

WASHINGTON, JOSEPH G.: Age 28; Private; came to Texas from Tennessee in January of 1836. He was a member of the Tennessee Mounted Volunteers (Crockett's men.) Sources: Milam 932, 1079, 1602; I Milam 1243; Muster Rolls, pp. 2, 114. G. W. Bailey to William Steele, March 6, 1876, also, W. P. Orndorff to William Steele. February 21, 1876, *Adjutant General's Miscellaneous Papers*, Texas State Library.

WATERS, THOMAS: Age 24; Private; native of England; immigrated to Texas from Louisiana. Sources: I Bexar 376; Muster Rolls, pp. 25, 29; Court of Claims Applications No. 183, File (S-Z); the name on the fourth column of the Alamo monument is simply Waters.

WELLS, WILLIAM: Age 22; Private; came to Texas from Hall County, Georgia. Sources: Bastrop 33; San Patricio 145; Bexar 235; I Bastrop 218; I Bexar 379; CMSR, No. 733; Muster Rolls, 29; *Telegraph and Texas Register*, March 24, 1836.

WHITE, ISAAC: Private; came to Texas from Kentucky. Sources: Fannin 1482; Bexar 250; Muster Rolls, pp. 3, 39; *Telegraph and Texas Register*, March 24, 1836; Court of Claims Vouchers, No. 869, File (S-Z).

WHITE, ROBERT: Age 30; Lieutenant; resident of Gonzales, and entered the Alamo on March 1, 1836. Sources: Bexar 220; Muster Rolls, pp. 2, 20; *Telegraph and Texas Register*, March 24, 1836; Court of Claims Vouchers, No. 1215, File (S-Z); Miles S. Bennett, *Texas Historical Quarterly*, II, 315; Rather, *Ibid.*, VIII, 159.

WILLIAMSON, HIRAM J.: Age 26; Sergeant-Major; came to Texas from Philadelphia. Sources: Montgomery 120, 137. In these certificates the name is written "H. S. Williamson," but they give the description as above and state definitely that the man died at the Alamo. The administrator of Williamson's estate, Thomas S. Saul, clears up the obscurity in the name by a statement that he made before the Land Board of Washington County, February 6, 1838. Saul said that H. S. and H. J. were variants of the initials of the same man, and that the error was on the part of a recorder. He furthermore stated that the name should be written "Hiram J. Williamson." This statement is enclosed with I Fannin 1757. Williamson was an unmarried man.

WILSON, DAVID L.: Age 29; Private; native of Scotland, resident of Nacogdoches. Sources: Milam 781, 788; Nacogdoches 662; 640; 641; I Robertson 413; Muster Rolls, pp. 2, 29; *Telegraph and Texas Register*, March 24, 1836; Court of Claims Vouchers, No. 893, File (S-Z). This man's widow married Albert Henning. She acted as administrator of his estate.

WILSON, JOHN: Age 32; Private; came to Texas from Pennsylvania through Tennessee. Sources: Milam 1620; San Patricio 88; Court of Claims Vouchers, No. 183, File (S-Z). There were six John Wilsons in the Texan army in 1836. Most of them used distinguishing middle initials, but even so, it is confusing to trace them through the documents. The documents, cited above, make it clear, however, that but <u>one</u> John Wilson was massacred at the Alamo with Travis.

WOLFE, ANTONY: Private; native of England, resident of Nacogdoches. Sources: Nacogdoches 137; Muster Rolls, pp. 20, 29; Memorial No. 2, File 88, Archives of the Department of State.

WRIGHT, CLAIBORNE: Age 26; Private; native of North Carolina, resident of Gonzales, and went to the Alamo on March 1, 1836. Sources: Milam 775, 784; I Fannin 1727; Muster Rolls, pp. 4, 29; *Telegraph and Texas Register,* March 24, 1836; CMSR, No. 3423; Miles S. Bennett, *Texas Historical Quarterly*, March 24, 1836; *Ibid.*, VIII, 159.

ZANCO, CHARLES: Age 28; Lieutenant; native of Denmark, resident of Bexar. Sources: Lamar 61, 85, 95; I San Patricio 81; Court of Claims Vouchers, No. 37, File (S-Z); Muster Rolls, p. 3, the name is incorrectly written Charles "Danor." On page 20 it is written "Charles Lance"; on page 30 it is "Charles Zanor." At each place the Christian name is Charles, and the place of nativity is Denmark; it is evident, therefore, that all refer to the same man. The certificates for land are all to Charles Zanco, and the lists in both the *Telegraph and Texas Register*, March 24, 1836, and *Texas Almanac*, 1860, give the name correctly.

_____, JOHN, the negro slave boy who belonged to Francis De Sauque, was left at the Alamo by his master. He died there. Why he was not spared as were the other negroes is not known. All lists of Alamo victims include this name, but no certificate for land to his heirs, if he had any, can be found.

ANNOTATED LIST OF POSSIBLE VICTIMS

ANDERSON,_____: This name Anderson appears on all lists. The Muster Rolls, p. 20 ("Neill's Return of the Soldiers left by him at the Alamo, February 12, 1836"), gives the name A. Anderson. All lists record the rank of this man as that of Assistant Quartermaster. The Bounty and Donation files, Bexar 1735, 1750, and Harris 10, show that one Holland Anderson, a corporal, served in the Texan army at the storming of Bexar in December, 1835, and was honorably discharged on January 19, 1836. I believe that it was this Holland Anderson, or H. Anderson, as his name is generally recorded, that Neill's return lists, for the capital H and capital A are easily confused in manuscript if they stand alone in initials. One weakness in such a guess is that this man was discharged before Neill made his return, but there are a good many indications that Neill's list was actually made out some time before February 12 (the date he left the Alamo). If this supposition be true then the Anderson listed by Neill's return should be eliminated from the Alamo victim roll.

Among the Court of Claims Applications, numbers 1757 (dated August 20, 1858) and 161 (dated October 9, 1860), File (A-B), applications for land were made by attorneys in behalf of the heirs of one George Washington Anderson. They claimed that lands were due this soldier for service in the Texan army in 1836, and stated that the man was massacred at the Alamo. They pointed out the fact that his name appeared on the muster rolls as Anderson. These heirs lived in Georgia. Each time they made application for land due their dead relative, the claims were postponed by the Land Board because of insufficient proof of heirship, and because of a complication due to the fact that there were several George Washington Andersons in the Texas army in 1836, and the Land Board could not determine whether the claims made by the Georgia people were valid. It is absolutely clear that two George Washington Andersons fought at the battle of San Jacinto (see Milam 1309, and San Patricio 97), and if there were a George Washington Anderson who died at the Alamo, he was the third man by that name in the Texan army in 1836. After 1860 the people in Georgia did not press their claims—why they did not could not be ascertained—and so no lands were granted to them. These findings, however, leave a probability that this name may belong on the Alamo roll. In my opinion this probability is strengthened by another document, Muster Rolls. p. 25 ("Breece's Company before Bexar and what became of it"). On this roll the Quartermaster sergeant is named George Andrews, and he is listed as "died at the Alamo." Since it is a proved fact that the majority of Breece's men were Alamo victims, I verified this entire roll to test its accuracy, and found it to be unusually correct for a muster roll document. I found land certificates or other documents concerning all the names on the roll, except for John Spratt, George Andrews, and _____ Kedison. Only a few errors had been made in the report of what had become of these men.

One variant that I am reasonably sure of which occurs in this roll is that of the name "James Dickens" for that of "James Dimpkins." This leads me to suspect that the George Andrews of the roll should be George Anderson. In view of the fact that so many of the early lists included the name of Anderson as the quartermaster, together with the above stated facts, I have been forced to the tentative opinion that one George Washington Anderson did die at the Alamo, but I have no conclusive proof of the fact, so place the name on the list of probable victims.

AYERS (AYRES), _____: This name does not appear on the Muster Rolls, pp. 2-4 (Roll of those who died at the Alamo) nor on the lists made of Alamo victims, made by writers contemporaneous with the event. The Bounty and Donation files were searched in vain for certificates of land issued to a man named Ayers for Alamo service. The headright files I Nacogdoches 770, and I Fannin 1211, show the heirs of Henry C. Ayers getting land due him for service in 1836, the certificates stating that the man was killed in the service in 1836, but not when or where he died. The name, Henry Ayres, does not appear on the muster rolls of either the Goliad men, or the San Jacinto men, and it is therefore possible that he was an Alamo victim. My opinion is against this supposition.

The headright certificate of Joseph Ayres and that of Thomas Ayres are equally uncertain. No bounty certificate was found for either man. Both "died in the service" during 1836; their names are not on the Goliad or San Jacinto rolls. J. J. Linn, E. M. Pease, Frank Templeton, Alamo Monument, and other rolls include this name, Ayres, as an Alamo victim. Frank Templeton writes the name "George Ayres." That is an error, for George Ayres (Harris 11) was living in 1838. Indeed, it is my opinion that the name Ayres should be excluded from the list of Alamo heroes, but I did not prove that it does not belong there.

BURNELL, _____: This name is found on Muster Rolls, p. 2, and on every list of Alamo victims—except my own—that has ever been made. I have made a most painstaking search among the Land Office documents and all other available materials, but have found no record of a Burnell who died at the Alamo. Some lists record the name "John Burnell," others as "A. A. Burnell." In a former study concerning this name I was misled into reading the name Alexander A. Burnett as Burnell, for the final t's of the name of the document are looped and so faintly crossed that it required the aid of a reading glass to discern the fact. While the headright certificate of this Alexandre A. Burnett states that the man died in the service in 1836, it does not definitely say that he was an Alamo victim.

Gray's Alamo victim roll gives this name as "John Burnell." On the *Register of the District Clerks' Reports*, General Land Office, there is an entry, pp. 8-9, showing that the fall term of the District Court of Harris County (1847) granted to the heirs of John Burnell relief in the amount of 320 acres of land. No service was stated. The Land Commissioner himself became interested in this problem and spent almost an entire day, assisted by several clerks, trying to run this reference through the various files for further information, but that one entry was all that could be found concerning John Burnell. Considering these facts, I am of the opinion that it is probable that a Burnell, or Burnett, died at the Alamo. I am inclined to believe that it is more probable that the man's name was Alexandre A. Burnett than that it was John Burnell. Future findings will, perhaps, clear up this problem.

KEDISON, _____: This name is listed on Muster Rolls, pp. 2, 4, 25, and on all former rolls, made of Alamo victims. No further information has been found.

GEORGE, WILLIAM: In the files of the Court of Claims, File No. 195 (E-G), there is to be found an application filed by Margaret Hood, Rachel Brown, and Matilda Alexander, daughters of James George, for lands due to their uncle, William George, who along with their father died at the Alamo. They make affidavit that William George was a young brother of James George who had just arrived in Texas as his brother was starting for the Alamo and so went along with him and died there. They represent William George as an unmarried man about nineteen years old. The claim was filed by Graves and Slack, attorneys. It was "postponed for further information," but no further information could be found concerning it. This claim, however, shows a possibility of one William George having died at the Alamo.

JACKSON, JOHN: It is possible that one John Jackson died at the Alamo. The records show some half dozen John Jacksons in the Texas army in 1836. John N. Jackson and another John Jackson can be identified as Goliad victims, but another John Jackson—not a Fannin man—was killed in the service in 1836 (see I Gonzales 484), but the document concerning him does not definitely state that he died at the Alamo. The name J. Jackson appears on a number of the former rolls of Alamo victims. Some of these rolls give merely the surname Jackson.

INGRAM, _____: Muster Rolls, pp. 2-4, and all lists of Alamo victims, formerly made, include this name. Some rolls give the name "J. Ingram." All land certificates and all other available documents have been carefully investigated, but they give no definite evidence of an Ingram having died with Travis. At the storming of Bexar there was one John Ingram, a native of England, but his bounty files (Fannin, 1594) show that he was honorably discharged on January 6, 1836, while Bexar 777, shows that he was living in 1857.

Among the *Adjutant General's Miscellaneous Papers*, Texas State Library, there is a letter from W. P. Zuber to General William Steele, September 24, 1877, in which the following extracts may be found: "Of those who fell in the Alamo, I was personally acquainted with Col. W. B. Travis, C. Grimes, John Harris, Holland & Lewis Johnson. I knew something by hearsay of Col. James Bowie, James B. Bonham, David Crockett, Albert Martin, and John Pixon, whose name is not on Gov. Pease's list...A few years ago Ingram had a brother, John Ingram, living in Bastrop who can give you the full name of his brother. John Pixon was a transient man who never had a home from his boyhood; my father knew him in Georgia before I was born."

Court of Claims Applications, No. 1777, File (H-L), reads as follows:

Application:

To the Hon. Court of Claims Application is hereby made for land, or land certificates, or duplicates due to the heirs of H. Ingram who fell at the Alamo.

William Echols Hollowell
Agent - August 2, 1858

On the face of the jacket of this document, in pencil, is written "Ingram" without a Christian name. It is thus on the Muster Rolls, but there is no evidence that this application was for the man on the Rolls. The document is marked "rejected."

OLAMIO, GEORGE: George Olamio, from Georgia, took the oath of allegiance to the Texas government before John Forbes at Nacogdoches, January 14, 1836 (Muster Rolls, p. 117). Except for this record of enlistment no trace can be found of this man in any document or source for Texas history. He enlisted along with Crockett's men, and it is possible that he joined Crockett's band of soldiers when they left Nacogdoches and that he died with them at the Alamo. Almost all lists of Alamo victims give the name "Lanio," sometimes it is written "Lamio." The only two names for which this can be a variant are those of Peter Lanio, and George Olamio. Peter Lanio was still living in 1869. It is possible that George Olamio was indeed an Alamo victim.

PIXON, JOHN: Several lists give the name of "John Nixon." W. P. Zuber to William Steele, September 24, 1877, *Adjutant General's Miscellaneous Papers* (also see notes under entry for "Ingram" here), says this name is "John Pixon." Nothing further has been found concerning either John Pixon, or John Nixon.

ROBBINS, GEORGE S.: Native of Kentucky, came to Texas via New Orleans. This name does not appear on the Muster Rolls of the Alamo dead but Chester Newell, Telegraph and Texas Register of March 24, 1836, W. F. Gray and others list it. CMSR, No. 1878 shows his wife, Cynthia, as the administrator of his estate; I Montgomery 422 and Court of Claims Vouchers, No. 171, File (M-R) show the same. These documents state that he was killed in the service during 1836, but fail to prove conclusively that he perished at the Alamo.

SPRATT, JOHN: On some lists this name is given as "William Spratt." Gray gives simply "Spratt." Muster Rolls, p. 25 ("Breece's Men and what became of them"), shows John Spratt as an Alamo victim. No further information has been found. It is possible, though I believe hardly probable, that one Spratt fell at the Alamo.

WARNER, _____: It is also possible that one Thomas S. Warner fell at the Alamo. The surname Warner is listed by the *Telegraph and Texas Register*, March 24, 1836, by E. M. Pease in 1878, by J. J. Linn in 1881, and by others. Frank Templeton gives the name as Stanley Warner, and I San Augustine 42, seems to indicate that he was right, but the evidence is not definite, and no other document or statement has been found to verify the inference.

ANNOTATED LIST OF COURIERS FROM THE ALAMO
(VERIFIED & PROBABLE)

ALLEN, JAMES L.: This man came to Texas in the late days of 1835. He, along with other newly arrived soldiers, was equipped and mounted by the firm of McKinney and Williams and sent to various commands. Young Allen was given a very fleet horse and was sent to Travis at San Antonio. As he was young and slight, he was detailed on the courier squad. His biographers all claim that he was one of the last, if not the last, courier to leave the doomed fortress. He became a settler of Indianola, and there served as county judge, town mayor, and later as justice of the peace, and during the Civil War he served as assessor and collector of taxes. The Land Office records do not show that James L. Allen ever received any land for his services in the Texan army.

BASTION, SAMUEL G.: Johns Henry Brown (*Indian Wars and Pioneers of Southwest Texas*, 137-138) tells of one Samuel G. Bastian who published his reminiscences in a Philadelphia newspaper in 1891. In these reminiscences Bastian claimed that he was one of the couriers sent from the Alamo on February 23, with a message to Gonzales. Brown denounces Bastian's account as "notoriously false," and one is inclined to think that Brown may be right, for Travis would hardly have sent Bastian to Gonzales on the same day that Sutherland and Smith were sent there. Moreover, no evidence can be found at the Land Office, or in other official documents that have been examined during the work of this study, which show that any man by the name of Bastian was in the Texas army in 1836. This is not definitive proof that the statement in his reminiscences that he was a courier from the Alamo is not true, so I include his name in this list.

BAYLOR, JOHN W.: The date upon which Baylor was sent out from the Alamo is not ascertained. Mrs. Mary Austin Holley wrote a letter to her daughter on March 24, 1837 (see Mrs. Holley's MS. notes and letters, University of Texas Archives), from Mobile, Alabama. In this letter she wrote:

> Mrs. Baylor's oldest son was a cadet of West Point. He joined the army of Texas and was with Travis at the Alamo, but was sent out on some service and thereby escaped the massacre at the time of its fall. He was then with Fannin's corps but was one of those who escaped the massacre; and after all these perils, he died ingloriously of disease soon afterwards. His whole soul was devoted to Texas, so his sister says.

Mrs. Holley's information was not quite accurate concerning Baylor's service at Goliad, for Memorial No. 37, File 5, shows R. E. Baylor, a nephew of John W.

Baylor, petitioning for land due his uncle for his services in the Texan army. In his affidavit he says:

> Dr. John W. Baylor of Alabama enlisted in Captain Dimmitt's Company, October 5, 1835. He was at the taking of Goliad, the storming of Bexar, and later participated in the Battle of San Jacinto. He died a short time after this battle at his home in Cahaba, Alabama, being at the time of his death on furlough.

Another fact that makes it believable that Mrs. Holley was correctly informed about Baylor's being a messenger from the Alamo is that Dimmitt and a squad of his soldiers were a part of the force at the Alamo when the Mexicans arrived. Dimmitt left with Nat Lewis soon after the arrival of the enemy at Bexar, but his soldiers remained at the Alamo and died there. So Mrs. Holley's letter is fairly conclusive information concerning this matter.

BONHAM, JAMES BUTLER: James Butler Bonham acted twice as a messenger from Travis to Fannin. He first went out before the arrival of the Mexicans, that is on February 16, 1836. He returned to the Alamo on February 23, after the arrival of the Mexicans,[1] but was sent out again on, or about February 27 (date not certain), and returned again on March 3.[2]

BROWN, ROBERT: It is certain that this man either died at the Alamo or was sent out as a messenger, for on February 25, Travis in his letter to Houston, gives him special mention for bravery in going out under the enemy's fire to set fire to *jacals* that were giving cover to the Mexican sharpshooters. The registers at the Land Office list but one "Robert Brown" in the Texan army in 1836, and his certificates—Milam 257, 409, and I Bexar 343—show that he was a single man who came to Texas in October, 1835, and that he rendered service during the San Jacinto campaign by guarding baggage at Harrisburg. My research through other sources has not discovered any Robert Brown who died at the Alamo, so my supposition is that at sometime after February 25, 1836, the Robert Brown mentioned by Travis was sent out as a messenger, and that he later participated in the San Jacinto campaign. No other information concerning this name has been found, but it certainly belongs on the list of verified Alamo victims, or here on this list of Alamo couriers.

CRUZ Y AROCHA, ANTONIO: Left the Alamo with Juan N. Seguin on the night of February 29. (See entry and notes for Juan N. Seguin in this section.)

1 DeShields (ed.), "John Sutherland's Account of the Alamo," *Dallas News*, February 5, 1911; John
   S. Ford's *Journal* (MS.), University of Texas Archives.
2 Wooten (ed.), *Comprehensive History of Texas*, I, 645.

DE SAUQUE, FRANCIS: See notes under entry for "W. K. Simpson" below.

GARZA, ALEXANDRO DE LA: This man was one of the nine soldiers who went to the Alamo with Travis under the immediate command of Captain Juan N. Seguin. Seguin told R. M. Potter that this man was sent out as a messenger (see note in Alamo victim list under entry for "Juan Abamillo.") The records do not give the date on which Garza left the Alamo, but the inference is that he did not go with Seguin and Arocha or that fact would probably have been mentioned by Seguin, either in his *Memoirs* or in his letter to Potter.

HIGHSMITH, BENJAMIN F.: This man was sent out of the Alamo on the night of February 24 with a second message to Fannin.[3]

JOHNSON, _____: Dr. John Sutherland says that at the same time that he and Smith were sent to Gonzales with the note to Andrew Ponton, a young man named Johnson was dispatched to Fannin to announce the arrival of the Mexicans at Bexar and again to ask for help.[4] I have not been able to ascertain the Christian name of this man.

LOCKHART, BYRD: Lockhart left the Alamo with Andrew Sowell just before the fall to try to bring in supplies for the soldiers and do what he could to hurry reinforcements.[5]

MARTIN, ALBERT: Albert Martin carried out, on the night of February 24, the famous letter addressed "To the People of Texas and All Americans in the World." On the back of that letter he wrote in pencil:

> Since the above was written I have heard a very heavy cannonade during the whole day. I think there must have been an attack made upon the Alamo. We were short of ammunition when I left. Hurry on all the men you can get in haste.

NAVAN, GERALD: In a letter from Green B. James to General Sam Houston on January 18, 1836 (*Army Papers,* Texas State Library) we find this paragraph:

> I have one other subject which interests me some; to ask of you, if it is not too late, that is to recommend to your notice Capt. G. Navan, who is clerk in my department, for the appointment of suttler of this

---

3 McCall, "William T. Malone," *Texas Historical Quarterly*, XIV, 326.

4 DeShields (ed.), "John Sutherland's Account of the Fall of the Alamo," *Dallas News*, February 5, 1911; John S. Ford's *Journal* (MS.), Archives of the University of Texas.

5 Sowell, *Rangers and Pioneers of Texas*, 136.

Post as he is in every way qualified to fill the office. I know of no man who merits it more than he does; as an evidence of his patriotism he has absented himself from his family when he was also receiving a salary of $1800 per annum to aid us in our difficulties.

I did not discover whether or not Gerald Navan received the appointment as sutler of the post, but his name is on the return that Neill made to the Provisional Government when he left the Alamo on February 14, 1836. On that list this man is designated as "engineer of dept." The editors of the *Telegraph and Texas Register*, in the issue of March 24, 1836 state that John W. Smith and Mr. Navan had helped to compile the list of Alamo victims that was published in that issue.

OURY, WILLIAM S.: Oury was sent out of the Alamo with a message to Houston on or about February 29. See CMSR Nos. 2332, 6155 and Harris 111.

PATTON, CAPTAIN WILLIAM: Captain Patton carried a company of soldiers to the Alamo on January 18, 1836. He left the Alamo either immediately before or immediately after the arrival of the Mexican forces. The exact date of Patton's departure from the Alamo was not ascertained but very probably he should be on the roll of messengers.

SEGUIN, JUAN N.: Seguin left the Alamo on the night of February 29. In his *Memoirs* he tells that Travis called for volunteers for courier service. He got no response, so lots were cast to determine who should go. The die fell upon Seguin. Still Travis demurred, for Seguin was one of his strongest supporters, but the soldiery began to grumble, so Travis sent him out with the dispatches.[6] His corporal, Antonio Cruz y Arocha, accompanied him.

SIMPSON, W. K.: This name appears on the Alamo monument and on many other lists of Alamo victims, but the bounty and donation certificates, issued to the heirs of William K. Simpson for land due him, cites service at Goliad with Fannin. On the muster rolls of Fannin's men the name is "W. E. Simpson." The records at the Land Office, and the CMSR, as well as various other documents, show that there were several William Simpsons and one Wilson Simpson in the Texan army in 1836. Among the CMSR, there was an unnumbered and unclassified document, a requisition on the Provisional Government for $31.60 to be paid for beeves bought by Francis De Sauque to be delivered to William Simpson. Since it has been established that De Sauque left the Alamo on, or about February 22, for the purpose of gathering food supplies for the fort; and since Simpson's

6 Potter, "The Fall of the Alamo," 9, Reprint from the *American Historical Magazine*, January 1878; Seguin, *Memoirs*, 5, University of Texas Archives.

name appears on most all of the lists of Alamo dead, and since a man of the same name died at Goliad, the inference is that William K. Simpson left the Alamo with De Sauque, and that, cut off from the Alamo, they joined Fannin at Goliad. At any rate, both these men died with Fannin and his men. De Sauque, certainly, Simpson, probably, was a messenger from the Alamo. They left the fort, however, most likely the day before the investment began, a fact that should possibly exclude their names from the list of messengers.

SMITH, JOHN W.: Smith twice a messenger from the Alamo. He first went out on February 23, in company with Dr. John Sutherland. These two men carried the first message to Gonzales. This is a fact that is accepted by all Texas historians, as is also the fact of common information that Smith served as guide to the Gonzales band who reinforced Travis on March 1. Smith again left the Alamo on the night of March 3. He carried Travis's last dispatches and was the last courier to leave the doomed fortress.[7]

SMITHERS, LANCELOT: Among the papers of the late C. H. Raguet of Marshall, Texas, there are letters which prove that Lancelot Smithers was a messenger from the Alamo, sent out on February 23, 1836. The first of these letters reads:

> Gonzales
> February 24, 1836
>
> In a few words, there is 2,000 Mexican soldiers in Bexar, and 150 Americans in the Alamo. Sesma is at the head of them, and from the best accounts that can be obtained, they intend to show no quarter. If every man cannot turn out to a man, every man in the Alamo will be murdered.
>
> They have not more than 8 or 10 days provisions. They say they will defend it or die on the ground. Provisions, ammunition and Men, or you suffer your men to be murdered in the Fort. If you do not turn out Texas is gone. I left Bexar on the 23rd at 4 p.m.
>
> By Order of
> W. B. Travis
>
> L. Smithers

---

7 DeShields (ed.), "John Sutherland's Account of the Fall of the Alamo," *Dallas News*, February 5, 1911; John S. Ford's *Journal* (MS.), 54, University of Texas Archives.

Upon receipt of this message, Colonel Henry Raguet, chairman of the Committee of Vigilance and Safety at Nacogdoches, sent it on to Dr. Sibley who was Chairman of the Committee of Vigilance and Safety for Texas Affairs at Nachitoches. Colonel Raguet says:

> As Chairman of the Committee of Vigilance and Safety of this place, I beg to enclose to you a copy of a letter from Colonel Travis, the commanding officer of the Post at San Antonio, by which you will perceive the situation of our brave countryman and his small but patriotic band on the frontier. In addition to this astounding intelligence we have information which cannot be doubted, that Mexican troops are pouring in from all quarters, with the determination to make simultaneous attacks on various points, thereby compelling the troops of this unfortunate country to defend with a mere handful of men, those posts on the maintenance of which our existence as a people depends. Our situation, as you perceive, is truly critical; nothing, in fact, can save us but a continuance of your generous aid which has already been extended to us with a liberality unprecedented in any country and which never can be obliterated from the memory of a grateful, oppressed and struggling country people. We implore you, therefore, by everything you hold dear—by your "happy homes and altars free"—to make one more effort on our behalf to save us from the devouring grasp of a ruthless tyrant, and to enable us to live in peace and happiness in the land of our adoption.
>
> We earnestly beg you to give publicity to this statement to every well-wisher to our cause, to communicate the intelligence to our friends in New Orleans. I assure you that the truth of this message may be relied on...
>
> Your friend,
>
> Henry Raguet
> Chairman Com. Vig. and Safety

In addition to these letters from the *Raguet Papers* there is further proof that Smithers was zealous in transmitting messages from the Alamo. It is clear that Travis's letter of February 24, the letter that Albert Martin brought out, passed through his hands, for on the back of that letter, under Martin's note, Smithers wrote:

> I hope that every one will [rendezvous] at Gonzales as soon as possible as these brave soldiers are suffering. Don't neglect them. Powder is very scarce and some should not be delayed one moment. -L. Smithers

SOWELL, ANDREW: Sowell accompanied Byrd Lockhart. (See entry for "Byrd Lockhart" in the preceding pages.)

SUTHERLAND, JOHN: Dr. John Sutherland went out with John Smith to Gonzales on February 23, 1836.[8]

WARNELL (WORNEL), HENRY: Warnell's name appears on the verified roll of Alamo victims because of the preponderance of evidence found saying that he died at the Alamo. There is, however, evidence that indicates he died elsewhere from wounds received leaving the Alamo to carry a message from Travis. For this reason, his name also appears here with the couriers. Court of Claims Voucher No. 1579, File (S-Z), which is not dated, indicates that he was an inmate at the Alamo but escaped alive and died several months later at Port Lavaca from the wounds sustained there. Another document in the augmentation files of the General Land Office, filed by Warnell's heirs, indicates that he was wounded on February 28 or 29 leaving the Alamo with Travis's final message to Houston at San Felipe. The message arrived on March 4 and Warnell died several weeks later from his wounds. It is possible that Warnell's name belongs here more so than the roll of verified victims but there is conflicting evidence enough to land him on both this list and the former.

---

8 Memorial No. 131, File 82, Archives of the State Department; DeShields (ed.), "John Sutherland's Account of the Fall of the Alamo," *Dallas News*, February 5, 1911.

BIBLIOGRAPHY

A. PRIMARY SOURCES—MANUSCRIPTS

I. Manuscripts in the State Library

1) Army Papers of the Texas Revolution, 1835-1837.
2) Comptroller's Military Service Records, 1835-1842.
3) Domestic Correspondence, 1835-1838.
4) Fretelliere Papers.
5) Governor and Council Papers, 1835-1836.
6) The Consultation Papers, 1835-1836.
7) The Nacogdoches Archives, 1790-1836.
8) Miscellaneous (various letters and photostats.)

II. Manuscripts at the General Land Office

1) Bounty and Donation Register.
2) Bounty and Donation Files, 18,000.
3) Court of Claims Register (index to Court of Claims files.)
4) Court of Claims Files - Applications, Vouchers, Letters, Special Acts.
5) Headright Registers.
6) Lost Book of Harris.
7) Muster Roll Books.
8) The Spanish Archives - Empresario Registers, The Spanish Files.

III. Manuscripts in the Department of State

1) Memorials of Congress.
2) Book No. 3, Letters 1835-1836.
3) File Case of Alamo Records (regarding the State's purchase of the Alamo.)

IV. Manuscripts in the Archives of the University of Texas

1) Adriance (John) Papers, 1831-1910.
2) Archive General de Mexico, Secretaria de Guerra y Marina, 1834-1837.
3) Asbury-Bonham-Travis Correspondence.
4) Bexar Archives, 1835-1836.
5) Documentos para la Historia de la Provencia de Texas, Vol. XXVII & XXVIII.
6) Fontaine (Winston W.) Papers.

7) Franklin (Judge Benjamin) Papers

8) Mary Austin Holley Letters and Manuscript Notes

9) Reminiscences of J. H. Jenkins, Jr.

10) John S. Ford's Journal, 1836-1892, which contains:

    a) John Sutherland's "Fall of the Alamo"

    b) Juan N. Seguin's Reminiscences

    c) Mrs. Juana Alsbury's "Recollections of the Alamo Massacre."

11) Santa Anna's Memoirs, 1872. Original.

12) Santa Anna's Memoirs, Translated by Willye Ward Watkins, M. A. Thesis, 1922, MS.

V. Manuscripts in the Archives of the Daughters of the Republic of Texas

1) Five letters written by Mrs. Mollie Grissett DeCaussey, granddaughter of W. B. Travis.

2) Letter written by Mrs. Helen Marr Kirby describing Travis's son and daughter.

3) Miscellaneous reports and letters.

VI. Letters in Answer to Questionnaire

1) About one hundred letters, information mostly negative.

B. Printed Sources

I. American Historical Association Reports

1) *Austin Papers*, ed. by E. C. Barker, 2 vols., Vol. II (in two parts), 1919; Vol. II, 1922.

2) Diplomatic Correspondence of the Republic of Texas, ed. by G. P. Garrison, 2 vols., Vol. II (in two parts), Washington 1908-1911.

II. *Austin Papers*, ed. by E. C. Barker, Vol. III, University of Texas Press, 1924.

III. *Lamar Papers*, ed. by Gulick, Elliott, Allen and Smither, 6 vols., Austin, 1919, 1920, 1922, 1923-25, 1927, 1928.

IV. *Southwestern Historical Quarterly*, 34 Vols., Austin. The first sixteen volumes are entitled *The Texas Historical Quarterly*. The fol-

lowing volumes were used: I, II, III, IV, V, VI, VII, VIII, IX, X, XI, XIII, XIV, XV, XVI, XVII, XX, XXI, XXII, XXIII. References to specific articles appear in the footnotes.

V. Gammel, H. P. N., *Laws of Texas*, 11 vols., Vol. I used.

VI. Manuel Dublan y Jose Maria Lozano, *Legislacion Mexicano o Coleccion Completa de las Disposiciones Legislativas Expeditas desde la Independencia de la Republica*, 19 vols., Mexico, 1876-1890.

VII. *Texas Almanac*, 1856, 1858, 1859, 1860, 1862, 1868, 1870, 1873.

VIII. Newspapers and Magazines.

1) *The Telegraph and Texas Register*

a) January 9, 16, 23, 30 of 1836
b) February 20, 27 of 1836
c) March 12, 24 of 1836
d) March 28, 1837
e) March 23, 1842
f) July 26, 1843

2) *The Texas Republican*

a) July 5, 1834
b) July 25, 1835
c) August 22, 29 of 1835
d) September 19, 1835
e) October 31, 1835
f) November 14, 1835

3) *El Correo Atlantico*

a) April 11, 18 of 1836
b) June 13, 1836
c) August 1, 1836

4) *Austin City Gazette*

a) April 14, 1841
b) July 17, 1874

5) *Dallas Daily News*

    a) July 27, 1888
    b) February 21, 1897
    c) February 5, 12 of 1911

6) *Houston Daily Post*

    a) September 2, 1906
    b) March 10, 1907

7) *Galveston Daily News*

    a) June 10, 1803

8) *San Antonio Express*

    a) November 24, 1901
    b) March 7, 1880
    c) August 28, 1904
    d) January 22, 29 of 1905
    e) February 5, 15 of 1905
    f) May 28, 1905
    g) May 12, 1907
    h) February 18, 1912
    i) September 8, 1912

9) *Texas Field and National Guardsman,* May 1912

10) *El Mosquito Mexicano*

    a) January 22, 1836
    b) February 6, 1836
    c) March 4, 1836
    d) April 5, 1836

11) *Texas Magazine,* 1896-1897

    a) C. W. Raines, *Life of Santa Anna*

12) The W. B. Travis Family Bible, State Library

C. Secondary Sources

Baker, D. W. C., *Texas Scrap Book*, New York, 1907.

Bancroft, Herbert Howe, *History of Mexico*, 6 vols., San Francisco, 1886-1888.

Bancroft, Herbert Howe, *The North Mexican States and Texas*, 2 vols., San Francisco, 1886-1889.

Barker, Eugene C., *The Life of Stephen F. Austin*, Dallas, 1925

Barker, Eugene C., *Mexico and Texas, 1821-1835*, Dallas, 1928

Barker, Eugene C. *Readings in Texas History*, Dallas, 1929

Barnes, Charles Merritt, *Combats and Conquests of Immortal Heroes*, San Antonio, 1910

Bowie, Walter Worthington, *The Bowies and Their Kindred*, Washington, 1889

Brady, Cyrus T., *Border Fights and Fighters*, New York, 1902

Brown, John Henry, *The History of Texas*, 2 vols., St. Louis, 1893
              Life and Times of Henry Smith, Dallas, 1887

Calcott, Wilfred H., *Church and State in Mexico, 1832-1857*, Durham, 1926

Caro, Ramón Martinez, *Verdadera Idea de la Primera Campana de Tejas y Sucesos Ocurridos despues de la Accion de San Jacinto*, Mexico, 1837

Castañeda, C. E. (ed.), *The Mexican Side of the Texas Revolution*, 1836, Dallas, 1929

Clairborne, Airie M., *The Story of the Alamo*

Colquitt, O. B., *Message to the Thirty-third Legislature Relative to the Alamo Property*, Austin, 1913

Crockett, David (ed. by John Potter), *Autobiography*, Philadelphia, 1869

Crockett, David (ed. by J. Linbird), *Autobiography*, London, 1834

Crockett, David (ed. by McNeill Everett), *Autobiography*, New York, 1908

DeWees, W. B., *Letters from an Early Settler of Texas* (compiled by Cora Cardelle), Louisville, 1852

Dixon, Sam Houston, *Romance and Tragedy of Texas History*

Duval, John C., *Adventures of Big Foot Wallace, the Texas Ranger and Hunter*, Philadelphia, 1873

Duval, John C., *Early Times in Texas*, Austin, 1892

Edward, David B., *The History of Texas*, Cincinnati, 1836

Espinosa, Isadoro Felix de, *Chronica Apostolica*, 1746

Filisola, Vicente, *Memorias para la Historia de la Guerra de Tejas*, Mexico, 1848-49

Filisola, Vicente, *Defensa de* (an address to the President of Mexico defending his conduct in Texas with substantiating documents.) No Title page, 1836

Foote, Henry Stuart, *Texas and Texans*, 2 vols., Philadelphia, 1841

Ford, John S., *Origin and Fall of the Alamo*, San Antonio, 1896

Gouge, William M., *The Fiscal History of Texas*, Philadelphia, 1852

Gould, Stephen, *Alamo Guide*, Library of Congress, Washington, 1882

Gray, A. C., *From Virginia to Texas—Diary of W. F. Gray 1835-1836*, New York, 1909

Hefley, W. T., *The Graves of the Alamo Heroes*, Cameron, TX, 1913

Hammond, John Martin, *Quaint and Historical Forts of North America*, Philadelphia, 1915

Holley, Mrs. Mary Austin, *Texas*, Lexington, 1836

Houstoun, M. C., *Texas and the Gulf of Mexico*, 2 vols., London, 1844

Johnson, Francis White (ed. by E. C. Barker), *A History of Texas and Texans*, New York, 1916

Kennedy, William, *Texas: The Rise, Progress and Prospects of the Republic of Texas*, New York, 1841

Lester, C. Edwards, *Sam Houston and His Republic*, New York, 1846

Linn, John J., *Reminiscences of Fifty Years in Texas*, New York, 1883

Lundy, Benjamin, *The War in Texas*, Philadelphia, 1874

Maillard, N. Doran, *History of the Republic of Texas*, London, 1842

Morphis, J. M., *History of Texas*, New York, 1874

Newell, Chester, *History of the Revolution of Texas*, New York, 1838

Niles, John M., *History of South America and Mexico*, Hartford, 1884

Palacio, Vicente Riva (ed.), *Mexico a Traves de los Siglos*, 5 vols., Mexico, 1887-89

Portillo, Esteban L., *Apuntes para Historia Antigua de Coahuila y Texas*, Mexico, 1886

Potter, Reuben M., *The Fall of the Alamo*, Reprint from *American History Magazine*, May 1878

Priestley, Herbert, *The Mexican Nation*, New York, 1923

Rives, George Lockhart, *The United States and Mexico, 1821-1848*, New York, 1913

Rodrigues, J. M., *Memories of Early Texas*, San Antonio, 1913

Shepard, Seth, *The Fall of the Alamo*, Oration given at San Marcos, 1889

Smith, Justin, *Annexation of Texas*, New York, 1911

Sowell, A. J., *Rangers and Pioneers of Texas*, San Antonio, 1884

Sprague, William Cyrus, *David Crockett*, Houston, 1915

Stiff, Col. Edward, *Texas Emigrant*, Louisville, 1840

Templeton, Frank, *Margaret Ballentine, or, The Fall of the Alamo*, Houston, 1890

Thrall, Homer S., *A Pictorial History of Texas,* St. Louis, 1878

Urrea, Jose, *Diario de las Operaciones Militares de le Division que la manda del General Jose Urrea hizo la Campana de Tejas,* Mexico, 1838

Williams, Alfred M., *Sam Houston and the War of Independence in Texas,* New York, 1893

Winkler, E. W., *The Alamo,* 1916

Wooten, Dudley G., *A Comprehensive History of Texas from 1685 to 1897,* Dallas, 1898

Wright, Ione, *San Antonio: Historical, Traditional, Legendary,* Austin, 1916

Yoakum, Henderson, *History of Texas from Settlement, 1685, to Annexation to the United States, 1846,* 2 vols., New York, 1855

CPSIA information can be obtained at www.ICGtesting.com
Printed in the USA
LVOW091647120312

272348LV00002BA/2/P